GHASTLY
MURDER
IN THE EAST-END.
DREADFUL MUTILATION OF A WOMAN.

Capture : Leather Apron

Another murder of a character even more diabolical than that perpetrated in Buck's Row, on Friday week, was discovered in the same neighbourhood, on Saturday morning. At about six o'clock a woman was found lying in a back yard at the foot of a passage leading to a lodging-house in a Old Brown's Lane, Spitalfields. The house is occupied by a Mrs. Richardson, who lets it out to lodgers, and the door which admits to this passage, at the foot of which lies the yard where the body was found, is always open for the convenience of lodgers. A lodger named Davis was going down to work at the time mentioned and found the woman lying on her back close to the flight of steps leading into the yard. Her throat was cut in a fearful manner. The woman's body had been completely ripped open, and the heart and other organs laying about the place, and portions of the entrails round the victim's neck. An excited crowd gathered in front of Mrs. Richardson's house and also round the mortuary in old Montague Street, whither the body was quickly conveyed. As the body lies in the rough coffin in which it has been placed in the mortuary —the same coffin in which the unfortunate Mrs. Nicholls was first placed—it presents a tearful sight. The body is that of a woman about 45 years of age. The height is exactly five feet. The complexion is fair, with wavy dark brown hair; the eyes are blue, and two lower teeth have been knocked out. The nose is rather large and prominent.

THE NEMESIS OF NEGLECT.

"THERE FLOATS A PHANTOM ON THE SLUM'S FOUL AIR,
    SHAPING, TO EYES WHICH HAVE THE GIFT OF SEEING,
INTO THE SPECTRE OF THAT LOATHLY LAIR.
    FACE IT—FOR VAIN IS FLEEING!
RED-HANDED, RUTHLESS, FURTIVE, UNERECT,
'TIS MURDEROUS CRIME—THE NEMESIS OF NEGLECT!"

Sanitary Inspection: One inspector found seven people living in one basement kitchen, with a little child lying dead in the same room.

CHILDREN WAIFS

"PLEASE GIVE US A HA'PENNY TO GET A HA'PENNY DINNER SIR"

THE COMPLETE JACK THE RIPPER

Donald Rumbelow

Introduction by

Colin Wilson

NEW YORK GRAPHIC SOCIETY
Boston, Massachusetts

First published in England by W.H. Allen & Co. Ltd.
First published in 1975 in the United States by New York Graphic Society Ltd.
11 Beacon Street, Boston, Massachusetts 02108

Printed in the United States of America

To Colin Wilson, Dan Farson,
Tom Cullen, Robin Odell, and 'Ripperologists'—
not forgetting JACK who brought
us together

CONTENTS

ACKNOWLEDGMENTS

This book owes a great deal to the generous help of many friends. I should particularly like to single out Colin Wilson who has not only written the introduction but has helped me out in so many other ways that I shall never be able adequately to repay his kindness; Robin Odell who read the draft manuscript; and Tom Cullen and Dan Farson who generously helped me out with illustrations and in many other ways too numerous to mention.

I should also like to thank for their help and assistance David Anderson, Dale Wilkinson, Peter Simmons, Philip Loftus, Joe Gaute, David Brass, Richard Whittington-Egan, Professor J. M. Cameron of the London Hospital, Bill Tidy, the Half Moon Theatre Company, the Bubble Theatre Company, Hammer Films, the British Broadcasting Corporation, the ladies of the Metropolitan Police Library, New Scotland Yard, the Commissioner of the City of London Police, the Commissioner of the Metropolitan Police, and the Society of Authors on behalf of the Bernard Shaw Estate for permission to reproduce a letter from the Collected Letters 1874–1897, edited by Dan H. Laurence and published by Max Reinhardt, 1965.

My final acknowledgment is once again to my wife who has patiently deciphered my mutilated and mangled manuscripts not once but many times.

Among the people who have kindly placed their picture collections at my disposal and whom I should like to thank for their more than generous help are Robin Odell, Tom Cullen and Dan Farson. Equally generous was the late Professor Francis Camps, who spent one particularly fascinating afternoon with Dan Farson and myself arguing the Druitt theory, and a special mention, too, must be made of Philip Loftus who very kindly provided me with some illustrations.

INTRODUCTION

The first full-length book on Jack the Ripper—*The Mystery of Jack the Ripper* by Leonard Matters—appeared in 1929, forty-one years after the Whitechapel murders. Since then five more have appeared, each writer advocating his own theory. Donald Rumbelow's is the seventh—a traditionally lucky number—and so far the most exhaustive. He has no theory of his own, but he summarises all the known facts and all the known theories with a thoroughness and impartiality that were often lacking in the earlier volumes. He also compares the Ripper's crimes with others that had similar features—notably the murders of Peter Kürten, the Düsseldorf 'Ripper', and those of 'Jack the Stripper', the Thames Nude killer of the 1960s. What emerges is not a theory of the Ripper's identity, but a dim, shadowy picture of the *kind* of person who could have committed the Whitechapel murders.

One of the oddest aspects of the Ripper murders is that the Victorians did not recognise them as sex crimes. Nowadays we take it for granted, being familiar with a dozen or so similar cases, from Heath and Christie to Dean Corll (the homosexual mass-murderer of Texas). Sir Melville Macnaghten, chief source for the Druitt theory of the killer's identity, said that Montague John Druitt was 'sexually insane'—an odd phrase, implying that he was sane in other departments—and many other people at the time suggested a sexual motive. But it was not generally recognised as a series of sex crimes for a simple reason: the Ripper killings were the first case of sex crime in the sense that we understand it today.

This must be immediately qualified. The child-murders committed by Gilles de Rais, Marshal of France, in the 13th century, were obviously sex crimes; so were the murders of the sadistic Countess Elizabeth Báthory in 16th century Hungary (she was accused of causing the death of some 650 girls, in order to take baths in their blood). In 1867, Frederick Baker, a clerk of Alton, Hampshire, abducted seven-year-old Fanny Adams and dismembered her body in a kind of frenzy; he was executed in the same year. In Paris in 1880 twenty-year-old Louis Menesclou lured a four-year-old girl, Louise Dreux, into his room and strangled her. He slept overnight with the body under his mattress, then dismembered it and tried to burn it; he was caught when neighbours reported the smell. Menesclou denied violating the child; but his crime, like Baker's, is obviously sexual in origin. These cases, then, are the exceptions. But it nevertheless remains fundamentally true to say that Jack the Ripper inaugurated the age of sex crime.

The Victorians were aware that something new and strange was happening. Of course, they were accustomed to all kinds of violence, particularly in their slums; but this was the result of poverty and drunkenness. (Donald Rumbelow has some horrifying pages on conditions in the East End at the time.) The poor sometimes broke the windows of the rich; and even in the West End there was a certain amount of daylight robbery. (Mugging is not a modern invention.) All this was understandable. But these Ripper murders, with their nightmarish mutilations, simply went beyond normal comprehension. It was as if the killer wanted to *shock* the whole community, to fling the murders in its face like a hysterical insult.

And to understand the impact they made one has only to read the novels of Dickens or Thackeray or Trollope. The Victorians were great sentimentalists, and eternally hopeful idealists. They may have treated their poor very badly (as you can see from Gustav Doré's engravings of London), but they had the best intentions in the world. And the poor themselves 'knew their place'; they might commit burglary or robbery with violence, but they would have been deeply shocked by Karl Marx's proposals for a classless society. All literate Victorians, whether rich or poor, wept at the death of Little Nell, and reacted with indignation to Scrooge's: 'Christmas, humbug!' They all gasped with horror in the theatre as William Corder shot Maria Marten in the Red Barn, or when Colleen Bawn was murdered by her heartless playboy husband. (Both plays, incidentally, were based on true murder cases.) Victorian society might be divided by class barriers; but where sentiment was concerned, it was one big, happy family. Marx talked of the phenomenon of alienation, for he himself was an alienated man, an 'outsider' who had rejected his own class (the upper middle-class) and been rejected by it, a man who lived in pov-

erty on the edge of a society he loathed, and to whose overthrow he
was dedicated. But in spite of Marx, there was very little alienation
in Victorian London or Liverpool. The poor might wish they had a
better place in society; but they didn't feel alienated from it.

Marx died five years before the Ripper murders, but *he* would have
understood them. Here was a man who was really 'alienated', who
wandered around among his fellow human beings like a man from
some other civilisation, or like Swift's Gulliver when he returned
from the land of the Yahoos, and found himself unable to bear the
stink of London crowds. Jack the Ripper did not believe in the message of Dickens's *Christmas Carol;* he didn't believe in the brother-
hood of man. He was a sick man, a man twisted with hatred and
wracked by sadistic cravings. Neither did he believe, like Marx, in
taking advantage of the democratic process to express his loathing in
some socially acceptable way. He was like a man who insists on
shouting obscenities in church, or lowering his trousers in the middle
of a royal garden party. Donald Rumbelow's account of the Miller's
Court murder brings home this element of savage, almost blasphe-
mous violence—the nose cut off, the legs stripped of flesh, the entrails
torn out. (This is the first complete description of the mutilations that
has appeared in a book; I included one in the typescript of my *Casebook of Murder,* but the publisher toned it down as too horrific.)
The reaction was more than shock; people were stunned and winded,
as if by a blow. And a deep, instinctive disquiet stirred inside them.

In considering the impact of the murders, we also have to take into
account the famous Victorian prudery. This was of fairly recent origin; up to the 1860s, men and women had bathed naked at respectable
seaside resorts. A quarter of a century later, the glimpse of a lady's
ankle was regarded as indecent; and even table legs were kept covered. The Whitechapel victims were all prostitutes, and by that time
—1888—the very idea of prostitution was enough to cause morbid
shudders in most Victorians. Even in our enlightened society there
are newspapers that achieve wide circulation by assuming that most
people are avidly curious about adultery, seduction and rape—dem-
onstrating that the public's obsession with sex does not change
much from age to age. The Victorians called prostitutes 'daughters of
joy', apparently under the delusion that they were nymphomaniacs
who had chosen their trade because they were sexually insatiable. If
Jack the Ripper had murdered nursemaids or suburban housewives,
it would have been shocking enough; but his choice of prostitutes
touched the deepest springs of Victorian morbidity.

But this, I think, was secondary. What is more important was the instinctive recognition that something strange was happening, that some basic change was being signalled. Until Jack the Ripper, nearly all crime had been 'economic' in origin. Look through the two hundred or so cases recorded in the Newgate Calendar: dozens of robberies, assaults, burglaries, a few ordinary rapes committed by drunks (for which the sentences were often remarkably light)—nothing to suggest the manic violence of a man *at war with society*. The first criminal case that bears a superficial resemblance to the Ripper case is that of the Ratcliffe Highway murders of December 1811, when on two separate evenings two East End families were violently slaughtered with a hammer and a sharp knife; even a baby in its cradle was battered to death. The motive was apparently robbery—there are many puzzling features in the case—and a sailor named John Williams was convicted. No sexual assault was involved. The extreme violence of these crimes produced a nationwide sensation very similar to that produced by Jack the Ripper. Again, in 1828, the activities of the body-snatchers Burke and Hare caused a similar sensation; they killed at least a dozen people, most of them prostitutes. The motive was purely economic; they sold the bodies to an anatomist—for about £8 each—for dissection.

In the sixty years following Burke and Hare, most of the best-known cases are of middle-class domestic murder: Dr Pritchard, William Palmer, Constance Kent, Charles Bravo. . . . But 'economic murder' continued unabated among the poor. In Whitechapel, murders were so commonplace that the newspapers did not even bother to report the murder of Emma Smith on Easter Monday, 1888, and sometimes claimed as the first Ripper killing. (She died of peritonitis from a stab wound in the stomach.)

Then came the Ripper, first in a long line of maniac killers—so many that Donald Rumbelow has not had space to refer to most of them: Vacher, the French Ripper (1897), Ludwig Tessnow (1901), who literally tore his child victims to pieces, Fritz Haarmann, Karl Denke, Adolf Seefeld, George Grossmann, Béla Kiss, Peter Kürten, the Cleveland Torso killer (never caught; he also dismembered his victims), Albert Fish, Bruno Lüdke, Sylvestre Matushka (who wrecked trains to achieve a sexual climax), Earle Nelson, Gordon Cummins (the 'Blackout Ripper'), William Heirens, Neville Heath, Reginald Christie, Harvey Glatman, Alfred Whiteway, Heinrich Pommerencke, Werner Boost. . . . In the past decade or so there has been a disturbing tendency in some sex killers—particularly in America—to torture the victims: the Texarkana 'moonlight murderer' of 1946 (uncaught), Jerry Brudos, Dean Corll. In many of these cases the mutilations resembled those made by Jack the Ripper, and often the killers committed far more murders than the Ripper. (The record is probably held by Bruno Lüdke, a mental defective who confessed to eighty-six murders.) The characteristic of most of these crimes is that the criminal felt himself to be *outside society*. In some cases—Vacher, Tessnow, Seefeld, Lüdke—he was a wandering journeyman or homeless vagrant—and it is easy to understand how such a person could feel alienated from society. But in the majority of cases it was simply a matter of an abnormally powerful sexual urge that was unable to achieve satisfaction through the socially accepted channels (i.e. wives, mistresses, prostitutes). Gerry Thomson, the Peoria murderer (executed 1935) had committed a hundred or so rapes before he was arrested for killing his final victim. In other cases the killer's sexual urge has simply been of a perverted nature: the sadism of Kürten, the necrophily of Christie and Ed Gein, Fish's desire for children. I entitled the final chapter of my *Casebook of Murder,* dealing with such cases, 'Chamber of Horrors'. The description is accurate. And the first exhibit in the Chamber of Horrors is Jack the Ripper.

But why? What caused this new aspect of crime in the final years of the 19th century? In *A New Theory of Human Evolution* Sir Arthur Keith suggests that man's earliest tribal ancestors had two basic codes of conduct, which he calls the code of amity and the code of enmity. They felt amity towards members of their own tribe, enmity towards strangers. Up to the time of the Ripper, the code of amity prevailed in English society—the code symbolised by the music-hall comedian with the battered top hat, pretending to be a 'toff' (Burlington Bertie from Bow, etc.). With Jack the Ripper, the code of enmity had suddenly arrived—with a vengeance.

The basic cause of the change was probably, as Marx recognised, the increasing industrialisation of society. A twelve-year-old child who worked fourteen hours a day in a damp cotton mill was less likely to have a sense of 'belonging' than a farm labourer living in a small village. Improvements in education also played an important part; as many harsh old Tories rightly divined, education only made the lower classes dissatisfied with their lot. Love of reading is not confined to any particular social group. There were bookish tinkers (like John Bunyan) and ploughmen (like John Clare) as well as bookish lawyers and stockbrokers. Dickens himself played a major

part in bringing about the new 'age of enmity', for his books penetrated into every type of household, and his denunciations of social
injustice influenced every class of reader.

Slowly, very slowly, the 19th century was creating a new type of
man. In October 1888, right in the midst of the Ripper murders, there
appeared in a Danish monthly magazine, *Ny Ford,* an anonymous
sketch called *Hunger*. The author was a twenty-nine-year-old Nor-
wegian named Knud Pedersen. It was a startling piece of work, about
a young would-be writer, of peasant origins, living in a bleak room
in Christiana, almost continually delirious from hunger. He sees the
world through different eyes from well-fed people. He is an 'exile
from existence'. Although he is among fellow human beings, he feels
as lost as would a city dweller in a jungle. No one cares what happens
to him; no one would notice if he died in an alleyway.

Knud Pedersen was a young peasant who had worked as a quarry-
man, navvy, shoemaker. Unable to find opportunities in Norway, he
had emigrated to America, but found society there equally hostile.
His love of reading lost him a job as a street-car conductor in Chicago.
So he went back to Norway and expanded the story into a short novel,
also called *Hunger,* which appeared in 1890. He now used a pen-
name—Knut Hamsun—and he went on to become his country's most
celebrated novelist. *Hunger* brought him recognition. But it is more
than the first novel of a remarkable writer. It is one of the first great
'outsider' documents, the first novel to catch that sense of total alienation from society, of a man with no sense of belonging. In fact, Knut
Hamsun was talented enough to force the world to accept him on his
own terms. But supposing he had not been talented enough? A mere
twenty years earlier, in 1869, an intelligent, bookish young homosexual named Jean-Baptiste Troppmann had lured the family of an
Alsatian businessman to a remote suburb of Paris and there murdered all eight of them with a spade. He was also of peasant origin;
he longed for a better life; the murders were committed to obtain
the money to emigrate to America. (He was guillotined in the following year.) There but for the grace of God went Hamsun.

Now I am not suggesting that Jack the Ripper was a potential Hamsun. But there *was* an important fundamental similarity: not just the
sense of not belonging, but a kind of raging appetite that could turn
to violence. Hamsun's early novels are remarkable for their stormy,
rebellious atmosphere, and an impressionistic prose that is reminis-
cent of black clouds flying in the wind. We know little of Jack the
Ripper except for what emerges from those jeering letters to the po-

lice (of which only two or three are likely to be genuine), and from the sickening violence of the murders, but always there is the feeling of a man totally cut off from society by raging desires that twist him like a leaf in a flame. 'From Hell, Mr Lusk', he gloats in a letter. It is curious that so many sadistic murderers have felt this compulsion to write to the police—Neill Cream, Peter Kürten, the uncaught Axeman of New Orleans. Or perhaps not so curious after all. Kürten liked to revisit the scene of his crimes shortly after the bodies were discovered, to gloat over the horror of the spectators. Alienation craves to *express* itself, because its ultimate aim is to cease to be alienated. It would hardly be too far-fetched to say that the letter-writing of the sadist is a twisted literary impulse.

But the central point I wish to make here is that 'alienation' tends to sharpen man's appetites—particularly the sexual appetite. It is physical hunger that cuts off Hamsun's hero from society; it was sexual hunger that cut off Jack the Ripper from society. By this I do not mean that he felt sexual desire for his victims; most of them were bedraggled objects, and even the youngest and most attractive, Mary Kelly, was a massive Irish woman who looked as if she could knock down a horse with an uppercut. But the strangest thing about sexual desire is that, left unsatisfied, it can completely alter its nature, as wine becomes vinegar. We should never underestimate the effect that sheer frustration of the urge to self-expression can have on even the most decent character. 'Sooner murder an infant in its cradle than nurse unacted desire' said the poet Blake, who understood such things. Peter Kürten was highly-sexed from the beginning; but it was solitary confinement—and the violent sexual fantasies he conjured up to while away the time—that turned him into a perverted killer. Perhaps what happens is that sexual desire somehow mingles with thoughts of revenge, until the desire changes its nature and becomes cruel. What *is* certain is that man needs the time to brood—in a room of his own—to be possessed by such fantasies. There was obviously some touch of sadism in the Ripper's composition from the beginning, as there was in Kürten's; but there must have been one point in his career when he had nothing to do but sit in a room and brood on that world outside, from which he felt alienated. Possibly some hatred of his mother played a part—this is suggested by his obsession with wombs, and his need to cut them open. He deliberately developed this appetite for violence, like fanning a spark. And for a long time before his first murder he must have been tormented by this desire every time he looked at a woman: the morbid craving to cut her open. Possibly his first victim was not Polly Nichols, the woman who died in Bucks Row. It *could* have been Emma Smith, or someone like her (Emma Smith said she had been attacked by a gang). Then the desire to actually mutilate became overpowering . . .

It is also necessary to recognise that certain men—and women—belong to the 'high dominance' group. It seems fairly certain that these highly dominant individuals make up about 5 per cent of the population—not just among human beings, but in all animal groups. This 'dominant 5 per cent' is not made up of geniuses, or men of unusual talent—although these certainly belong to it. The dominant male—or female—may be merely a vicious bully, utterly stupid. But it seems generally true that most of these dominant people are highly sexed. The psychologist Abraham Maslow did researches into dominance and sexuality in women in the mid-1930s, and discovered that dominant females were promiscuous, sexually experimental (*i.e.,* had experimented with 'abnormal sex'), and liked rather brutal males who would hurl them on a bed and make love without sentimentality. In short, they liked highly dominant males. Maslow did not research into dominant males; but this since has been conducted (by Humphrey Knipe and George Maclay, for example, who publish their findings in *The Dominant Man*), and it reveals that male dominance patterns are basically similar. But what has not yet been fully investigated is the matter of relative dominance. Even within the 'dominant 5 per cent', there are obviously three clear groupings: averagely dominant people who stand out among their fellows and achieve some degree of leadership (foreman, shop-steward, sergeant-major . . .); unusually talented and dominant men, who actually achieve 'eminence'—Hamsun is a good example, and so are hundreds of other men you would find in reference books on literature, science, technology; finally, the tiny group of unusual men such as appear only once in a generation: Caesar, Beethoven, Einstein, Dante. But there are many males who, though not unusually talented, yet seem to belong by right to the second group—or perhaps just below it. For example a great many founders of crank religious organisations seem to belong to this group. There was the Rev. Henry Prince, who, in the early 19th century, announced he was the prophet Elijah, bought an estate near Bridgewater with money supplied by disciples, and set up a religious cult whose chief distinction was that all attractive female disciples were regarded as part of his harem. Prince's successor, John Smyth-Piggott, took over the church and also the 'pastoral' duties. In America in 1903, Franz Creffield announced that he was the prophet Joshua, established a 'Garden of Eden' facing the Pacific, and bestowed his sexual favours on the female adorers. After World War II, an ex-boilermaker named Francis Pencovic established The Fountain of the World in the San Fernando Valley; he was finally blown up by two disgruntled ex-followers whose wives he had seduced. And the French magazine *Detective* for June 1974 reports on the case of Paul Baumann, Grand Master of the religious order of Methernitha; his followers were housed in a multitude of chalets near Linden, in Switzerland, and he paid particular attention to the purification of teenage female followers—which involved licking them from head to foot, then making love to them. One such girl reports that he had made love to at least fifty girls between twelve and fifteen years of age.

Am I, then, suggesting that Jack the Ripper was another unbalanced messiah? Not quite. I am only trying to point out that there is a certain class of dominant male—to which the Ripper probably belonged—for whom sex is all-important, and who will go to very considerable lengths to get it. They belong to the 'medium' group of the dominant 5 per cent, but they are not possessors of unusual talent. It is as important for them to *dominate* as to achieve sexual intercourse; this is why the sub-group of promiscuous messiahs is so interesting, for it typifies this type of character. There *are* other males of this group who go in for simpler forms of conquest and dominance: the 'burning car murderer', Alfred Rouse, is an example. A commercial traveller, he finally became entangled with so many women that he had to 'disappear'—hence the plot to murder a stranger that led to his execution. Even more extraordinary is the Heidelberg hypnosis case of 1936; a confidence trickster, Franz Walter, who posed as a doctor, met a housewife on a train, and almost immediately hypnotised her, without her consent. On a subsequent occasion, he placed her in a trance, led her to his room, and raped her. He then induced her to sell herself to men and took her earnings, and later ordered her to make half a dozen attempts on her husband's life. Walter then ordered her to forget all her criminal acts. A hypnotist working for the police, Dr Ludwig Mayer, had the utmost difficulty in 'unlocking' her memory and untying Walter's complicated psychological knots. Walter was sentenced to ten years in prison. Mayer remarks that Walter was not an intelligent man, but a coarse commercial-traveller type with 'a gift of the gab'. That is to say, he was not *quite* talented or distinguished, but had an overpowering conviction that he ought to be.

All this is not as irrelevant as it may seem; it enables us to form some notion of the type of man who could have committed the Whitechapel murders. The old theory that he was a doctor reveals how little the Ripper's contemporaries understood of such things. In all the annals of sex-crime, I can recall only one—somewhat doubt-ful—example of a sadistic doctor: Neill Cream. But Cream was in-sane from an early stage. There have been several cases of doctors and dentists who have seduced patients under hypnosis or anaes-thetic, but these crimes are as unlike those of Jack the Ripper as can be. (It is for this reason that I would dismiss Sir William Gull as a suspect.) Leonard Matters, the Member of Parliament who wrote the first book on the Ripper, almost certainly invented his Dr Stanley theory (see Chapter 7); no shred of evidence for it has ever appeared. But again, it demonstrates the working of the ordinary, non-criminological imagination in trying to envisage the man who muti-lated Mary Kelly.

So, on the above evidence, what *can* we say about Jack the Ripper? That he was dominant, but not particularly intelligent or talented, and that he was also 'highly sexed'. A study of killers like Neill Cream and Béla Kiss enables us to form a more accurate picture of the kind of man who would have been capable of the Whitechapel murders. Both were 'satyrs' (the male version of a nymphomaniac). Cream told one prostitute that he lived only to indulge in women. And this is how Paul Tabori describes Kiss:

'Kiss was obviously a man of very strong sexual appetites, verging on satyriasis. It was his main preoccupation, and he needed a woman every day, if not several times a day. His potency must have been quite unusual; his entire life centred on the pursuit of feminine flesh.'

In the brothel quarter of Budapest, Kiss proved to be well-known, and no one had any complaints about him; he struck no one as ab-normal. Tabori goes on:

'He was a man of great physical strength . . . and almost finicky habits, washing his hands frequently, brushing his clothes, wiping his shoes as if being immaculate was the most important thing in his life. . . . He knew some poetry by heart and had a pleasant voice in which he sang snatches of ballads or sentimental hits. . . .'

Yet this was the man who murdered twenty or so women at his house in Cinkota, and put seven of them into petrol drums. Which raises the interesting question: how does a 'satyr' become a mass murderer? Kiss was never caught, so we cannot give the answer with any confidence; yet if we try to put ourselves into Kiss's state of mind, we begin to understand. Every female form that passes him in the street —from the age of ten to fifty—stirs his desire. He cannot exchange a word with any woman—a shopkeeper, a dentist's assistant, a lottery ticket seller—without forming a mental image of her removing her clothes for him. It often occurs to him that the world is full of millions of women he will never possess, and the thought causes a burning sensation in his stomach. . . .

In such a man, sexual desire always borders on the violent, because he regards women as 'throwaways'. The anonymous author of the book *Ravished Armenia*—describing the Turkish deportation and massacre of Armenians during World War I—relates a revealing incident. At an early stage in the deportation the Turks announced that any Armenian girls who chose to give themselves to Turkish officers would be spared. Many girls shamefacedly made their way to the officers' quarters. The next day they did not reappear, and their disembowelled bodies were subsequently found in the nearby river. They were also 'throwaways', and the killing constituted the final act of possession by the men who had ravished them. The same was true of Kiss, and probably of the American mass sex-killer H. H. Holmes, who murdered a long series of mistresses in his 'horror castle' in Chicago. Another interesting touch is the obsession with neatness—also characteristic of Holmes, Cream and Peter Kürten. It suggests what Freud calls an 'anal erotic', a man obsessed by trivial details because of some deep insecurity.

Finally, it is worth drawing attention to the Victorian underground classic *My Secret Life,* the anonymous autobiography of 'Walter', who thought of nothing but sex. These memoirs not only give us a chance to grasp how easy it was for a man to pick up women in any slum area of Victorian London; they also make us aware that there are some human beings who never grow up, never evolve, who spend their whole lives marking time on the one spot. Walter is by no means a sadist; but he is a coarse brute who stalks around the East End like a tiger looking for prey. Add a sadistic obsession with slashing bellies, and you have an accurate notion of the kind of man the Ripper *could* have been, and probably was.

In order to understand how a man like 'Walter'—or Béla Kiss— becomes transformed into a Ripper, we have to suppose that he is twisted with frustration and resentment, that at some point his self-esteem has been badly wounded. Perhaps when he leaves school he finds himself expected to earn a living without his having any particular qualifications to do so. He is what Shaw calls a 'downstart', someone whose natural path is down rather than up. Like Anthony Trollope—another downstart—he may even be forced to accept the lowest kind of clerkship in a City office or in the public service. (I think the City location likely, for it would have given him the opportunity to develop his obsession with Whitechapel, with its doss houses and low dives and cheap brothels.) And at some point he has a great deal of time on his hands, time to brood and fantasise so that his resentments swell to paranoid proportions. An interesting hypothesis presents itself—although it is nothing more than that. The place where such a man might have a great deal of time to brood is prison. What would he be doing in prison? Well, many sex killers have also been petty criminals—Vacher, Kürten, Heirens, Heath, Ian Brady. The Whitechapel killer may have committed some petty theft or swindle. But another possibility that suggests itself is that he had committed some offence against a prostitute. 'I am down on whores' says one of the letters that seems to be genuine, 'and I shant quit ripping them till I do get buckled.' Why? We might recall that the lifelong troubles of the Marquis de Sade began when he picked up a girl named Rose Keller, took her back to his country home, and flogged her. She escaped from an upper window with a rope of knotted sheets, and Sade went to prison and had to pay her a hundred louis; and again, three years later, another session with three prostitutes led to his arrest on a charge of sodomy and poisoning (with Spanish fly); he was sentenced to death, but escaped. De Sade poured his frustrations into writing while he was in prison. The Ripper undoubtedly possessed no gift for self-expression; his paranoid hatred came to centre on whores.

This is my own suggestion, and I regard it as no more than 'educated guesswork'. Still, if Mr Rumbelow, in his researches through the police archives, should come across the case of a man who spent some time in prison in 1887 for an offence against a prostitute, I would suggest that the matter deserves closer investigation. . . .

And what about those various suspects: Dr Stanley, Druitt, 'Jill the Ripper', the Jewish slaughterman, J. K. Stephen and the rest? Druitt *could* fit the 'psychological portrait' I have tried to draw. He was certainly a 'downstart', he had plenty of time for brooding in his rooms, waiting for clients who never came. We know that Druitt was

Macnaghten's chief suspect, and it seems clear from Macnaghten's notes (quoted by Rumbelow, for the first time in full) that Druitt's own family—probably his cousin Lionel—tipped off the police that he might be the Ripper. Dan Farson speaks of a pamphlet, 'Jack the Ripper—I Knew Him', by Lionel Druitt, printed in Australia. No copy has so far been found (I have even hired a researcher myself); but even if it *is* found, it will presumably only present Lionel Druitt's reasons for *suspecting* his cousin. Lionel could not have had proof, otherwise he would have offered it to the police. And Lionel's reasons may have been simply that his cousin behaved rather oddly—which is not surprising since he was shortly to commit suicide. There is no real evidence against Druitt so far.

J. K. Stephen, the Duke of Clarence's ex-tutor, is a more likely suspect: at least, the evidence against him is stronger. In his book *Clarence* Michael Harrison quotes several of Stephen's poems in full, and the hatred that boils out of them is definitely pathological. This was certainly a man who was twisted with an almost insane resentment. One poem describes a man on a train who accidentally stood on Stephen's foot, and the poem ends:

> May fiends with glowing pincers rend thy brain,
> And beetles batten on thy blackened face.

And the long poem about the woman he met walking—'loose-hipped, big-boned, disjointed, angular . . .'—is an incomprehensible scream of rage:

> I did not like her; and I should not mind
> If she were done away with, killed or ploughed.

It brings to mind similar stories of the mass-poisoner Graham Young, told by his sister, about the loathing of 'commonplace' people, especially women. Young committed several murders, for no particular motive, and once described himself as 'your friendly neighbourhood Frankenstein'. This is certainly getting altogether closer to the psychology of the pathological killer. And if we also take into account that Stephen suffered fits after a fall from a horse, and that he died insane, I think that he is certainly one of the likeliest suspects yet. On the other hand, there is once again no evidence whatever. . . .

And this is, perhaps, the real trouble with all the theories so far. The suspects may 'fit', but without that definite piece of evidence, this means nothing whatever. Let me conclude by giving a brief preview of the latest theories. The originator of one is Mr Thomas Toughill of Glasgow. Mr Toughill's researches have led him to conclude that the Ripper was Frank Miles, a homosexual artist who at one time lived with Oscar Wilde. He and Wilde separated in 1881, after Miles had got into some kind of fairly serious trouble, and Wilde had helped get him out of it. Robert Sherard told Hesketh Pearson that Miles was an exhibitionist who had a predilection for displaying himself to small girls. At the time he and Wilde separated Miles was on his way to becoming a highly successful and fashionable painter; but for some reason, his work 'failed to retain its hold on the fickle public' (in the words of one biographer), and he began to suffer from some sort of brain disease. He was committed to an asylum near Bristol in December 1887, and in the March of the following year the *Magazine of Art* announced his death. This would seem to settle the matter, since the Ripper murders began later the same year. In fact, Mr Toughill has established that Miles died of general paralysis of the insane in July 1891. He has established some curious connections between Miles and the Duke of Clarence—Frank's cousin was the Duke's equerry—and also, oddly enough, with Montague Druitt, whose brother was in Miles's regiment, and Sir Melville Macnaghten was a neighbour of Wilde—and of Miles—in Tite Street.

But where is the *evidence* that Miles could have been the Ripper? It is true that he was known for his habit of picking up young women off the streets as models, but this does not make him a murderer. Mr Toughill turns to Wilde's novel *The Picture of Dorian Gray* (1891), and argues—very persuasively—that Dorian was based on Miles (who died in the year the book was published) and that Wilde knew Miles to be Jack the Ripper, and dropped clues about it in the novel—for example, Dorian's murder of the painter Basil Hallward with a knife. I shall not offer more detail here, for Mr Toughill intends to publish his theory himself. But it seems to me that the old objection still applies: that no matter how much 'corroborative evidence' can be supplied, it *must* be inconclusive unless one can prove some definite connection between the suspect and one of those bodies in Whitechapel. It seems to me that identifying suspects who *could* have been Jack the Ripper is a waste of time, since London at the time must have been full of people who could have been the Ripper. Perhaps the right approach is to study other cases of sadistic murder for parallels to the Ripper case, to attempt to draw a composite portrait of the Ripper, and *then* look for someone to fit it.

And finally—only a few days before this book goes to press—there is news of a theory that could provide the solution of the mystery of the Ripper. The theory, which is to be published in Nigel Morland's magazine *The Criminologist,* is not quite new; the candidate is the poisoner Neill Cream, whose last words on the gallows were: 'I am Jack the . . .'—at which point the trap fell. As Mr Rumbelow has pointed out, the objection to the Cream theory is that Cream was at the time serving a prison sentence in Chicago.

The new theory apparently disputes this. The Chicago of 1888 was a notoriously corrupt city; Cream would have had no difficulty bribing his way out of jail. But perhaps the most interesting corroboration of the theory comes from Donald Davis, one of Britain's leading handwriting experts. Davis has examined Cream's handwriting, and the handwriting on two of the Ripper letters—including the one beginning 'From Hell, Mr Lusk', and has asserted that he has no doubt whatever that they were written by the same hand.

Of course, even if this were proved beyond all doubt, it would still not prove that Cream was the Ripper. But it would certainly make him the most likely suspect so far.

I do not wish to be discouraging, but I think we should also bear in mind that if Peter Kürten, Fritz Haarmann, Charles Manson, had escaped detection, we could discuss their crimes forever without getting any closer to their identity. They would retain their anonymity. The Ripper may have been a nondescript little man of whose existence nothing is now known.

In conclusion, I should tell the reader something about the remarkable man who is the author of this book. He has already established a permanent place for himself in the ranks of literary detectives since he solved the 'Sidney Street case'. Ever since that famous siege, and the trial of anarchists that followed, it has been doubtful whether the men who died in the burning building were the men who killed three policemen when escaping from Houndsditch a month earlier; in his book *The Houndsditch Murders,* Mr Rumbelow finally established that the chief culprit *was* acquitted, and subsequently became one of Stalin's chief hatchet men. He was able to do this by taking advantage of his position as a member of the City Police force to inspect the archives and review all the known facts.

I first heard of this literary criminologist from Dan Farson, who told me that Don Rumbelow had accidentally saved the morgue photographs of the Ripper's victims from destruction, and that they had been published in a police journal. A week or so later, I met him —on a late-night television programme, when we joined Dan Farson and Michael Harrison to discuss Harrison's newly published theory that Stephen was Jack the Ripper. I expected him to be one of those middle-aged, square-jawed detectives who write books with titles like *My Years at the Yard,* so I was surprised to meet a young, powerfully-built man with a good-natured face and an easy social charm.

Like most people who have just been introduced to him, I asked him how he became a writer. The story was amusing. He was on night duty one night in 1966 down by the Mermaid Theatre, and as he passed each locked door, he placed his hand against it and shoved it gently—the standard test to see if some miscreant has forced it open and is now lurking inside. After the fiftieth time or so, he became careless and shoved too hard. The door flew open, and he found himself sprawling across the threshold of Sally Miles, the daughter of Bernard Miles. She and her husband Gerald Frow, were unalarmed at the sudden apparition, and offered him a cup of tea. They became friendly, met often, and finally the Frows suggested that he might string together some of his anecdotes about cops and robbers into a play. The play, called *Lobsters and Bowmen,* was produced at the Horseshoe Wharf Club in 1966. Someone in the force then suggested that he might write a history of the City police force—after all, England's police force originated in the City of London. The result was his first book, *I Spy Blue,* a delightful and skilful piece of work that reveals him as a born writer. The classic *Houndsditch Murders* followed, and the present book is his third. The fact that he is a policeman gives him an unusual insight into the crime he is writing about and, as far as I know, makes him quite unique among literary criminologists. Many detectives have written good books about their own cases, but these have been basically autobiographical. It seems that most people who write about crime—like myself—are amateur criminologists who approach it from a rather literary point of view, and most policemen look on this approach with kindly contempt. Crime writers do not resent this; I think that most of us have a slight inferiority complex in the face of the down-to-earth realism of the policeman. Donald Rumbelow has become a kind of liaison officer between the two worlds: an arrangement which should be to the benefit of both. I do not know how high he will rise in the police hierarchy; but I think he is set to become one of the most interesting and authoritative criminologists of our time.

COLIN WILSON.

July, 1974.

1

OUTCAST LONDON

'This street is in the East End': so begins Arthur Morrison's *Tales of Mean Streets,* which is about life at the end of the nineteenth century. 'There is no need to say in the East End of what. The East End is a vast city, as famous in its way as any the hand of man has made. But who knows the East End? It is down through Cornhill and out beyond Leadenhall Street and Aldgate Pump, one will say; a shocking place, where he once went with a curate; an evil plexus of slums that hide human creeping things; where filthy men and women live on penn'orths of gin, where collars and clean shirts are decencies unknown, where every citizen wears a black eye, and none ever combs his hair. The East End is a place, says another, which is given over to the Unemployed. And the Unemployed is a race whose token is a clay pipe, and whose enemy is soap; now and again it migrates bodily to Hyde Park with banners, and furnishes adjacent police courts with disorderly drunks. Still another knows the East End only as the place whence begging letters come; there are coal and blanket funds there, all perennially insolvent, and everybody else wants a day in the country. Many and misty are people's notions of the East End; and each is commonly but the distorted shadow of a minor feature.'

It is a place as foreign to us now as it was to the average Victorian. Nine hundred thousand slum dwellers existed east of Aldgate Pump. The East End was outcast London. There was a feeling that it was separated topographically from the rest of the metropolis as well as spiritually and economically. Its people were as strange as the African pygmies and the Polynesian natives with whom they were often equated by journalists and sociologists who wished to draw attention to its problems. So little was known about them, until slumming became fashionable in the 1870s and 1880s, that an educated woman who was visiting St George's-in-the-East in the seventies remarked with some astonishment on the fact that the people didn't sleep

squatting against a wall, and that they lived in houses and not in railway carriages, as she had expected!

For the greater part of Victoria's reign, the East End was ignored
by the Church. Occasional lip service was paid to the needs of the
'lapsed masses' but very little practical help was ever given them. An
impact was beginning to be made on some of the area's major social
problems by philanthropists and private charities when the Rev
Samuel Barnett and his wife moved to St Jude's vicarage in 1873. The
previous incumbent was still in residence and too ill to be moved,
so they were forced to take temporary lodgings nearby. The landlady had some careless habits: she apologised one day for not serving Mr Barnett his usual rice pudding as a mouse had drowned in it!
Many years later, there was still a rasp in Mrs Barnett's voice when
she retold the story for her memoirs.

Their church, St Jude's was an isolated and empty one. At the
first Sunday service there was a congregation of six or seven old
women who all expected some dole for attending. The newly hired
organist played tunes on a damp stained piano and Mrs Barnett, who
could not sing a note in tune, led the hymn singing. Most of their
parishioners had been lured away by the Sunday street market in
Middlesex Street (Petticoat Lane), where card sharps, thimble rig-
gers and swindlers of all sorts, as well as men seeking casual work,
went in their thousands hoping to get enough money to see them
through the week. Equally disgraceful to Mrs Barnett were the herds
of cattle goaded through the streets of Whitechapel each week to the
slaughterhouses in and around Aldgate. Sometimes the horns would
catch in the spokes of moving wheels, the animals, maddened with
pain and fear, would scramble onto the pavement scattering the
crowds. At the slaughterhouses, which were often ordinary shops,
the sheep would be dragged in backwards by their legs and the bul-
locks hounded in by dogs and blows, while small boys clustered ex-
citedly round the door and passers-by stepped their way as best they
could through the blood and urine flooding the pavement.

Mr Barnett's parish was bounded by the City on the west and
Whitechapel High Street, where there were forty shopkeepers and
their families, on the south. Apart from the lessees of some large
warehouses in Commercial Street and several rows of well kept cottages tenanted by Jews, the bulk of his parishioners were crowded
into a network of courts and alleys, none of which was intersected
by any roads. All these courts stank from the accumulated piles of
rags and rubbish and a miasma of liquid sewage that flooded the

cellars of each house. At the end of each court there might be a solitary standpipe to provide the only source of fresh water.

Most of the rooms in these houses were let out to single families at eightpence a night. In 1883 the chairman of the London School Board reported that out of three schools that were surveyed of children from 1129 families, 871 families had only one room to live in and in the majority of cases the number of people sharing with them was as many as five and, in some cases, as high as nine. The broken windows were frequently stuffed with rags or covered with papers (they were rarely opened because of the smells outside, and because the wretches who lived in them were badly clothed and couldn't be exposed to draughts. In Wentworth Street, a daily procession of waggons carted their uncovered piles of rubbish to the dust destructor which Mrs Barnett renamed the dust distributor because of the clouds of dust it vomited out and the way it choked the drains.) In some cases, these 'repairs' might be enough to justify the landlord's charging an extra threepence a week for rent! The average number of people in each room was generally between five and seven. In the house at 35 Hanbury Street, typical of the parish, there were seven people in each room with adult sons and daughters sleeping on the floor. In none of the rooms was there more than one bedstead, and the only w.c. was on the ground floor. This was normally in such a filthy state that the tenants used their chamber pots which, said the Rev R. C. Billing, giving evidence to a House of Commons Select Committee, were left in the rooms for a very long time before being taken down and emptied in the yard. Staircase bannisters had often been removed for firewood and it was a common sight to see vermin-infested wallpaper hanging in strips from the walls. What furniture there was might consist of the broken-down remains of an old bedstead or table but was more likely a wooden board across some bricks, or an old hamper or box turned upside down; the bed might be a sack of flea-infested straw.

Andrew Mearns in *The Bitter Cry of Outcast London* pulled few punches:

Every room in these rotten and reeking tenements houses a family, often two. In one cellar a sanitary inspector reports finding a father, mother, three children, and four pigs! In another room a missionary found a man ill with small-pox, his wife just recovering from her eighth confinement, and the children running about half naked and covered with dirt. Here are seven people living in one underground kitchen, and a little dead child lying in the same room. Elsewhere is a poor widow, her three children, and a child who had been dead thirteen days. Her husband, who was a cabman, had shortly before committed suicide. Here lives a widow and her six children, two of them who are ill with scarlet fever. In another, nine brothers and sisters, from 29 years of age downwards, live, eat and sleep together. Here is a mother who turns her children into the street in the early evening because she lets her room for immoral purposes until long after midnight, when the poor little wretches creep back again if they have not found some miserable shelter elsewhere. Where there are beds they are simply heaps of dirty rags, shavings or straw, but for the most part these miserable beings find rest only upon the filthy boards. The tenant of this room is a widow, who herself occupies the only bed, and lets the floor to a married couple for 2s. 6d. per week. In many cases matters are made worse by the unhealthy occupations followed by those who dwell in these habitations. Here you are choked as you enter by the air laden with particles of the superfluous fur pulled from the skins of rabbits, rats, dogs and other animals in their preparation for the furrier. Here the smell of paste and of drying match-boxes, mingling with other sickly odours, overpowers you; or it may be the fragrance of stale fish or vegetables, not sold on the previous day, and kept in the room overnight. Even when it is possible to do so the people seldom open their windows, but if they did it is questionable whether much would be gained, for the external air is scarcely less heavily charged with poison than the atmosphere within.

The population for Whitechapel was about 80,000 people. For the East End as a whole the figure was about 900,000. Charles Booth broke these figures down into several categories. At the bottom were the occasional labourers, loafers and semi-criminals. Above them were the 'very poor' and the 'poor'. The word 'poor' he defined as those who had a meagre but regular income of between 18 shillings and 21 shillings a week, and the 'very poor' were those whose income fell below this level. The former struggled to make both ends meet and the latter lived in a state of chronic want. The condition of the lowest class of all, which doesn't get a rating, can be imagined. At a rough guess there were about 11,000 of them—about 1¼ per cent of the total population. This figure includes the 'dossers' and the homeless outcasts who slept on staircases, in doorways and even in dustbins and lavatories for warmth. Their lives, Booth said, were the lives of savages, 'with vicissitudes of extreme hardship and occasional excess.' Their food was of the coarsest, and their only luxury was drink. It was not easy to say how they lived. When they could not find threepence for a night's lodging they were turned out into the street. Booth wrote of them: 'They render no useful service, they create no wealth; more often they destroy it. They degrade whatever they touch, and as individuals are perhaps incapable of improvement. . . .' Their children were often the ragged street arabs who might be found, separated from their parents, in pauper schools or in homes such as Dr Barnardo's.

The 'very poor' added up to about 100,000 or 11¼ per cent of the total population. Three-quarters of them were women and children; children under 15 numbered about 38,000 and young persons aged between 15 and 20 about 9,000. This category lay between the hammer and the anvil of the outcast poor and the poor. When trade was bad the market was flooded with labour from the categories above, so the casual earnings for which they fought to exist were liable to disappear completely. The women often worked for people as poor as themselves, scrubbing floors, washing and doing needlework.

The 'poor' numbered about 75,000 persons or 8 per cent of the population. This category consisted of men whose jobs were seasonal, such as builders who could only work eight or nine months in the year, or dockers, who might get only one or two days' work a week. Included too were the other victims of a competitive market, the poorer artisans, street sellers and small shopkeepers. Some of the men on casual work could earn as much as 15 or 20 shillings a week by heaving coal, carrying grain or carting timber, but often this was done at the cost of great physical exhaustion resulting in very heavy eating and drinking and with little money left over at the end of the day to take home. Booth wrote:

The poor fellows are miserably clad, scarcely with a boot on their foot, in a most miserable state; and they cannot run, their boots would not permit them. . . . there are men who come on to work in our docks (and if with us, to a much greater extent elsewhere) who have come on without having a bit of food in their stomachs, perhaps since the previous day; they have worked for an hour and have earned 5d. in order that they may get food, perhaps the first food they have had for 24 hours. Many people complain about dock labourers that they will not work after four o'clock. But really, if you consider, it is natural. These poor men come on work without a farthing in their pockets; they have not anything to eat in the middle of the day; some of them will raise or have a penny, and buy a little fried fish, and by 4 p.m. their strength is utterly gone; they pay themselves off; it is absolute necessity that compels them.

The commonest work was sweat shop tailoring. For trouser finishing (sewing) linings, making button holes and stitching on the buttons a woman might get twopence ha'penny a pair and have to buy her own thread. For making men's shorts they were paid tenpence a dozen, lawn tennis aprons threepence a dozen, and babies' hoods from 1s. 6d. to 2s. 6d. a dozen. In St George's-in-the-East women and children, some only seven years old, were employed as sackmakers and earning a farthing for each one they made. Sometimes women could earn a penny or twopence a peck by shelling peas, or twopence farthing a gross matchbox making, but out of this they would have to buy the string and the paste. None of these earnings would give them more than tenpence or a shilling a day, and might mean seventeen hours' work.

Life in such circumstances had to be lived on a day-to-day or, better still, an hourly basis. Food was bought for immediate consumption. In one family, Booth found, they would buy nothing until it was actually needed. 'They go to their shop as an ordinary housewife to her canisters; twice a day they buy tea, or three times if they make it so often; in 35 days they made 72 purchases of tea, amounting in all to 5s. 2¾d., and all most carefully noted down. The "pinch of tea" costs ¾d. [no doubt this was ½ oz. at 2s. per lb.]. Of sugar there were 77 purchases in the same time.'

Couples could struggle along on a hand to mouth existence until children came along. (The most common forms of contraception were syringeing, the vaginal sponge, coitus interruptus and the safe period.) Most children were physically and mentally underdeveloped —that is, those who did not die in childbirth. Fifty-five per cent of East End children died before they were five. One-tenth of elementary school children were estimated later to be mentally defective or unnaturally dull. Children frequently came to school crying with hunger and fell off their seats from exhaustion. In winter they could not learn because they were too cold.

Some sort of financial relief was always expected from the church when times were hardest. The Rev Barnett made it plain from the beginning that this accustomed palliative could not be expected from him. Indiscriminate charity, he argued, was one of the curses of London. He went so far as to claim that the poor starved 'because of the alms they receive'. Demands for money were often accompanied by lies and followed by threats of violence when it was not forthcoming. Sometimes the applicants would stop passers-by and crowds would gather outside the vicarage. Frequently the vicarage was under siege and had its windows broken with stones. Eventually a door had to be cut into the church so that the vicar could have an escape route to fetch police reinforcements. His inflexibility on this point was based on a firm-held belief that suffering would be reduced not by indiscriminately handing out money but only by making a realistic appraisal of each man's problems and then giving practical help to meet them. In its simplest form, this was an exhortation to thrift and better money management but, as Jack London angrily pointed out in *The People of the Abyss,* to be thrifty the man had 'to spend less than his income—in other words, to live on less.' He went on:

This is equivalent to a lowering of the standard of living. In the competition for a chance to work, the man with a lower standard of living will underbid the man with a higher standard. And a small group of such thrifty workers in any overcrowded industry will permanently lower the wages of that industry. And the thrifty ones will no longer be thrifty, for their income will have been reduced till it balances their expenditure. In short, thrift negates thrift. . . . And anyway, it is sheer bosh and nonsense to preach thrift to the 1,800,000 London workers who are divided into families which have a total income of less than 21s. per week, one-quarter to one-half of which must be paid for rent.

A start was made on the problems of overcrowding with the passing of the Artisans Dwelling Act in 1875. This Act empowered the two governing bodies for London, the City of London Corporation (for the one square mile only) and the Metropolitan Board to buy up slum property, demolish it and resell the land for working-class accommodation. The actual financing of the new properties was left to the commercial dwelling companies and private philanthropists. In no way was the scheme meant to impinge on the widely held belief that it was wrong for the state to finance schemes for people who, for whatever reason, hadn't imbibed and practised the principles of self-help.

The next year, in Whitechapel alone, four thousand homes were condemned as uninhabitable. Demolitions did not take place for another four and, in the meantime, until they were evicted, the tenants suffered even more than usual as their living conditions steadily deteriorated and the landlords refused to carry out repairs. Ironically, it was soon realised that the Act, instead of penalising the slum landlords, would leave them even better off than before. Profits were so great that there was a rash of speculation in slum property which even tempted some of the reformers who had been urging for years that the properties they were now buying should be pulled down. Compensation had to take into account all the factors affecting the value. This was an open incitement to the landlords to cram even more people into their crumbling tenements and to claim even more by way of lost rents. In the Goulston Street scheme in Whitechapel, the property and land was bought for £371,600 but, because of the conditions imposed by Parliament under which it had to be sold, the auction price when it was resold was a meagre £87,600. The overall loss was catastrophic. Forty-two acres had been bought for £1,661,-372. The loss, because the land was sold for homes and not for offices, was a staggering £1,100,000!

Within a very short time, both the City of London Corporation and the Metropolitan Board were urging that the terms of the Act should be changed and that they should not have to sell the land for unprofitable housing. In two years the City had cleared out nearly two thousand people from the slums on the north fringe of the City; these were people so bad, it was said, that no policeman would dare go among them at night. The sites were left vacant. The City refused to sell them for housing because the commercial value was so high.

In 1879 the Act was amended to allow the two authorities to rehouse those that they had evicted elsewhere. In reality, they only added to the overcrowding.

In the meantime, private philanthropists such as Octavia Hill were buying up properties and finding ways of making them yield a steady 5 per cent return. There was still the same gross overcrowding in these properties but there was at least a security of tenure for the better-off artisan. But this was dependent on prompt payment of rent. Failure to pay, for any reason, meant instant eviction. Yet it was only by occasionally evading payment or going hungry that they could afford to buy clothes and necessary household items. The philanthropists viewed the problem quite differently. They thought that these ruthless methods would force the tenants to practise those principles of thrift that were always being advocated by Mr Barnett and the lady rent collectors who called each week. Unfortunately it did not allow for the frequent periods when the men were laid off work, not through any fault of their own, but through trade recession or seasonal slackness. For the better-off artisan, there was a chance that, in the long term, he would be able to move out of his one room and into two, and that his children could be trained for something better. This was the only level at which this scheme may have worked. No figures are available for the number of failures and evictions. Probably they were quite high. Others who tried to work the same scheme did not have much success. One landlord complained bitterly of the dirty and destructive habits of the low strata of humanity which he had been forced to accept as tenants. Lamentably, none of them had absorbed the principles of self help.

Most of those who had been displaced by the redevelopments and clearances were dockers, costermongers, watermen and lightermen. Some were offered accommodation in the model Peabody dwellings but few of them could pay the high rents of four shillings a week. Instead they were forced to pack into already overcrowded accommodations or live on the streets and sleep, when they had the money, in the common lodging houses or seek refuge in the workhouse. In the summer months many of them slept out of doors, but between November and April the streets were generally clear. Even then, there was always a residue left—as Jack London discovered when he visited Christchurch Gardens, Spitalfields, nearly thirty years later: 'A chill, raw wind was blowing, and these creatures huddled there in their rags, sleeping for the most part, or trying to sleep. Here were a dozen women, ranging in age from twenty years to seventy. Next a babe, possibly of nine months, lying asleep, flat on the hard bench, with neither pillow nor covering, nor with anyone looking after it. Next half-a-dozen men, sleeping bolt upright or leaning against one another in their sleep. In one place a family group, a child asleep in its sleeping mother's arms, and the husband (or male mate) clumsily mending a dilapidated shoe. On another bench a woman trimming the frayed strips of her rags with a knife, and another woman, with thread and needle, sewing up rents. Adjoining, a man holding a sleeping woman in his arms. Farther on, a man, his clothing caked with gutter mud, asleep, with head in the lap of a woman, not more than twenty-five years old, and also asleep.'

The women, his guide told him, would sell themselves 'for thru'pence, or tu'pence, or a loaf of stale bread'.

The Lancet, in fact, had estimated that in 1857 one house in every sixty in London was a brothel and one woman in every sixteen a whore. If true, this meant that there were six thousand brothels in the capital and about eighty thousand prostitutes.

In October 1888, the Metropolitan Police estimated that there were about twelve hundred prostitutes, of a very low class, in Whitechapel. From figures supplied by the beat men they thought that there were about sixty-two brothels. Probably there was an even greater number of houses that were being used intermittently for the same purpose. Until fairly recently it had always been customary for several prostitutes to share the cost of hiring a lodging-house room to which they could take their men. In 1851 a new Act made such hirings almost impossible, since its terms gave the police the right to search the common lodging houses. If exposed, the owners and lodging-house keepers risked criminal charges of keeping or permitting a disorderly house. Although prostitutes continued to take customers to the lodging houses, things weren't quite so blatant as before. Generally couples just shared a double bed. They had very little privacy. The beds were in the dormitories and had screens or partitions, which were open at the top and bottom, pulled around them. Naturally the women preferred renting a room in a private house, if they could afford it, as—privacy apart—the police did not have immediate right of entry into private property. Any prosecutions had to be carried out by the local vestries. As this could be a very expensive business few of them ever did so. The only vestry which made any attempt to suppress the brothels in its area was Mile End, where a police pensioner was hired to collect the evidence and prosecute the owners. Two streets were cleared of brothels in this way but in the long term the only result it brought about was to increase sharply the number of prostitutes who harried and molested men in the streets.

The crude economic necessity that drove women to 'sail along on their bottoms' was generally glossed over with a wishy-washy sentiment that they had fallen because they had been betrayed by a wealthy seducer. A survey carried out by a prison chaplain in 1890 found that, of the sixteen thousand women the chaplain had interviewed, over eleven thousand had taken the plunge deliberately and only 4 per cent—less than seven hundred—had been seduced. The age of consent was then thirteen, but prior to 1875 it had been twelve. (In Hanbury Street, Whitechapel, there was a Salvation Army refuge for young girls, many of them ten, eleven and twelve.)

Given the overcrowded homes incest was inevitable and common. Generally it was between father and daughter or brother and sister. Lord Salisbury told the story of a friend who was going down a slum court when he 'saw on the pavement two children of tender years, of ten or eleven years old, endeavouring to have sexual connection on the pathway. He ran and seized the lad, and pulled him off, and the only remark of the lad was, "Why do you take hold of me? There are a dozen of them at it down there." You must perceive that that could not arise from sexual tendencies, and that it must have been bred by imitation of what they saw.'

Not many couples bothered to get married. Often it was a question of simple economics. Much to Mr Barnett's disgust the 'Red Church', as he called it, in Bethnal Green Road was prepared to marry couples free of charge. His objection was that it was wrong to start married life with a lie, for couples had to say that they lived in the parish and this—in most cases—was simply not true. On a more light-hearted occasion, a lady philanthropist had finally managed to persuade a common law husband and wife to get married, as much for their own sake as for the sake of their children, and made the arrangements for their wedding. On the day of the ceremony the couple didn't turn up and, in a towering rage, she went to their house to find out why not. The woman told her that her man had been offered five shillings for a carting job and that that was much more important.

Couples, married or not, often lived for years in the lodging houses on a day-to-day basis. There were 233 common lodging houses in Whitechapel accommodating 8,500 persons. Often they were 'the resorts of thieves and vagabonds of the lowest type, and some are kept by receivers of stolen goods. In the kitchen men and women may be seen cooking their food, washing their clothes, or lolling about smoking and gambling. In the sleeping room are long rows of beds on each side, sometimes sixty or eighty in one room'. Generally these were a mixture of single and double beds for both men and women. A double bed was eightpence a night and a single bed fourpence. In some lodging houses there was the compromise of a twopenny rope lean-to; this was a rope stretched across the room for the men to lean on and on which they had to sleep as best as they could! If the women hadn't earned enough money by selling flowers, washing clothes, or scrubbing floors, but had enough money for their bread and beer, but not enough for a bed, they could generally count on finding someone who would let them sleep with them in return for some casual sex.

Each lodging house was generally visited once a week by a lodging-house police sergeant. He might just as well have stayed away. The time of his visit was always known in advance and it was always in the daytime, when the dormitories were empty—never at night when they were crowded with 'dossers' and with mattresses laid out on the floors between the beds. During his inspection he had to count the number of beds, see that the rooms were tidied and dusted and that the slops had been emptied. The lodging-house owners nearly always lived elsewhere in the vicinity. During the daytime they stored any extra beds and blankets in their houses. A deputy, who was generally a ticket-of-leave man, was left in nominal charge. In spite of these inspections, the conditions inside the lodging houses were often quite grim. In one a police inspector reported that 'The place was swarming with vermin, large blocks of creeping things having been taken out from the walls and ceilings. The bedsteads and bedding were also swarming with insects, and disgusting in the extreme.'

Most 'dossers' had casual jobs, and any work they did was generally badly done. Such money as they earned was spent on basics such as bread, margarine, tea and sugar. Meals cost on average a penny threefarthings a head. In late summer, some thirty thousand Londoners went hop picking in Sussex and Kent. Some went by train and others 'padded the hoof'. Generally the period when they went coincided with the slack period in the docks. It was the nearest thing that most of them ever had to a holiday. It also coincided with the August slackness in many other trades. Better still the work was family work. Every child who could walk was wanted. Those over twelve could easily earn 1s. 6d. to 2s. 6d. a day for three weeks' work.

Even when they had some money, few of them would try to put any by for the hard times that followed the next day or the next week. As well as being a brutal and rootless way of life, it was also a careless existence, with tomorrow never coming. Life as they lived it was boldly set out in a statement made by a seaman, James Saddler, when he was arrested for the murder of a prostitute, Frances Coles, in Whitechapel in 1891. As she had been ripped in the by now familiar manner, he was suspected of being not only her murderer but also Jack the Ripper.

In the statement made after his arrest, he said that he had been discharged from his ship at 7 p.m. on 11 February and, after a drink, had fixed up some lodgings. He had then gone to the 'Princess Alice' where he saw a prostitute named Frances Coles. He'd picked her up in Whitechapel Road some eighteen months earlier, on another shore leave, and had spent the night with her at a lodging house in Thrawl Street. Beckoning her over he asked her to have a drink. She said she would rather go on somewhere else because whenever she was flush the other 'Princess Alice' customers expected her to spend the money with them. After an evening's drinking in other pubs in the area and buying half a pint of whisky to take home with them (Saddler later got twopence worth of drink for returning the bottle), they finished the night in an eightpenny double, and stayed in the lodging house until almost noon the next day.

Drinking was resumed as soon as they got up. They visited several more pubs, including 'The Bell' in Middlesex Street where they stayed for about two hours, drinking and laughing. Frances had by now wheedled out of Saddler a promise to buy her a hat. At the shop in Baker's Row he gave her half a crown and waited for her while she went inside to buy it. As some elastic had to be stitched on before the hat was ready for wear, they waited in a nearby pub and had some more drinks until it was time for Frances to return and collect it.

At this point there was some suspicion that she arranged for Saddler to be mugged later that afternoon and, in the circumstances, it seems more than likely that this was so.

When she returned with the hat Saddler made her try it on. He told her to throw her old hat away but this she wouldn't do and she pinned it instead to her dress. It was still hanging there when her body was later found that night with the throat cut and the stomach disembowelled.

By now Saddler was beginning to feel somewhat drunk. They continued drinking in the 'Marlborough Head' in Brick Lane and afterwards he remembered that the landlady objected to Frances being there but he could not say why. It was soon afterwards, as they were walking down Thrawl Street, that he was mugged. A woman in a red shawl hit him on the head and knocked him down. As he tried to get up he was surrounded by several men who put the boot in and robbed him of his money and watch. They escaped by running into a lodging house. Saddler, when he managed to stagger to his feet, had a raging quarrel with Frances (it was this that led to his arrest) as he thought that the least she could have done was to help him when he was down.

As he was now penniless and had not got the money to pay for a bed, he went back to the docks to try and get on board his ship. He was in a foul mood and swore at the men on the dock gates and at some passing dockers who threatened to give him a good hiding if the young policeman who was standing nearby would only turn his back. He did more than that. He walked away and after he had turned the corner one of the dockers, to whom Saddler had been particularly abusive, made a dead set at him. Saddler was knocked down and kicked and would have been badly injured if his attacker had not been forcibly restrained from doing him further injury. Saddler managed to stagger to a lodging house in East Smithfield, where he was known, and begged and pleaded with the night porter to let him have a bed. When he saw that pleading was useless, he hobbled back to the lodging house in Dorset Street where he'd spent the night before with Frances, and found her in the kitchen with her head on her arms. She was fuddled with drink and, like himself, didn't have any money, not even a farthing, to pay for a bed. Hopefully, Saddler told her that he had £4 15s. ship money coming to him. But when he tried to persuade the lodging-house deputy to let him have a bed on the strength of it, he was thrown out of the lodging although Frances was allowed to stay there.

Saddler set off for the London Hospital to have his injuries seen to. En route he was stopped by a policeman who told him that he looked a pretty pickle. Saddler grumbled that he'd had 'two doings over' that day and that he'd been cut and knocked about with a knife or bottle. Immediately he mentioned the word 'knife' the constable said 'Oh, have you a knife about you?' and searched him in spite of Saddler's protests that he never carried one. Afterwards the policeman helped him across the road to the hospital gate! The porter hummed and hawed about letting him in but eventually did so in spite of the abuse that Saddler hurled at his head. His head was bandaged up and he was allowed to spend the rest of the night on a couch in the Accident Ward until morning when he was turned out. Once more he went to his regular lodgings and begged yet again for the loan of a few pence. Again he was unlucky. He had to wait until the shipping office was open before he could get the £4 15s. that he was owed. The first thing he did was to pay for a bed. He slept and moodily drank by himself and didn't go out for the next twenty-four hours until he was arrested and accused of murdering Frances the night before.

Without any money, anyone who was down and out had no choice but to go into the workhouse if he wanted to live. In spite of the unpleasant regime it did offer a chance of survival. Queuing usually began early in the day and the admissions, starting in the afternoon, were taken in three at a time. Jack London's experiences in 1902, as related in *The People of the Abyss,* were of the system *after* it had been improved and not, as might easily be supposed from his account of the conditions, as they were *before.* On entering he was given a loaf of bread which, he says, felt like a brick, and was searched for knives, matches and tobacco which casuals such as he were not permitted to have. In the cellar to which he was first sent, the light was very dim. Most of the men were wearily taking off their shoes and unwrapping the bandages from their blistered feet. For food he was given a pannikin three-quarters filled with skilly, a mixture of Indian corn and hot water. He gave it away as the sight and smell of it turned his stomach. He had no better luck with his bread. It was so hard that he had to soften it with water before he could bite it. Most of the men, when they came to eat their own, dipped it into the piles of salt that were scattered about the dirty tables.

At 7 p.m. they were forced to take their baths in pairs. Twenty-two men washed in the same tub of water. London blanched when he saw that one man's back was 'a mass of blood from attacks of vermin and retaliatory scratching'. Afterwards his clothes were taken away and he was given a night-shirt and a couple of blankets to roll up in. In a long narrow dormitory lengths of canvas were stretched between two iron rails on the ground, each strip about six inches apart and eight inches off the floor. These were the beds. London tried unsuccessfully to sleep. He listened wistfully to the children playing outside in the street, and then dozed off about midnight but was woken up by a rat on his chest. His shouts woke everyone else up and he was roundly cursed by them all.

At 6 a.m. they were made to get up and after a further meal of skilly, which London again gave away, the men were given various jobs to do. In some workhouses the work was both punitive and mindless. Stone might have to be pounded into a fine dust and sieved through a grill in the wall at the end of the room. London was included in the work party that was sent to the Whitechapel Infirmary to do scavenger work.

'Don't touch it mate, the nurse sez it deadly', warned one of the men as London held open a sack into which a garbage can was being emptied. Waste food had to be collected from the sick wards, and London had to carry the sackloads down five flights of stairs and empty them into waste bins which were immediately sprinkled with disinfectant. When the work was done they were given tea and some

scraps of food that London unable to conceal his disgust, described
as

> . . . heaped high on a huge platter in an indescribable mess—
> pieces of bread, chunks of grease and fat pork, the burnt skin
> from the outside of roasted joints, bones, in short, all the leavings
> from the fingers and mouths of the sick ones suffering from all
> manners of disease. Into this mess the men plunged their hands,
> digging, pawing, turning over, examining, rejecting and scrambling
> for. It wasn't pretty. Pigs couldn't have done worse. But the poor
> devils were hungry, and they ate ravenously of the swill, and when
> they could eat no more they bundled what was left into their hand-
> kerchiefs and thrust it inside their shirts.
>   'Once, when I was 'ere before, wot did I find out there but a
> 'ole lot of pork ribs,' said Ginger to me. By 'out there' he meant
> the place where the corruption was dumped and sprinkled with
> strong disinfectant. 'They was a prime lot, no end of meat on them,
> and I ad'em in my arms and was out of the gate and down the
> street lookin' for some'un to gi'em to. Couldn't see a soul, and I
> was runnin round clean crazy, the bloke runnin' after me and
> thinkin' I was slingin' my 'ook. But just before 'e got me I got an
> 'ole woman and poked em into 'er apron.'

London couldn't take any more. He fled to a hot bath, a decent bed
and food.

In the 1870s there had been a general impression that the working
class was becoming better off. It was a shock to learn that overcrowding, bad sanitation and prolonged periods of unemployment were
beginning to blur uncomfortably the distinctions between the respectable working class and the thousands who were 'physically, mentally
and morally unfit' to live and for whom the state could do nothing
except let die by leaving them alone. There was also the growing
fear that the two might combine to overwhelm the established order.

'This mighty mob,' George Sims wrote in *How the Poor Live,* 'of
famished, diseased and filthy helots is getting dangerous, physically,
morally, politically dangerous. The barriers which have kept it back
are rotten and giving way, and it may do the state a mischief if it be
not looked to in time. Its fevers and its filth may spread to the homes
of the wealthy; its lawless armies may sally forth and give us the
taste of the lesson the mob has tried to teach now and again in Paris,
when long years of neglect have done their work.'

Another pamphleteer, Arnold White, wrote in *The Problems of a*

Great City: 'How much more repugnant is it to reason and to instinct that the strong should be overwhelmed by the feeble, ailing and unfit!'

The events of 1886 and 1887 only intensified these fears. The winter of 1885–86 was the coldest for thirty years. Men and women with haggard faces and thin worn bodies, crowded into the relief offices. Even Mrs Barnett came near to jettisoning her principles for the sight of some temporary happiness in 'those sad faces' with the 'gift of nice bright half crowns all round' except that he, Mr Barnett, 'ever wishful to redeem character stood resolute.' Mrs Barnett could still wince, many years later, as she recalled the reproaches of a broken-hearted mother who had sobbed, as she wept over her baby whose life might have been saved: 'They said it was no use a-sending to the Church, for you didn't never give nothing though you spoke kind.'

Even jobs as scavengers were beyond the physical capabilities of most of the men.

A mass meeting of unemployed dockers and labourers was held in Trafalgar Square that winter, and afterwards some of the crowd marched to Hyde Park where they intended to disperse. In Pall Mall there was some provocation from clubmen and the march turned into riot. About three thousand demonstrators rioted and looted their way through Piccadilly and Mayfair to Oxford Street where they were eventually dispersed by the police. In the aftermath, the Home Secretary appointed a committee of inquiry to look into the conduct of the police and he took the unusual step of presiding over it himself. As he was chairman this meant that he presented the committee's findings to himself! The Metropolitan Police Commissioner, Colonel Sir Edmund Henderson, was made scapegoat for the debacle and he resigned.

His successor was Sir Charles Warren. The appointment of another soldier caused a few lifted eyebrows, but the feeling was that his appointment might give the force the discipline it seemed to be lacking. Already trouble was being fomented inside the force from outside agitators urging them to strike, and there were genuine grievances over pay and punishments.

1887 was Victoria's Jubilee year. Trade was slack but the weather was fine and throughout the summer a great many unemployed workers slept in Trafalgar Square and St James's Park. In October the weather changed, but by now camping out—in Trafalgar Square especially—had almost become a permanent way of life. Charities and well-meaning individuals had got into the habit of taking food and clothes to the Square, which was described by one writer as a 'foul camp of vagrants', and by another as consisting of the 'scum of London'. Sir Charles Warren also complained that he had to employ two thousand men to shepherd workers' demonstrations through the West End, while the City Police, with far fewer men and outside the scope of Home Office control, had broken up similar size crowds. There was one law, it seemed, for the City and one for the metropolis. Warren cleared Trafalgar Square of its ragged army of squatters but his action brought him into direct conflict with the Home Secretary, who subsequently rescinded his original order empowering him to do so. West End shopkeepers now publicly threatened to take the law into their own hands and to hire armed bands to clear the square themselves if the police didn't do so. Warren demanded additional powers to control a situation that was rapidly getting out of hand. With the Home Secretary's approval, he banned the use of the square on certain days. His challenge was taken up and on 13 November the battle of 'Bloody Sunday' was fought in the square.

Altogether four thousand constables, three hundred mounted constables, three hundred Grenadiers and three hundred Life Guards, as well as seven thousand constables held in reserve, were used to break up the giant mob of demonstrators that struggled to break through to the square. Many of them were armed with iron bars, sticks and knives. At the end of the day more than a hundred and fifty of the crowd had had to be treated for injuries and nearly three hundred more had been arrested. Some were sentenced to imprisonment with hard labour, for one, two, three or six months.

Warren's high-handed action was both censured and praised. Working-class hatred for him was perhaps epitomised by one of the many anonymous personal threats which he subsequently received: 'Beware of your life you dog. Don't venture out too fur. Look out. This is yours'. This was followed by a crudely drawn coffin. Other threatened demonstrations against 'police rule in London' never materialised, and Warren was able to bask in the glow of official approval. The following month the Queen conferred upon him a Knight Commandership of the Bath.

As fears of mob rule began to recede, so criticisms of the police, and of Warren in particular, began to increase. Within a year, the scorn and abuse which had been hurled at the Trafalgar Square mobs only twelve months earlier, had been turned against the police who, from being the champions of liberty, had become the downtreaders

of the suffering poor. George Bernard Shaw was not slow to point out
how quickly attitudes had changed:

> Less than a year ago the West End press was literally clamouring
> for the blood of the people—hounding Sir Charles Warren to thrash
> and muzzle the scum who dared to complain that they were starv-
> ing . . . behaving, in short, as the propertied class always does
> behave when the workers throw it into a frenzy of terror by ven-
> turing to show their teeth.
>
> Whilst we conventional Social Democrats were wasting our time
> on education, agitation and organization, some independent genius
> has taken the matter in hand. . . .

He was to be known as Jack the Ripper!

2
BLOODY KNIFE

When George Cross walked through dark and empty Buck's Row on his way to work shortly before 4 o'clock on the morning of Friday, 31 August 1888, the only light was a solitary gas lamp at the far end of the street. On one side of the street was a warehouse wall, and on the other some terrace houses which were occupied for the most part by better-class tradesmen. He was opposite these houses when, in a gateway leading to some stables, between the houses and the board school, he saw a bundle that he at first thought was a tarpaulin. It was only when he crossed over for a closer look that he realised the bundle was in fact a woman. She was lying on her back with one hand nearly touching the stable gate and the other her black straw bonnet, which was lying close by. Her skirt was pushed up almost to her waist. His first thought was that she had been raped and was still unconscious from the attack; and his next that he might have disturbed her attacker. Normally there was a great deal of noise in the street, but at that hour of the morning it was unusually quiet and although he listened carefully for any strange noises he could hear none. If he had disturbed the woman's attacker he must have heard his footsteps as he escaped or, supposing that the woman had been brought there in a cab and dumped, the rattle of wheels as he drove off. He was still by the body when he heard footsteps behind him.

John Paul, also a market porter, was likewise on his way to work when he saw Cross standing in the roadway. He stepped off the pavement to avoid him, but as he did so Cross touched him on the shoulder and said 'Come and look at this woman.' Paul cautiously did so but when Cross suggested that he should give him a hand to lift the woman to her feet, thinking she was only drunk, Paul refused to help him. Instead he knelt down and felt the woman's face and hands which were already cold. He said that he thought she was dead but, as he straightened her clothes to make her a little more decent, he felt her heart and thought that he could detect a slight movement. Both men thought that the best thing they could do was to find a policeman, and they walked off together in search of one. Because it was so dark, neither had noticed the blood, now concealed by the skirt, coagulating on the pavement between the woman's legs.

Police Constable 97J John Neil missed seeing them by minutes. Nearly half an hour had passed since he had last walked through Buck's Row, although his beat was a short one and could be covered at a brisk walk in twelve minutes. Shining his bull's-eye lamp into the stable gateway he saw what the two men had not been able to see, that the woman had been murdered. Blood was oozing from an ugly gash in her throat which had been cut almost from ear to ear.

The windpipe and gullet had been completely severed, cut back to the spinal cord. Her eyes were open, and her skirt was rumpled above her knees; though her hands and wrists were cold, her arms—which he knelt down and felt—were still warm from the elbow upwards. The flashing of his lamp as he examined the body attracted the constable on an adjoining beat, and Neil called to him to run and fetch a doctor. There was a surgery close by and within a quarter of an hour a Dr Llewellyn had been roused and was at the scene. He made a cursory examination of the body, watched by several policemen who obligingly shone their lamps on the body, and two or three men who having just finished work at a nearby slaughterhouse were on their way home.

On the left side of the neck, about an inch below the jaw, there was an incision about four inches long starting from a point immediately below the ear. On the same side, but an inch below, and beginning an inch in front of it, was a second incision which ended at a point about three inches below the right jaw. This second incision, about eight inches long, had cut the throat back to the vertebrae.

The main arteries had been severed but there seemed to be very little arterial blood on the ground. Most of it, the police realised when they lifted the body on to the ambulance, had soaked into the woman's clothes as it had flowed down her back from her neck to her waist. In spite of her posture and the massive loss of blood, her legs were still warm. From his preliminary examination the doctor guessed that she had not been dead more than half an hour. On his instructions the body was taken to the mortuary adjoining the local workhouse, as the area did not have a mortuary of its own, and a bucket of water was thrown over the blood, about six inches in diameter, that was left on the pavement and running down to the gutter. By daylight, most of it had been washed away and there were only some stains between the paving stones to show where the body had been. The body was left in the yard until two pauper inmates, one of them subject to fits, had had their breakfast and were ready to start stripping the body. The police inspector who was present jotted down a list of the clothing as they took it off—a reddish-brown ulster, somewhat the worse for wear, a brown linsey frock and black ribbed wool stockings. The woman was wearing two petticoats, one of grey flannel and the other of wool, which had to be cut through the bands to be taken off. As the attendant tore them down with his hands, exposing the brown stays, the inspector saw in the lower part of the abdomen, two or three inches from the left side, a deep jagged incision and other mutilations. He hurriedly summoned Dr Llewellyn who came at once and made a thorough post mortem examination of the body, which was that of a woman of about 40 or 45. There was some bruising along the lower edge of the jaw on the right side of the face that might have been caused by a punch or thumb pressure. On the other side of the face was a circular bruise, which again might have been caused by finger pressure. Apart from the injuries to the throat and to the abdomen, which have already been mentioned, there were several other incisions running across the abdomen as well as several downward slashes on the right side of the body. The abdomen had been cut open from the centre of the bottom of the ribs along the right side, under the pelvis to the left of the stomach—there the wound was jagged; the omentum or fatty membrane which covers the front of the stomach was cut in several places and there were two small stab wounds on the vagina. From the angle of the wounds, which were from left to right, Dr Llewellyn thought that these mutilations might have been done by a left-handed person using a stout-backed knife—such as a cork-cutter or a shoemaker might use—with a blade about six to eight inches long.

The first problem was to identify the woman. Her only possessions were a comb, white pocket handkerchief and a broken mirror. But stencilled on the bands of her two flannel petticoats was the mark of Lambeth Workhouse. The police hoped that the matron of the workhouse might be able to identify the woman, but this she was unable to do. Nor could she identify the clothing, which could have been issued at any time in the previous two or three years. The broken mirror was a good indication that the woman had been dossing in a common lodging house where mirrors were a luxury not normally provided. As the police started to question the lodging-house keepers and news of the murder spread, first one woman and then another came forward to try to identify the body. It was soon learned that a woman answering the description of the murdered woman had been living in a common lodging house at 18 Thrawl Street, Spitalfields. Women were fetched and they identified her as 'Polly'. She had been sleeping at the lodging house for about six weeks up until the last eight to ten days. A girl who had been sharing her bed had last seen her alive about an hour before her body was found. Earlier that same evening she had staggered back to the lodging house from the Frying Pan public house in Brick Lane but had been turned away because she had not got the 4d. doss money for a bed.

'I'll soon get my doss money,' she had laughed. 'See what a jolly bonnet I've got now.'

She had been wearing a new black straw bonnet trimmed with black velvet. She was 42 years old, 5'2" tall, with brown hair turning grey and five front teeth missing; her clothes were shabby and stained and the boots she was wearing had the uppers cut and steel tips on the heels. After she had left the lodging house she was seen about an hour later in the Whitechapel Road staggering drunkenly against a wall. Her friend had tried to persuade her to come back to the lodging house with her. Instead Polly boasted that she had had her lodging-house money three times that day but had spent it, that she was going to get some more money for her lodgings and that she would soon be back. She was last seen staggering drunkenly eastward down Whitechapel Road. At 3.45 a.m., about an hour and a quarter later, she was found with her throat cut not three-quarters of a mile distant from the spot where she had last been seen.

An inmate of the Lambeth Workhouse who was taken to the mortuary within a day or two of the killing identified the body as Mary Ann Nichols or Polly Nichols. William Nichols, her husband, was living in the Old Kent Road. He had not seen his wife for three years. They had five children, the oldest (now 21) was lodging with his grandfather and the youngest (eight or nine) was living at home. They had separated several times because of her drunken habits but each time he took her back she got drunk again and eventually the break became final. For some time the husband had allowed her five shillings a week from his wages. In 1882 he learned that she was living the life of a prostitute and had discontinued the allowance. In consequence she became chargeable to the Guardians of the Parish of Lambeth who summonsed the husband to show cause why he should not contribute to her support. They dismissed the summons when they learned the grounds on which he had discontinued the allowance. Since then, after three or four years of intermittent living and quarrelling with her father, she had drabbed her way through workhouses in Edmonton, the City of London, Holborn and Lambeth. She had tried to make a new start and left the Lambeth Workhouse on 12 May for a job as a domestic servant in Wandsworth. She stuck it for two months and then absconded with clothing worth £3 10s., which she probably pawned, and since then had been living in the lodging house in Thrawl Street and a similar one in Flower and Dean Street close by.

There was no apparent motive for her murder. An early theory was that she was a victim of a gang, allegedly terrorising and ill-treating prostitutes who did not hand over part of their earnings to them. There was some evidence for this theory. Two prostitutes had already been mutilated in a similar manner—murdered within three hundred yards of Polly Nichols' body.

The first had been Emma Elizabeth Smith, a common prostitute of the lowest type, living at 18 George Street, Spitalfields. She was supposed to be a widow with a son and daughter living somewhere in the neighbourhood of Finsbury Park as she was often heard to say that she thought they ought to do something for her.

She had been living in George Street for about eighteen months. Generally she left the lodging house between six and seven in the evening, returning home at all hours. When she was drunk she fought and behaved like a madwoman and it was quite a common sight to see her with a black eye and other injuries which she would explain away by saying that she had been fighting or had fallen down.

She had left the lodging house at the usual hour on 2 April and at 12.15 a.m. the next day she was seen talking to a man dressed in dark clothes and a white scarf in Fairance Street, Limehouse. She was not seen again until she staggered into the house some four hours later and told the deputy that she had been assaulted and robbed in Osborn Street. Much against her will she was taken to the London Hospital by the deputy and another lodger.

She said that she had been attacked by four men but either she could not or was in no condition to describe them. Her face was bloody and her ear was cut but the worst injuries had been internally inflicted. Something, not a knife, had been inserted into her vagina with such force that it had broken, but not cut, the partition between the front and back passage. Next day she died of peritonitis.

The police were not informed of the attack until 6 April, when the Coroner's Officer told them that the inquest was to take place the next day.

After such a time lapse there was very little for the police to look into, although they went through the motions of investigating. The place where Emma Smith had been attacked was pointed out to them by the lodger who had taken her to hospital. There were no blood-stains to be seen on the pavement but an examination of her clothing showed that her woollen shoulder wrap was saturated with blood. She had apparently taken it off and put it between her legs to soak up the blood when she realised how badly she had been injured. The rest of her clothing was in such a dirty and ragged condition that it was impossible to tell if any part of it had been freshly torn.

One puzzling factor was that after the attack she must have walked nearly a quarter of a mile to George Street and from there half a mile to the London Hospital. In doing so she must have walked past a number of police constables on duty in Brick Lane, Osborn Street itself and Whitechapel Road. Since she must have been in great pain and walked with considerable difficulty, why did she not ask for help? Why was she so reluctant to go to hospital? Had the police been told earlier they might have got some answers to these questions.

The second victim had been Martha Tabram whose body was found at 3 a.m. on Tuesday, 7 August on the first-floor landing of George Yard Buildings with thirty-nine puncture wounds in her body. In neither case had the killer been caught. The foreman of the Coroner's Inquest jury subsequently alleged class bias and said that, if a re-ward had been offered for the George Yard murderer, neither this nor the murder that was shortly to follow would have happened. Regula-tions to the contrary notwithstanding, he was convinced that a sub-stantial reward would have been offered for the killer if the victim had been rich.

Equally baffling was the apparent ease with which the murder had been committed and the killer escaped. The circumstances in which the body was found proved conclusively that Nichols had been killed where she was found. It was equally apparent that she must have met her death without a cry or shout for help—for the spot was almost under the windows of Mrs Green, a light sleeper, and was opposite the bedroom of Mrs Purkiss, who was awake at the time. Worse from the investigating point of view, was that as well as the beat policemen there were three watchmen close by, none of whom had heard any screams. It seemed astonishing that the killer could have escaped, because he must have had blood on his hands or clothes. However, there were so many slaughterhouses in the area that people would take little note of bloodstained hands and clothing, which would explain why he failed to attract attention as he disappeared into the twilight of the Whitechapel Road and lost himself in the early morning's market traffic.

Not only was there no motive but there was no suspect. Robbery and jealousy as motives were out. Police inquiries in the locality from the people living and working close by, of the policemen on the adjoining beats and in every quarter where it was thought that there might be a lead, failed to throw up an atom of evidence to connect anyone with the crime. The inquiries did reveal that a man named Jack Pizer, nicknamed Leather Apron, had been ill-treating prostitutes in this and other parts of the metropolis for some time and a fruitless search was made to find him and eliminate him from the inquiry, although there was nothing to connect him with the murders. Suspicion that he was the killer, however, hardened into near certainty when a second body was discovered eight days later with a piece of leather apron close by.

The second body was found shortly after 6 a.m. on Saturday 8 September, at the back of a lodging house at 29 Hanbury Street, less than a half a mile away from Buck's Row. The house, like hundreds of others in the area, had been built for the Spitalfields weavers, but when steam power had driven out the looms they had been taken over as cheap lodging houses. Seventeen people slept in the house, from a woman and her son in a cat's-meat shop on the ground floor to the five adults in the room in the attic. There was a yard at the back and a side hall or passage giving access to the stairs. As the house was let by rooms it was customary to leave the front and back doors of the passage open. The local prostitutes knew this and used the yard for their casual pick-ups. John Davis—his mother ran a small business from the first floor making packing cases—subsequently told the coroner's inquest that at night he often found prostitutes and their clients in the yard and on the first-floor landing and didn't hesitate to turn them out.

The dead woman was last seen alive at 5.30 a.m. by a park keeper's wife on her way to early morning market. She remembered seeing a man and a woman outside the house, apparently haggling. She was certain of the time because the brewer's clock was striking the half hour. Subsequently she identified the body as that of the woman she had seen standing with her back to the shutters. The only description she could give of the man was that he was dark, apparently a foreigner, aged about 40, of a shabby genteel appearance and wearing a deerstalker hat, probably brown. She had not seen his face as he was standing with his back towards her. As she had walked past them she had heard him ask 'Will you?' and the woman's reply 'Yes'. She had not looked back and, in the noise and bustle of carts, nobody saw them go into the passage and close the door behind them.

A lodger found the woman's mutilated body about half an hour later. No attempt had been made to conceal it. The passage was about four feet above ground level and had three stone steps down to the yard. To the right of the steps there was a small recess and to the left a wooden fence about five and a half feet high. The woman was about six inches in front of the bottom step, lying parallel to the fence, with her feet pointing towards a small wood-shed. According to the coroner's reconstruction of what had probably happened, they had entered the yard and closed the back door. 'The wretch must have then seized the deceased, perhaps with Judas like approaches. He seized her by the chin. He pressed her throat, and while thus preventing the slightest cry, he at the same time produced insensibility and suffocation. There was no evidence of any struggle. The clothes were not torn. . . . The deceased was then lowered to the ground and laid on her back; and although in doing so she may have fallen slightly against the fence, the movement was probably effected with care. Her throat was then cut in two places with savage determination, and the injuries to the abdomen commenced.'

The body was found by one of the lodgers, the elderly John Davis, who had only been living in the house for two weeks. He had been awake from about three to five o'clock and then had slept for half an hour. He had got up at about quarter to six and come downstairs just as the church clock was striking six o'clock. The yard door was closed, although whether it had been on the latch or not he couldn't say. When he had pushed it open and had started down the steps he had seen the body.

Some men from a case-maker's shop nearby had seen him stumble into the street with his trouser belt in his hands and heard him call them to come and look in the yard. Out of curiosity they had followed him through the passage but none of them would go down the steps. Nor would any of the crowd that soon began to gather outside in the street as the news of the murder began to spread. Some workmen ran off to fetch the police; one of them, after swallowing some brandy, fetched a tarpaulin to throw over the mutilated remains.

From the steps the woman's face was clearly visible. Her hands were raised with the palms upward as though she had fought for the throat. Her hands and face were smeared with blood as though she had been struggling. Her legs were drawn up with the feet resting on the ground and the knees turned outwards. Her long black coat and skirt had been pushed up over her bloodstained stockings and she had been disembowelled. According to the staccato police report she was 'lying on her back, dead, left arm resting on left breast, legs drawn up, abducted, small intestines and flap of the abdomen lying on right side above right shoulder attached by a cord with the rest of the intestines inside the body; two flaps of skin from the lower part of the abdomen lying in a large quantity of blood above the left shoulder; throat cut deeply from left and back in jagged manner right around the throat.'

There was a handkerchief of some kind tied around the neck. The throat had been so savagely cut that it had almost severed the head from the body. According to some newspapers the handkerchief had been tied on by the killer to stop the head from rolling away. Later evidence showed that the woman had been wearing the handkerchief as a neck scarf and that she was wearing it when she was murdered.

Inspector Joseph Chandler was on duty in Commercial Street when he saw several men running down Hanbury Street towards him. Beckoning one of them over he was told what had happened and hurried to the house. He arrived there within a few minutes of the discovery of the body. Already a crowd, some reports say a mob, had built up outside the house and he had to force his way through. As soon as reinforcements arrived he cleared the passage of sightseers and refused to allow anyone into the yard until the body had been examined by the divisional surgeon who had been sent for. He hastily arranged for telegrams to be sent to Detective Inspector Frederick Abberline at New Scotland Yard, who had been called in to assist in the Buck's Row murder, and to several other officers informing them of what had happened.

While he waited for the surgeon to arrive, Inspector Chandler made a preliminary search of the ground. He was watched by the scores of faces that were craning out of the back windows for a view. For some days afterwards the tenants did a brisk business charging sightseers for a look from their windows. He covered the body with some sacking and examined the ground for signs of a struggle. The yard had not been properly paved and it was a patchwork of stones and earth. He could not detect any signs of a struggle, nor of anyone having climbed over the temporarily erected fence. None of the palings was broken but there were some bloodstains on the fence about fourteen inches above the ground and immediately above the blood that had flowed from the woman's cut throat. The only other bloodstains, varying in size from a sixpenny piece to a pin-point, were on the back wall of the house, at the head of the body.

The police had no scientific advisers other than the divisional surgeons, whose role was very much that of today's scenes-of-crime officer. Divisional surgeons like Dr George Bagster Phillips, with twenty years practical experience to draw on, were invaluable to an investigation. After formally certifying that the woman was dead he ordered the body to be taken to the mortuary. Ironically, it was carried away in the same shell that had been used for Polly Nichols the week before.

Phillips made a thorough search of the yard, which yielded several clues. Several items had been deliberately placed or scattered about the yard. The woman's clothing had not been torn but the pocket that she had carried under her skirt had been cut open at the front and at the side. A piece of muslin and a comb and a paper case were lying close to the body. As if he was taking part in some elaborate ritual the killer had laid the two rings he had torn from her fingers, some pennies and two new farthings at the woman's feet. Near her head was a part of an envelope and a piece of paper containing two pills. On the back of the envelope was the seal of the Sussex regiment and on the other side the letter 'M' and a post office stamp 'London, 28 Aug., 1888'.

There was also a leather apron lying saturated with water about two feet from the water tap.

One popular rumour was that the murderer had scrawled, on the wall of the yard, 'Five; fifteen more and then I give myself up.' Equally dramatic was the story told by a young woman called Lyons the following day. She claimed to have met a strange man in Flower and Dean Street who asked her to meet him at half past six at the Queen's Head public house and have a drink with him. Having made her promise that she would meet him he disappeared, but met her at the appointed time. As they were drinking he startled her by saying, 'You are about the same style of woman as the one that's murdered.' When she asked him what he knew about her he muttered, 'You are beginning to smell a rat. Foxes hunt geese, but they don't always find 'em.' Having said this the man then hurriedly left the bar. The woman had followed him until they were near to Spitalfields Church when, suddenly realising that he was being followed, the man had rushed away and was lost sight of. The woman's description was identical with the published descriptions of the elusive Leather Apron. According to *The Times* the police had already searched more than two hundred common lodging houses for him.

Shortly before 2 p.m. on the Saturday afternoon Dr Phillips went to the mortuary to make the post mortem and was astonished to find that the body had been stripped, the blood washed off the chest and the clothes tossed into a corner of the shed except for the handkerchief which was still tied around the woman's neck. The clerk of the guardians had ordered this to be done and detailed two nurses for the work. Later, at the inquest, Phillips protested as he had done before, at the conditions in which he was forced to work. It was incredible that so large a borough did not have its own mortuary. Bodies dragged from the river had to be packed in boxes.

The body was soon identified as that of Annie Chapman, or Siffey. Among the men and women who had gone from the lodging house to the mortuary to try and identify her was her friend Amelia Farmer. She was one of the first witnesses at the inquest when it opened on Monday, 10 September at the Working Lad's Institute, Whitechapel Road.

She told the coroner, Mr Wynne E. Baxter, that for four years or more Annie Chapman had lived apart from her husband, who had been a coachman at Windsor. During that period she had lived in the lodging houses in and around Whitechapel and Spitalfields. About two years earlier she had been living in the same lodging house as herself at 30 Dorset Street, with a man who made iron sieves. It was for this reason that she called herself Siffey, or Sievey, because it was the name of his trade. At the same time she had been receiving an allowance of ten shillings a week from her husband. Some eighteen months prior to the murder, it had stopped being paid and Chapman had learned then that her husband was dead. Their children, who had been living with her husband, had been sent away to school; her boy, who was a cripple, had been sent to a Cripples' Home and her daughter to an unnamed institution in France.

Chapman, by all accounts, was a clever woman. Occasionally she tried to earn some money selling flowers or doing crochet work. Frequently she got drunk and as she was not fussy about how she earned her living, she went on the game.

Amelia Farmer had seen her two or three times in the week before she died. She had met her on the Monday when she had complained of feeling unwell. At the time she was sporting a black eye and had a badly bruised chest. This was the result of a drunken brawl with Liza Cooper, a prostitute Chapman had known for fifteen years. 'Dark Annie', as Chapman was also known, occasionally spent the weekend at the lodging house with a man locally known as The Pensioner. He lived only a short distance away in Osborn Street. The quarrel between the two women had started over a piece of soap that Dark Annie had borrowed for The Pensioner to wash with. She promised to return it but did not do so, and when she was asked for it the following week she contemptuously tossed a halfpenny to Liza and told her to go and buy some more. Later, they happened to meet in The Ringers public house. Liza was drunk—probably Dark Annie was also—and they started to quarrel. They were still quarrelling when they staggered back to the doss house kitchen. Dark Annie finally slapped the other woman's face and told her, 'Think yourself lucky I did not do more'. Now Annie was about 45 years old and a stout, well-proportioned woman; she was described as one who had seen better days. She was a small woman, only five feet tall, with dark brown wavy hair, blue eyes, a large thick nose and two teeth missing from her bottom jaw. She was a formidable opponent. Unfortunately she had badly underestimated Liza Cooper who mauled her and kicked her and blacked her eye and badly bruised her chest. When Amelia Farmer saw her some days later she was still creeping around like a sick cat. Next day, Tuesday 3 September, she had met her again by the side of Spitalfields Church. Dark Annie again complained of feeling unwell and said that she thought she would go to the casual ward for a day or two. She had had nothing to eat or drink that day except for a cup of tea. Amelia Farmer had given her twopence for a cup of tea and told her not to have any drink. She didn't see her again until 5 o'clock on the Friday afternoon when she asked her if she was going to Stratford. Annie again complained of feeling too ill to do anything. She was listless and didn't want to move but said, 'It's no use my giving way. I must pull myself together and go out and get some money, or I shall have no lodgings.' That was the last time Amelia Farmer had seen her alive.

The next witness was Timothy Donovan, the deputy of the common lodging house at 35 Dorset Street. He told the court that Annie Chapman had lived there for about the past four months except for the last week, during which time he had not seen her until the Friday evening. About 7 o'clock she had come into the lodging house and asked him if she could go into the kitchen.

Donovan had known her for about sixteen months and let her stay in the kitchen until nearly 2 a.m. when he was compelled to turn her out as it was obvious by then that she wasn't going to rent a bed. She told him that she had been ill and in the infirmary and asked him to trust her for the doss money. He told her that she knew the rules, and that she could not stay without paying. Normally Annie would get drunk on Saturday night, but not during the rest of the week. Tonight, however, she had been drinking, but she could walk straight. Donovan did not see which way she went out but, as she left, she told him that even though she had no money he was not to let her bed, which was still vacant, as she would soon be back.

Apart from an unconfirmed report that she had been serving at a public house in Spitalfields market less than half an hour before she was murdered, the last two people to see her alive were the night-watchman at the lodging house, who saw her walk away in the direction of Brushfield Street, and the park keeper's wife, who saw her talking to her killer.

Not all of Dr Bagster Phillips' evidence could be published in the newspapers. Some of it could only be reproduced in *The Lancet*. He began by saying that the woman's face and tongue were swollen and that there was bruising on the face and chest. There were abrasions on the ring finger where the brass rings that had been so carefully laid at her feet had been torn off. The incisions in the throat indicated that they had been made from the left side of the neck. There were two distinct cuts, parallel to each other, and about half an inch apart. From the way that the muscles had been worried it seemed as though the killer had tried to cut through the spine and take off the head. 'The abdomen had been entirely laid open and the intestines severed from their mesenteric attachments which had been lifted out and placed on the shoulder of the corpse; whilst from the pelvis, the uterus and its appendages with the upper portion of the vagina and the posterior two-thirds of the bladder had been entirely removed. Obviously the work was that of an expert—or one, at least, who had such knowledge of anatomical or pathological examinations as to be enabled to secure the pelvic organs with one sweep of the knife.' The cause of death, he concluded, was visible from the injuries he had described. From these appearances he was of the opinion that death arose from syncope, or failure of the heart's action in consequence of loss of blood caused by the severance of the throat.

Cross-examined by the coroner he thought that the murder weapon must have been a very sharp knife with a thin, narrow blade, at least six inches to eight inches long, probably longer. The injuries could not have been inflicted with a sword-bayonet or bayonet. They could have been done with a post mortem knife but the ordinary surgical cases might not contain such an instrument. Those knives used by slaughtermen, which were well ground down, were possible alternatives but those used in the leather trade would not be long enough in the blade. There were indications that the murderer had some anatomical knowledge. Even without a struggle he did not think that he could have committed all the injuries in under a quarter of an hour. Had he done them in a deliberate way, as a professional, it would probably have taken him the best part of an hour.

The leather apron which had been found he dismissed as of no importance. There had been no blood on it and from its appearance it had not been recently unfolded. Some staining on the wall of a nearby house which he had been shown looked like blood but on examination turned out to be urine. Referring again to the bruises on Dark Annie's face he said that those about the chin and the sides of the jaw were recent but those on the chest and temple were several days older. Clearly the latter were the result of the brawl with Liza Cooper. He thought that the killer had taken hold of Dark Annie by the chin and made his incision from left to right. To a suggestion that she might have been gagged he could only point to the swollen face and protruding tongue, both of which were signs of suffocation.

It seemed as if society as a whole had needed some horror such as this to awaken them to the fact that within a cab-hire distance of the palaces and mansions of the West End there were 'tens of thousands of fellow creatures begotten and reared in an atmosphere of godless brutality, a species of human sewage, the very drainage of the vilest production of ordinary vice; such sewage ever on the increase, and in its increase for ever developing fresh depths of degradation.'

An unknown moralist in a letter to *The Times* laid the blame for the killings squarely on society and not on the half-crazed monster terrorising the East End in its search for blood, whose legend was even then being created. They had sown the seed and must reap the harvest.

The Rev Samuel Barnett, Vicar of St Jude's, Whitechapel, more pragmatically thought that the Whitechapel horrors would not have been in vain if 'at last' the public conscience was awakened to the life that these horrors revealed. 'The murders were, it may almost be said, bound to come; generation could not follow generation in lawless intercourse, children could not be familiarised with scenes of degradation, community in crime could not be the bond of society and the end of all be peace.' As one of those who for years had known of the conditions that the killings had brought to the general attention of the public, he offered some practical remedies to these problems. He was careful to point out that these criminal haunts were of limited extent. The greater part of Whitechapel was as orderly as any part of London and the life of most of its inhabitants was as moral, if not more so, as that lived in some of the wealthier parts of the capital. Most of its evil was concentrated in an area of about a quarter of a mile square and to deal with it, or at least to bring it under control, he offered some practical suggestions:

> There should be more efficient police supervision. There had never been enough policemen to do anything more than to contain crime within certain areas. Rows, fights and thefts had been allowed to go unchecked in these rookeries of crime so long as the main thoroughfares were safe. More policemen were therefore needed to enforce the law in these areas.
>
> There should be, at least, adequate street lighting and cleaning. The back streets were gloomy and dirty and encouraged crime.

Barnett failed to point out that this was not the fault of the local authority. It was a simple question of economics. Because of the general poverty of the area, the amount of money that could be raised on the rates was simply not enough to pay for these basic services. Unless some sort of financial help was forthcoming from the richer boroughs, and the East End as a whole made London's responsibility, then the squalor and vice of Whitechapel could never be mitigated.

Yet neither the Rev Barnett nor *The Times,* in which there was some quite lengthy comment on his proposals, was bold enough to suggest that this was a matter of public responsibility rather than private charity. The most sensitive of the issues that the Rev Barnett raised had concerned private property and the fat profits that could be made by landlords and tenants who let, sub-let and sub-let again, piling lease upon lease until a situation was reached, as in 29 Hanbury Street, where seventeen people could exist in grossly overcrowded squalor. They could only express the pious hope that such properties would be bought by public-spirited philanthropists who would not batten on the easy profits that could be made from prostitution and gross overcrowding. Their final conclusion was that society had to make fresh and determined efforts to extirpate the existing evils which were an intolerable reproach to a Christian and civilised society. Either that or 'acquiesce in the desolating conclusion that our social organisation demands for its base a festering mass of unexplored and irredeemable iniquity.'

The police were adversely criticised by press and public for their incompetence. At Chapman's inquest one witness complained that when he had told a street constable that there had been a second murder similar to that at Buck's Row, the policeman had told him that he couldn't come and that he (the witness) must find someone else. An inspector's explanation to the coroner that constables on fixed points were not supposed to leave them but to send someone else did not revive his listeners' waning confidence.

Critics were equally scathing about the casualness of the investigation. Even the coroner voiced his criticisms. He wasn't provided with plans and had nothing to show where the body was found, not even a map of the street. Clearly, however, there were severe handicaps to the police investigation. Fingerprinting as a science had yet to be proved and accepted in the English courts, and twenty more years were to pass before the first conviction was obtained from them. Blood grouping was unknown. Pocket radios, telephones and wireless cars were for the future. Detection, in fact, relied very heavily on local knowledge, informers and an arrest at the time of the offence. According to Press Association reports, the police did not feel that they would get anywhere with their inquiries. No attempt was made to disguise the fact that such inquiries as had been made had been so fruitless as to produce in official minds a feeling almost of despair.

Tradesmen had so little confidence in the efforts being made that some of them formed a Vigilance Committee and published the following notice:

Finding that, in spite of murders being committed in our midst our police force is inadequate to discover the author or authors of the late atrocities, we the undersigned have formed ourselves into a committee and intend offering a substantial reward to any one, citizens or otherwise, who shall give such information as will be the means of bringing the murderer or murderers to justice.

Samuel Montague, the member of parliament, offered £500 reward for the capture of the murderer, and the police had been bombarded as a result with literally hundreds of letters from all parts of the country offering advice.

Early on the morning of Monday 10 September, the elusive John Pizer (Leather Apron) was traced to a house in Mulberry Street. Police suspicions of him had been intensified after Timothy Donovan, Annie Chapman's lodging-house keeper, said in an interview with a Press Association reporter that not only had he ejected Pizer from the lodging house a few months earlier for attacking or threatening a woman, but that both he and another witness, when they had last seen him, had noticed that Pizer was wearing a deerstalker hat similar to the one worn by Annie Chapman's killer.

Pizer was arrested by Sergeant Thicke, who told him that he was wanted for questioning in connection with the death of Annie Chapman. While searching the house they found five sharp long-bladed knives, which Pizer claimed that he used in his trade as a boot finisher. They also found several old hats, an unfortunate reminder that Pizer made hats and that Polly Nichols had boasted of her new hat shortly before she was murdered.

Pizer, protesting his innocence, was taken to Leman Street police station. The friends with whom he had been hiding accompanied him, and they insisted that he had not been out of the house since the previous Thursday and that he knew nothing of the affair.

The same afternoon there were crowds waiting outside Commercial Street police station when Detective Inspector Abberline arrived there from Gravesend with William Piggott, a suspect who closely resembled Leather Apron. Somebody had noticed his bloodstained clothing as he was drinking in a pub in Gravesend and had sent for the police. Piggott's behaviour when he was being questioned had been so erratic that he was arrested at once. On his hands were several recent wounds. In custody he made a rambling statement that he had been in Whitechapel, walking down Brick Lane, on the Saturday morning at about half past four, when he had seen a woman fall down in a fit. Yet when he tried to pick her up she had bitten his hand. Exasperated by her behaviour he had struck her across the face and then, seeing two policemen coming towards them, run away. None of this explained the bloodstained shirts in the bundle of clothing that he was carrying, nor the blood that had recently been wiped off his boots. In London, however, none of the police witnesses, such as Mrs Fiddymont, could identify him. Nevertheless, rather than let him go it was thought best to keep him in custody until something more could be found out about him. But after two hours in the cells his behaviour and speech became so strange and so incoherent that a doctor was called in at once to examine him and, on his advice, Piggott was declared insane and sent immediately to an asylum at Bow.

An important point, which had to be cleared up when the inquest resumed, was the exact time of Annie Chapman's murder. According to the evidence, she must have been murdered after 5.30 a.m. which, if correct, meant that the killer must have walked through the streets in daylight with blood on his hands and clothes. There was some corroborative evidence for this. According to a police statement, a dustman had seen a man with bloodstained clothing walking down the street at about this time.

Doubts had been raised over the time of the killing. Dr Bagster Phillips had thought she might have been dead for about two hours when he saw the body at 6.30 a.m. He subsequently admitted that the heavy loss of blood and the coldness of the morning might have caused him to miscalculate the time. Another witness, Mr Cadosh, who lived next door, said he was crossing the yard of 27 Hanbury Street at about 5.20 a.m. when he heard a woman's sharply uttered 'No' from the other side of the fence. A few minutes later he heard something fall against the fence. He could easily have misjudged the time as he said that he didn't get up until 5.15 a.m. and left for work at 5.30 a.m. His timing appears to be a little too rigid—a bit more flexibility might explain the discrepancy.

The first witness was John Richardson. His widowed mother rented the ground floor of 29 Hanbury Street as well as the workshop and yard at the back. It had used to be her habitual practice to leave her door open since she trusted her neighbours. But some time earlier the cellar in the yard had been broken into and a saw and a hammer stolen. Since then the cellar had been regularly padlocked at night. John Richardson used to check that the cellar flaps were secure whenever he was in the market. On the day of the murder he had gone to the house at between 4.40 and 4.45 a.m., only an hour before the body was discovered. The front door was closed and so was the yard door. He had not gone down the steps into the yard as he could see from where he was standing that the padlock was on. It was still dark but it was light enough for him to see all over the yard. The body hadn't been there then. Indeed, because one of his boots was hurting him he had sat down on the top step with his feet on the flags of the yard. Had the body been there they would have been resting on her head! He cut a piece of leather off his boot with a table knife that he had picked up by mistake that morning at his house and put in his pocket. The coroner pounced on this point and questioned him closely about the knife, which the witness said was about 5" long. He was sent home to fetch it. When he returned with it (it had been lying on the table where he had left it) the coroner handed it over to the police.

Another point that had raised certain doubts in the coroner's mind about John Richardson's innocence had centred on the leather apron found, by Dr Bagster Phillips, lying half in half out of a pan of water in the yard. John Richardson's widowed mother explained that her son normally wore it when he was working in the cellar. On the Thursday she had washed it, leaving it by the fence where the police had found it on the Saturday morning. The police had wrongly assumed that it belonged to Leather Apron.

This was John Pizer, a bootmaker. Detective Sergeant Thicke said that he had arrested him on Monday 10 September at 22 Mulberry Street where he was hiding. He had known Pizer for several years, and when anyone locally spoke of 'Leather Apron' they meant him.

Pizer was no longer in custody and had been called as a witness to give him a chance of publicly clearing himself. The police had confirmed his alibis and released him the next night. His alibi was that he had been hiding with his brother and stepmother for four days and hadn't stirred out of doors until he was arrested by Sergeant Thicke on Monday morning. His brother had advised him not to leave the house as he was the prime suspect. In other words he had an unshakeable alibi for Annie Chapman's murder. From Thursday 6 to Monday 10 September he had not moved out of the house.

It was equally important that he should have an alibi for the night that Polly Nichols was murdered. When questioned he told the coroner that he had spent the night at Crossman's common lodging house in the Holloway Road. It was called the 'Round-house'. At 11 p.m. he had had his supper and then gone out and walked as far as the Seven Sisters Road. Then he turned back and went down Holloway Road, from where he saw the glow of a large fire in the London Docks. Outside the lodging house, when he got back, he spoke to the lodging-house keeper and one or two constables who were talking together. When he asked them where the fire was they could only tell him that it was a long way off. One of them had then added that he thought that it was 'Down by the Albert Docks'. It was then about 1.30 a.m. as near as he could remember. He had then walked on as far as Highbury railway station before turning back to the lodging house. As it was after 11 p.m., when all the unoccupied beds were re-let, he paid the night duty attendant 4d. for another bed. Before turning in he sat on a form in the kitchen and smoked a clay pipe. Next morning, he was woken up by the day attendant who told him that he must get up as he wanted to make the bed. He did so and went downstairs to the kitchen.

The coroner said that he thought it only fair to point out that this statement could be corroborated.

Pizer left the court completely cleared of the allegations that had been made about him and free to begin the first of several court actions against those newspapers that had so grossly libelled him.

On 26 September Mr Wynne E. Baxter summed up the evidence. He reserved his bombshell for the end. Two things were missing from the body, he said. Chapman's rings, which had not been found, and the uterus, which had been taken from the abdomen. The body, he went on, had not been dissected but the injuries had been made by somebody with considerable anatomical skill and knowledge. There were no meaningless cuts. The amount that was missing would go into a breakfast cup, and had the post-mortem examination been less thorough it might easily have gone unnoticed. An unskilled person could not have performed such a deed nor, he added, pouring cold water on another popular theory, a mere slaughterer of animals: it must have been someone accustomed to the post-mortem room. It was impossible to escape the conclusion that a desire to possess the missing abdominal organ had been the object of the attack. If the object had been robbery, then the injuries to the viscera were meaningless, as death had resulted from the loss of blood from the cut throat. Moreover, when they found an easily accomplished theft of some paltry brass rings and an internal organ which it had taken a skilled person at least quarter of an hour to remove, they were driven to the conclusion that the object of the attack was the abstraction of the viscera, and the stealing of the rings a thinly concealed attempt to disguise the fact.

It was not necessary to assume that the murderer was a lunatic, because there was in fact a market for such organs. After the earlier medical evidence had been published in the newspapers, the sub-curator of the pathological museum attached to one of the great medical schools had informed him of an incident that could have a bearing on the case. Some months previously an American had asked him to procure a number of specimens of the missing organ, and for these he was willing to pay £20 each. He planned to issue an actual specimen with each copy of a publication on which he was then engaged! Even though he was told his request was impossible, the American had persisted in his demands, explaining that he wanted them preserved in glycerine to keep them flaccid. He had afterwards made the same request to a similar institution.

Mr Wynne Baxter told the jury that he had passed this information on to Scotland Yard, and asked if it was not feasible that somebody, having heard of the American's request, had been incited to commit a murder for gain.

This, as *The Times* pointed out in a leader the next day, not only threw a different light on the crime but attributed to it an appalling motive. Sixty years had passed since Burke and Hare committed the series of murders that had given a new word to the English language. A few years later another resurrectionist had been convicted of the same offence. The current price then for a body had been between £7 and £10, which, even allowing for the depreciation of money, was less than the sum the American was alleged to have offered. This fact, when coupled with the general conclusion that the murderer (a) had a special method of arresting consciousness in his victim and (b) was possessed of surgical skill, at once vastly narrowed the field of search. Obviously he was a class above the people he had killed, and considerably superior in education to the people whom the police first suspected. 'There is a perfect abundance of clues provided they are followed up. . . . The police will be expected to follow up with the keenest vigilance the valuable clue elicited through the Coroner's inquest, and, since the lines of their investigation are plainly chalked out by information which they themselves failed to collect, it will be a signal disgrace if they do not succeed.'

3
DOUBLE EVENT

After a lull of nearly two weeks, two more equally brutal murders were committed in the early hours of Sunday 30 September, within a quarter of an hour's walking distance of each other.

The first body was found just after 1 a.m. in a narrow court off Berner Street, then a quiet street running down from Commercial Street to the London, Tilbury & Southend railway. At the entrance to the court were two large gates, one of them fitted with a wicker gate that was used when the gates proper were closed. On the left of the court were some terrace cottages, occupied by sweat shop tailors and cigarette makers. Most of the residents had been in bed by midnight but some of them were kept awake by noise from the International Working Men's Educational Club on the other side of the court, where earlier in the evening there had been a heated debate followed by impromptu singing and dancing. Although it was after midnight, lights were still streaming out of the first-floor club windows, and onto the terrace windows and roofs of the facing cottages. Otherwise the court was in darkness, and the street lights were out as well. Anyone coming into the court, therefore, had to grope his way for eighteen to twenty feet through a shroud of darkness that lay between the blind walls just inside the gates.

The steward of the club was Louis Diemschutz. He was also a traveller in cheap costume jewellery, which meant that he left the day-to-day running of the club to his wife. It was 1 a.m. when he eventually turned his pony and costermonger's barrow into the court. As he did so the pony shied to the left and wouldn't pull straight. Diemschutz thought at first that some mud or rubbish must be in the way but, when the pony shied again, he peered about and saw the body. He still could not make out what it was and he poked it with his whip before getting down and striking a match. It was a windy night and the match was instantly snuffed out. In the spurt of light

Diemschutz saw that the object was a woman's body and that she was either dead or drunk. He hurried into the club and got a candle. Some of the club members came back with him and helped him to lift the woman's head and shoulders from the ground. The woman's musty black clothes were wet from the rain but her body was still warm. As they lifted her they saw that her hands were folded underneath her, one of them gripping a bag of cachous. Some red and white flowers were pinned to her black fur-trimmed jacket. Blood had coagulated on the cobbles by the gash in her throat and a lot more—about two quarts, they thought—had flowed down the cobbles towards the club door.

Several men immediately went off in search of a policeman. When they found one his whistle blasts soon brought others running to the courtyard and cottages, which were quickly sealed off. These and the club house were thoroughly searched, as were the outside closets and dung heap. Dr Bagster Phillips examined the body and pro- nounced life extinct. Putting his hand inside the top of the woman's bodice and jacket, which were undone, he was heard to tell one of the policemen that she was still warm. He then examined for blood- stains the hands and clothes of everyone who had been in the club or who was living in the court, much to their indignation. They were equally enraged when their homes were searched. Eventually the police abandoned their search about 5 a.m. By then, news was begin- ning to spread that there had been a second body found in Mitre Square in the City.

It had been a double event.

The Times thought that 'the assassin, if not suffering from insanity, appears to be free from any fear of interruption while on his dreadful work.' He had taken enormous risks. Mitre Square had three en- trances—one from Mitre Street and passages from Duke Street and St James's Place. On two sides of the square there were warehouses, belonging to Kearley and Tonge, with a watchman on night duty. On the third side, opposite where the body was found, there were two old houses, one of which was unoccupied and the other lived in by a policeman. On the fourth side were three empty houses. Every fif- teen minutes during the night the square was patrolled by a police constable: at 1.30 a.m. the square had been empty when he strolled through; at 1.45 a.m. he had found a body.

In a sense this fourth killing was unique. The victim was, as it turned out, the only one to be murdered in the City of London and the investigation, unlike those of the other murders, was in the hands of the City police. They, responsible for the one square mile only, were answerable to the Corporation of the City of London, whereas Sir Charles Warren and the Metropolitan Police were answerable to the Home Office. The Commissioner was Sir James Fraser but, as he was nearing retirement and had been absent for two months, the investigation itself was in the hands of the Assistant Commissioner, Lt. Col. Sir Henry Smith, described by a contemporary as a good raconteur and a good fellow. Since August he had been desperately keen to lay hands on the killer and, to guarantee success, had put nearly a third of the force into plain clothes, with instructions as he candidly admits in his memoirs 'to do everything which, under ordinary circumstances, a constable should not do. It was subversive of discipline; but I had them well supervised by the senior officers. The weather was lovely, and I have little doubt that they thoroughly enjoyed themselves, sitting on door-steps, smoking their pipes, hanging about public-houses, and gossiping with all and sundry.'

Smith was beginning to think that the killer had either gone abroad or had retired from business when he was woken up with the news of the Mitre Square murder. He had been spending an uncomfortable night in Cloak Lane Police Station, not far from Southwark Bridge. There was a railway goods depot in front of the station and a furrier's behind, which meant that the sickening smell from the skins was always present. Sleep was an impossibility, and it was a relief when the bell by his head rang violently. After being told what had happened he had dressed and was in the street within a couple of minutes and boarded a hansom, which he detested: 'This invention of the devil claims to be safe. It is neither safe nor pleasant. In winter you are frozen; in summer you are broiled. When the glass is let down your hat is generally smashed, your fingers caught between the doors, or half your front teeth loosened. Licensed to carry two, it did not take me long to discover that a fifteen stone Superintendent inside with me, and three detectives hanging on behind, added neither to its comfort nor to its safety. Although we rolled like a "seventy-four" in a gale, we got to our destination—Mitre Square—without an upset, where I found a small group of my men standing round the mutilated remains of a woman.'

She was lying on her back, with her left leg extended and her right leg bent. There was a large gash across her face from her nose to the right of the cheek and part of the right ear had been cut off. Her throat had been cut and she had been brutally mutilated. Her dress, with its pattern of Michaelmas daisies and golden lilies, had been pushed up to her waist and bunched up on her chest, together with her drab linsey skirt, her dark green alpaca petticoat and a grubby white chemise. She wore brown, ribbed knee-stockings, darned with white cotton, and a pair of men's laced boots. Her black cloth jacket had an imitation fur collar and three large metal buttons. Her black straw bonnet, trimmed with black beads and green and black velvet, was still tied to her head.

In her pockets she carried everything she owned: a white handkerchief with a red border, a match box containing cotton, a blunt table knife with a white bone handle, two short clay pipes, a red cigarette case with a white metal fitting, a printed handbill, five pieces of soap, a small tin box containing tea and sugar, a portion of a pair of spectacles, a three-cornered check handkerchief, a small comb, a red mitten and a ball of worsted.

Smith had given orders that every man and woman seen together after midnight was to be stopped and questioned. He was convinced that, if his orders were carried out the murderer would be caught. What galled him now was the knowledge that the woman, Catherine Eddowes, had been in police custody, in a City Police station, until a short while before her death.

At 8.30 p.m. on Saturday she had been found lying drunk on a pavement in Aldgate. P.c. 931 Robinson had picked her up and propped her against some shutters, but she had fallen down again. The police constable had taken her to Bishopsgate Police station and she had been put into a cell to sober up. She was carried in by two constables and the gaoler, who checked on her several times while she was sleeping to make sure that she was all right. At midnight he heard her singing and at about half past twelve she asked when she was going to be let out, as she was capable of looking after herself. It was normal policy, and a humane one, to let drunks out when they had sobered up rather than take them to court and punish them with a punitive fine that few of them could pay. She was let out and, with a ' 'Night old cock', she walked out of the station towards Houndsditch and Mitre Square, which was less than a quarter of a mile away.

Somewhere on this route she met the Ripper.

When she had been discharged she had given her name as Kate Kelly, of 6 Fashion Street, Spitalfields. In her pocket were two pawn tickets, one of them in the name of Kelly. Her married name was in fact, Conway but for the past seven years she had lived with a John Kelly. According to him they had been thrown together a good bit in the lodging house where they lived, which was why they had paired up. She used to get an occasional spot of charring and he picked up all the odd jobs he could get in the markets. She drank, he knew, but she was not troublesome. Most years they went hop-picking for a holiday and to make some money. They had not done too well this particular year and had walked back to town, arriving on Thursday 27 September. Luck, as usual, was against them. They had no cash, and the only thing of value that they possessed was a pair of boots, which Kelly told Kate to pop in order to get a bite to eat. They had pledged them for one shilling and sixpence, and also a man's flannel shirt for the same amount. Their first night in London they spent in the casual ward in Shoe Lane. On Friday Kelly managed to earn six-pence and wanted to spend it on food, but Kate told him to take four-pence and go to the lodging house where he could at least get a decent night's lodging. She took the remaining twopence and went to the casual ward at Mile End. Kelly had seen her next morning at 8 a.m., and again on the Saturday afternoon when she had told him that she was going to Bermondsey to try to find her daughter Annie, pre-sumably to borrow money from her. Later, he heard that she had been arrested and locked up because she'd had a drop of drink. Kelly didn't bother to go and ask about her because he was sure that she would turn up on the Sunday morning.

As the body of Eddowes-Kelly was being undressed in the mortu-ary, the detectives noticed that part of the bloodstained apron that was around her neck had been cut away. This missing piece was found soon afterwards in Goulston Street, which was about a third of a mile away and some ten minutes' walk from Mitre Square. The bloodstained scrap of material, which looked as if a knife had been wiped on it, had been discarded in a passageway to some flats. It was picked up by a patrolling policeman, Constable 254A Alfred Long, who immediately searched the adjoining staircase for bloodstains. As he was shining his lamp about he saw that a message had been scrawled across the black dado of the wall. The three-line message had been written in chalk—'in a good schoolboy hand', according to one witness—and read:

The Juwes are not the
men that will be blamed
for nothing.

He assumed that it must have been recently written because so many people were living in the flats that the words would certainly have been rubbed out soon after being written.

As soon as the constable had reported his discovery at Leman Street Police Station, and handed his find to Dr Phillips, detectives converged on the building. They searched the flats and surrounding neighbourhood but, as usual, they found nothing. One of the City detectives, Daniel Halse, stayed behind, sending a message to the City head of C.I.D., Mr MacWilliam, that he would wait by the passage until it was light enough for a photograph to be taken of the words. This was because Goulston Street was on Metropolitan Police ground, and Superintendent Arnold, who was in charge of that division, wanted the words rubbed out since he thought that if they were seen they might inflame local prejudices and aggravate the danger of anti-Jewish riots. However, he was not prepared to shoulder the responsibility for the destruction of such a vital piece of evidence. His solution was to send an Inspector to wait at the spot with a dry sponge!

Sir Charles Warren, however, had no doubts as to what must be done when he arrived at Leman Street Police Station shortly before 5 a.m. He hurried at once to Goulston Street and ordered the words to be rubbed out. Halse tried to persuade him to wait just one hour until it was light enough for a photograph to be taken. Warren afterwards in a letter of explanation to the Home Secretary, said that he thought that if they had waited as long as that the house might have been wrecked. Traders were just beginning to put out their stalls and before long the streets would be crowded.

Warren rejected a suggestion that the message be temporarily covered up, because he thought there was danger for as long as the message was in place. He also rejected various compromises—from Halse, that perhaps they rub out only the top line, and, from one of his own men (probably Superintendent Arnold), that it might be enough to rub out the word 'Juwes' only. According to Major Smith the words, once copied down, were rubbed out by Warren personally.

Smith had gone to bed by the time Warren called at City Police headquarters to tell them what he had done. It was left to his head of C.I.D., Mr MacWilliam, to tell Warren bluntly that he had made a bad mistake in destroying the writing, as a photograph might have yielded a clue.

Smith had roamed the station houses for most of the night, hoping in vain for an arrest. In Dorset Street his men had been so close on the killer's trail that he had arrived there in time to see the blood-stained water where the Ripper had washed his hands. Finally he had gone to bed about an hour before at 6 a.m., 'after a very harassing night' and feeling 'completely defeated'.

In the winter of 1887–88 relations between the Metropolitan Police Commissioner (Sir Charles Warren) and the Home Secretary (Henry Matthews) steadily worsened. Warren was also quarrelling with the Receiver, Sir Richard Pennefather, and the head of the C.I.D., James Monro. According to one contemporary, 'Pennefather was a very able man, but disagreeable to deal with; he rubbed everybody up the wrong way. Warren was the finest man we had in Whitehall, but probably the worst appointment, because he must be independent, and the Commissioner of Police is held in very tight bonds by the Home Office. Matthews was an exceedingly able lawyer, but quite incapable of dealing with men; he was a regular Gallio in his attitude to Warren's complaints. Later on he quarrelled with Bradford, and if you couldn't get on with Bradford you could get on with nobody.'

Warren's main quarrel with the Home Office was that it interfered too much in the internal administration of the force, and didn't give him the free hand to which he claimed the right under the statute appointing him Commissioner. Certainly he was justified in asking for an inquiry into the relations between the police and the Home Office. Faced with, and constantly referred to, memoranda and letters which he claimed that he had never seen, he could only take his stand and insist on the legal rights that he was entitled to.

His internal quarrel with Monro, who had been the head of C.I.D., since 1884, was over the claim of his department to be an independent department—a state within a state, in fact, and free of the Commissioner's control. *The Times* related that the information which Monro gave to Sir Charles was of the scantiest possible. Monro, although he was holding the rank of Assistant Commissioner, claimed to be independent of the Commissioner and responsible only to the Home Secretary; so much so that he refused to let Warren even see his correspondence. The Home Office played one off against the other, and Matthews annoyed Warren still more by writing to Monro direct. Such a state of affairs could not continue indefinitely and, in August 1888, Warren forced Monro to resign.

The officers of the Criminal Investigation Department, as Robert Anderson pointed out when he took over from Monro in September 1888, were already demoralised by the way that their former Chief had been treated. All sorts of rumours were being spread about his possible successor and for some 'occult reason' Anderson was sworn to secrecy not to make his appointment known. As he had been in the habit of frequently meeting with Monro to discuss other matters on which they were engaged for the Home Office, it was immediately —and wrongly—assumed, when Warren started to make frequent calls on him, that the Commissioner was spying on him because he was Monro's friend. Indignation was so great among the senior officers that it was with only the greatest difficulty that Anderson stopped his chief subordinate from sending in his resignation.

An already serious situation was complicated still further by the fact that Anderson himself was feeling the strain of long periods of overwork and was physically unfit for his new job. His doctor insisted that he should have two months' complete rest and told him that he would probably give him a certificate for a further two months' sick leave. Anderson said that was out of the question. He told the Home Secretary that, although 'greatly to his distress', he could not take up his new job until he had had a month's holiday in Switzerland. And so, after one week as head of C.I.D., he crossed the Channel.

The night before he left, Annie Chapman was murdered in Hanbury Street.

Soon the newspapers were beginning to comment on his absence.

Letters from Whitehall (presumably urging that he should return) forced Anderson to spend the last week of his holiday in Paris to be closer in touch with his office. He arrived in Paris on the night that the Berner Street and Mitre Square victims were murdered. Next day, an urgent appeal from the Home Secretary forced him to return to London.

He spent the day of his return and half the following night reinvestigating the case. The next day he held a conference with Matthews, the Home Secretary, and Sir Charles Warren. Matthews told him that they would hold him responsible for finding the murderer but Anderson shook his head in the negative.

'I hold myself responsible,' he said, 'to take all legitimate means to find him.'

He thought that the police methods so far had been 'wholly indefensible and scandalous, for these wretched women were plying their trade under definite police protection.' He suggested that all prostitutes found prowling the streets after midnight should either be arrested or warned that the police would not protect them! The first course was thought to be too drastic and, according to Anderson, the second was therefore adopted.

The Times reported that Warren sent 'every available man' into the East End in the hope of catching the killer red-handed.

In charge of the investigation was Inspector Abberline. He had been one of the fourteen 'appointments to divisions' when the C.I.D. was first formed. He was a soft-spoken man, rather portly, with the appearance of a bank manager or a solicitor. He had unrivalled knowledge of the East End and for many years had been the Detective Inspector or Local Inspector for the Whitechapel division which he had left only on promotion to the Yard. He was the best known of the squad of detectives out scouring Whitechapel. From 30 September his main aides were Inspectors Reid, Moore, and Nairn, with Sergeants Thicke (who was locally known as Johnny Upright because of his walk and his methods), Godley, McCarthy and Pearce (all of H division). Each of them had to follow up on average about thirty main enquiries each week in inner London and the suburbs.

After Emma Smith's murder people gossiped at street corners about her death, but nothing more—there were equally brutal crimes and other murders in Whitechapel. There was no hint of the panic and fear that was to come. Later, they began to walk about in groups, with sheer terror often reflected on their faces. But gradually, as the panic wore off, they would walk about in pairs and finally they could even joke about the murders to the local policeman, as he double patrolled Flower and Dean Street, and quip 'I'm the next for Jack'.

Instead of getting the newspapers to help them, Scotland Yard's policy was to keep the newsmen at arm's length. Inevitably, the press, with so few facts to work on, turned their attention to the police and individuals such as the Commissioner. However, none of them—including Abberline—was permitted to give interviews. This policy was wrong. As one policeman later wrote: 'I have always thought that the higher police authorities in ignoring the power of the Press deliberately flouted a great potential ally, and indeed might have turned that ally into an enemy.'

The first police theory was that the murderer was part of a gang who were levying blackmail on these unfortunates. This soon gave way to a more likely one that the murders were the work of one man. Once this was realised, it became much harder for the police to get information. People thought that if this theory were true then the personal risks to themselves were much greater because he had no accomplice to betray him. Rather than jeopardise their lives they withheld information which might possibly have led to the identification of the killer. Inevitably there was a continuous flow of information of sorts to the police. Some of it came from publicity seekers, who only wanted to see their names in the newspapers, and much of it was worthless.

Always there was the question of the killer's motive. Each of the victims was too poor to be worth robbing and with one or two exceptions, could not be thought of as sexually desirable.

The only common feature was that all were prostitutes.

The Home Office refused to issue rewards for the killer's capture. (One inquest jury pointed out with some vehemence that, if the victim had come from the West End, the reverse would have been the case.) Warren was himself in favour of offering a reward, but was overruled by the Home Secretary. There were good reasons for such a decision. Experience had shown that offering rewards was often too strong a temptation for quasi-policemen and vigilantes and led to the forming of Blood Money conspiracies. The last trials for such had been in 1816 and 1818. In practical terms this meant that the conspirators framed innocent men for the reward money. In 1772 alone this had resulted in the deaths and imprisonment of several people. Private individuals did, however, offer rewards. Samuel Montague, M.P., for example, offered £500 for the Ripper's capture.

As terror mounted, it was the not knowing who it was that broke down people's resistance to panic scares. Their blood lust and the lynching mood became sharper. Among the men concentrated in and around Hanbury Street was Walter Dew (who was later to achieve fame as the man who arrested Crippen). At this time he was only a uniformed constable. He was standing in Hanbury Street when he saw a local villain named Squibby who was wanted on an assault charge (he had been throwing bricks at a policeman when one of them missed and hit a child). Dew saw him on the morning after the Hanbury Street murder but, as he moved in closer to arrest him, Squibby dashed between the legs of a horse and ran off with the policeman in hot pursuit and pulling out his truncheon as he ran. Immediately the crowd jumped to the conclusion that the man he was chasing was Jack the Ripper.

'Jack the Ripper! Jack the Ripper! Lynch him!' they shouted.

The cry was quickly taken up and, as they ran along, Dew could hear hundreds of other feet running along behind him. As they reached Flower and Dean Street Squibby dashed into a lodging house and then into an adjoining building, where he was caught just as he tried to climb through a back window. Dew's immediate reaction was to prepare for a fight. Normally it took six or eight policemen to bring Squibby into the station, fighting all the way. This time, however, the man was shaking with fright. Suddenly Dew realised that he was afraid of the lynching. Outside the crowd were shouting 'Lynch him! Fetch him out!'

Other policemen fortunately reached the house in time and barricaded the door against the mob while others went to Leman Street and Commercial Street police stations for reinforcements. This only confirmed the crowd's suspicions that the police had arrested the killer, and the shouts of 'Lynch him, Murder him' and 'Get him' became even more insistent.

As the police tried to force their way out through the crowd the screams and shouts became even more furious. The crowd surged against the lines of policemen trying to hold them back and made determined efforts to take Squibby from them. Fortunately the police managed to bundle the prisoner into a four-wheeler cab and with an escort get him to the station. Even so it was nearly turned over. In Spitalfields market the police were forced to scramble out of the carriage and then to force their way through a double line of policemen to Commercial Street police station, through a 'yelling, hooting mob of frenzied people'. Even when they reached the police station the mob didn't give up hope of lynching the prisoner. Several times they stormed the building. All efforts to convince the mob that the man had nothing to do with the murders were to no avail, and it was several hours before the mob calmed down.

And all this, as Dew said, because some fool, seeing a man chased by the police had shouted 'Jack the Ripper!'

Later the following evening, on 1 October, the Berner Street victim was identified as Elizabeth Stride. One of the witnesses, who was taken to the mortuary to identify her, knew her also as Annie Fitzgerald. She was regularly arrested for drunkenness but whenever she was charged she always denied that she was drunk and said that she suffered from fits. The inquest was held in the Vestry Hall, Cable Street, before Mr Wynne E. Baxter. One of the witnesses, a lodger at 32 Flower and Dean Street who had known Stride for six years, said that she had always known the woman as 'Long Liz'. Another witness was the Rev Sven Olsson, pastor of the Swedish Church in Trinity Square, who had known her even longer, for about seventeen years. Her maiden name was Elizabeth Gustaafsdotter, he said. She had been born near Gottenberg on 27 November 1843, and, according to the local parish register where she had been entered on 10 July 1866, she had been registered as an unmarried woman. In 1869 she married John Thomas Stride, a carpenter at Sheerness. Elizabeth Stride had claimed that he had drowned in the 'Princess Alice' disaster with two of their nine children. If this was true, she would have been twenty-five when the 'Princess Alice' was run down by a collier on 3 September 1878, and so either this tale or the story that she had nine children by the marriage was a lie. Five hundred passengers were drowned in the so-called 'Great Thames disaster'. A check of the passenger list reveals that nobody of the name of Stride was on board at the time and the only case recorded of a father and two children drowning was that of an accountant with two sons aged ten and seven years old. Probably the truth was that she and her husband had separated and she invented the story as a face saving expedient.

For the past three years she had been living in Fashion Street with a waterside labourer named Michael Kidney. Occasionally she had earned some money by sewing and charring but, whenever the mood took her, or the restraints of their life together became too much for her, she would drift away from him for a while. During the three years they had been together they had separated altogether for about five months. The cause was always the same: drink. Kidney never went after her as he always knew that she would return to him in her own good time. On the previous Tuesday she had walked out on him. He didn't see her again until he identified her body in the mortuary. Afterwards he had gone away and got drunk. Later that night he had staggered into Leman Street police station and told the detectives that if he had been a policeman and the murder had occurred on his beat, he would have shot himself.

The inquest brought a few new surprises.

Dr Blackwell had been called at 1.10 a.m. on the Sunday morning to go to Berner Street. Stride's body was still warm when he examined it, apart from the hands, which were cold.

The right hand was lying on the chest, and was smeared inside and out with blood. It was quite open. The left hand was lying on the ground and was partially closed, and contained a small packet of cachous wrapped in tissue paper. There were no rings or marks of rings on the fingers. The appearance of the face was quite placid, and the mouth was slightly open. There was a check silk scarf round the neck, the bow of which was turned to the left side and pulled tightly. There was a long incision in the neck, which exactly corresponded with the lower border of the scarf. The lower edge of the scarf was slightly frayed, as if by a sharp knife. The incision in the neck commenced on the left side, 2½ in. below the angle of the jaw, and almost in a direct line with it. It nearly severed the vessels on the left side, cut the windpipe completely in two, and terminated on the opposite side 1½ in. below the angle of the right jaw, but without severing the vessels on that side.

He thought that the murderer had probably pulled her backwards by the scarf but whether she had been standing up when he cut her throat or lying down he could not say. She would not have been able to call out after her windpipe was cut and would probably have bled to death in about one to one and a half minutes. She had haemorrhaged through the partial severance of the left carotid artery.

Both Dr Blackwell and Dr Phillips had performed the post mortem at St George's mortuary on the Monday afternoon in the presence of two other doctors. Phillips said that apart from the injury to the throat there were no other marks on the body except some healing sores.

The stomach was large, and the mucous membrane only congested. It contained partly-digested food, apparently consisting of cheese, potatoes and farinaceous powder. All the teeth on the left lower jaw were absent. On Tuesday I again went to the mortuary to observe the marks on the shoulder. [There was bruising over both shoulders and under the collar bone on the front of the chest indicating that she had been seized by the shoulders and forced down onto the ground. From the bloodstains it was obvious that her throat wasn't cut until she was lying down.] I found in the pocket of the underskirt of the deceased the following articles—key as if belonging to a padlock, a small piece of lead pencil, a pocket comb, a broken piece of comb, a metal spoon, some buttons and a hook. Examining her jacket, I found that, while there was a small amount of mud on the right side, the left was well plastered with mud.

Both he and Dr Blackwell commented on a knife which had been found that same night in the Whitechapel Road by another witness, Thomas Coram, at 12.30 a.m. A policeman saw him find it outside a laundry shop where it was lying on the bottom step of the doorway. A bloodstained handkerchief was tied around the handle with string. The blade was dagger-shaped and about 9 to 10 inches long. It was a slicing knife and came from a chandler's shop. The blade was rounded at the point and both doctors thought it a highly unlikely weapon for the murderer to have used as it could only be used one way although it would have been capable of making the incisions in the neck.

The most important evidence to be heard was from three witnesses, one of them a policeman, who had seen Stride within an hour or so of the murder.

The first was William Marshall, a labourer in an indigo warehouse. Cross-examined, he said: 'On Sunday night I saw the body of deceased in the mortuary. I recognised it as that of a woman I saw on Saturday evening about three doors off from where I am living in Berner Street. That was about a quarter to twelve. She was standing talking to a man. I recognise her both by her face and dress. There was no lamp near and I did not see the face of the man she was talking to. He had on a small black coat and dark trousers. He seemed to me to be a middle-aged man.'

CORONER: What sort of cap was he wearing?
MARSHALL: A round cap with a small peak to it—something like what a sailor would wear.
CORONER: What height was he?
MARSHALL: About five feet six inches and he was stout. He was decently dressed, and I should say he worked at some light business and had more the appearance of a clerk than anything else.
CORONER: Did you see whether he had any whiskers?
MARSHALL: From what I saw of his face I do not think he had. He was not wearing gloves and he had no stick or anything in his hand.
CORONER: What sort of a coat was it?
MARSHALL: A cutaway one.
CORONER: Are you sure this is the woman?
MARSHALL: Yes, I am. I did not take much notice of them. I was standing at my door and what attracted my attention first was her standing there some time and he was kissing her. I heard the man say to deceased: 'You would say anything but your prayers.' He was mild speaking and appeared to be an educated man. They went down the street.

The next witness was Police constable 452H William Smith whose beat took in Berner Street on that particular night. Normally his patrol took him about half an hour, and it was about 12.30 a.m. when he saw a man and a woman talking together.

CORONER: Was the latter anything like the deceased?

W. SMITH: Yes, I saw her face. I have seen the deceased in the mortuary and I feel certain it is the same person.

CORONER: Did you see the man who was talking to her?

W. SMITH: Yes, I noticed he had a newspaper parcel in his hand. It was about eighteen inches in length and six or eight inches in width. He was about five feet seven inches as near as I could say. He had on a hard felt deerstalker hat of dark colour and dark clothes.

CORONER: What kind of a coat was it?

W. SMITH: An overcoat. He wore dark trousers.

CORONER: Can you give any idea as to his age.

W. SMITH: About twenty-eight years.

CORONER: Can you give any idea as to what he was?

W. SMITH: No sir, I cannot. He was of respectable appearance. I noticed the woman had a flower in her jacket.

The last witness was a boxmaker, James Brown, who went out at about 12.45 a.m. to get some supper from a chandler's shop in Berner Street. As he was crossing the road he saw a man and a woman standing up against the wall by the Board School. He heard the woman say, 'Not tonight, some other night,' which made him turn round and look at them. The man was leaning over the woman with his arm against the wall. Brown noticed that he was wearing a long dark coat which reached almost down to his heels. He took no further notice of them and went home.

'When I had nearly finished my supper I heard screams and shouts for the police—that would have been in about a quarter of an hour.'

There were several points of similarity between the two witnesses' descriptions. Marshall and Smith both agreed in general that the man they had seen was dressed in a black cutaway coat and that he was middle-aged in appearance. Where they differed was over his headgear. Smith said that he was wearing a deer-stalker hat and Marshall that he was wearing a round cap like a sailor's. They also disagreed as to whether he was carrying anything in his hand. Marshall said that he saw nothing and Smith that he was carrying a parcel about eighteen inches long and six to eight inches wide. Smith thought, too, that the man he had seen was wearing a coat down to his heels. Either Stride had been with more than one man in that last hour, which was not impossible, or else the descriptions were confused. Faced with these descriptive permutations of what was probably the same man the *Police Gazette* hedged their bets both ways and issued the following descriptions:

> At 12.35 a.m. 30th September, with Elizabeth Stride found murdered on the same date in Berner Street at 1 a.m., a man, age 28, height 5 feet 8 inches, complexion dark, small dark moustache; dress, black diagonal coat, hard felt hat, collar and tie, respectable appearance, carried a parcel wrapped up in newspaper.

> At 12.45 a.m., 30th, with the same woman in Berner Street, a man, age about 30, height 5 feet 5 inches; complexion fair, hair dark, small brown moustache, full face, broad shoulders; dress, dark jacket and trousers, black cap with peak.

In his summing up the Coroner asked to know precisely how Stride had met her death.

> There were no signs of any struggle; the clothes were neither torn nor disturbed. It was true that there were marks over both shoulders, produced by pressure of two hands, but the position of the body suggested that she lay down or allowed herself to be laid down where she was found. Only the soles of her boots were visible. She was still holding in her hand a packet of cachous, and there was a bunch of flowers still pinned to her dress front. If she had been forcibly placed on the ground, it was difficult to understand how she failed to attract attention, as it was clear from the appearance of the blood on the ground that the throat was not cut until after she was actually on her back. There were no marks of gagging, no bruises on the face, and no trace of any anaesthetic or narcotic in the stomach, while the presence of the cachous in her hand showed that she did not make use of it in self-defence.

The marks on the shoulder to which the coroner had referred suggest that some pressure was applied from behind in order to push her down onto the ground. Clearly the attack must have come from behind, since she would otherwise have dropped the bag of cachous which she evidently gripped in her final spasm. Indeed it is very possible that she was dead before the throat was cut.

Within twenty-four hours of the 'double event' the public were clamouring for the resignation of Sir Charles Warren and the Home Secretary. At a meeting of nearly a thousand people in Victoria Park, the crowd passed a resolution calling on them to resign and make way for men who would leave no stone unturned to find the murderer. At four other meetings on Mile End waste there were similar resolutions passed.

A petition was presented to the Queen by George Lusk, head of the Whitechapel Vigilance Committee, on behalf of the inhabitants of Whitechapel, asking for Her Government to offer a reward for the capture of the murderer. Warren had already tried to persuade the Home Secretary to agree to this but Matthews had refused to countenance such a step. He similarly advised the Queen that it would be bad policy to agree to this measure now. Fortunately the City of London Corporation did not come under Home Office control and within twenty-four hours of the murders Colonel Fraser, the City Police Commissioner, offered a reward of £500 for information leading to the capture of the Whitechapel murderer.

A petition more to the Queen's liking was organised within the three days following the murders and forwarded to her by Mrs Barnett, who had managed to collect between 4000 and 5000 signatures:

To our Most Gracious Sovereign Lady Queen Victoria.

Madam—We, the women of East London, feel horror at the dreadful sins that have been lately committed in our midst and grief because of the shame that has fallen on our neighbourhood.

By the facts which have come out in the inquests, we have learnt much of the lives of those of our sisters who have lost a firm hold on goodness and who are living sad and degraded lives.

While each woman of us will do all she can to make men feel with horror the sins of impurity which cause such wicked lives to be led, we would also beg that your Majesty will call on your servants in authority and bid them put the law which already exists in motion to close bad houses within whose walls such wickedness is done and men and women ruined in body and soul.

We are, Madam, your loyal and humble servants.

In vain, a harassed Warren pointed out that he had drafted as many police reinforcements into the East End as he could spare. In a long and detailed letter, which was published in *The Times* on 4 October, he refuted point by point the allegations that he had switched experienced detectives from one district to another where they had no local knowledge to help them; that he had not changed the old system of beat patrols but had kept the same one that had been in existence for the past twenty years. But the public was wanting a scapegoat and it did not matter what he said or did. The mounting opposition to him was completely summed up in one newspaper headline—'War on Warren'.

He was heaped with ridicule when he negotiated with Mr Edwin Brough of Scarborough for the use of two champion bloodhounds named Barnaby and Burgho. Burgho was a black and tan with a head nearly 12 inches long. On Monday 8 October they gave a demonstration of their tracking powers in Regent's Park at 7 a.m. on ground thickly coated with frost. They hunted a man for about a mile after he had been given a fifteen-minute start. They were tested again that night, when it was dark, and again the next morning, when half a dozen runs were made. Warren himself was present and took the part of the hunted man on two of them.

But he could not make up his mind whether to use them or not. There was never any agreement made with the owner that they would be. It was this general misunderstanding that led then and now to the story that the bloodhounds were tested again at Tooting and became lost in a fog. Barnaby's keeper took him to Hemel Hempstead for some exercise on the same day that a sheep was killed on Tooting Common. The local police telegraphed him for the bloodhounds to be sent but he did not receive this message until later that evening when he returned home. Because they did not turn up somebody said that they were missing and this was magnified into a story that they had been lost. Burgho was down at Scarborough!

The inquest on Catherine Eddowes (Kate Kelly) opened on Thursday 4 October. As the hearing was within the jurisdiction of the City of London, it took place at the Golden Lane mortuary and was presided over by the City Coroner, Mr S. F. Langham.

P.c. 881 Watkins, who had found the body, said that his beat normally took him between twelve and fourteen minutes to patrol. He had walked through the square at 1.30 a.m. and again at 1.44 a.m. On the first occasion he had shone his bull's-eye lamp into the dark corners and passages but had seen nothing unusual, and the second time had seen the body as soon as he entered the square. Shining his light on it he saw that she had been ripped up, like a 'pig in the market', he said, and her entrails 'flung in a heap about her neck'.

He had run across to Kearley and Tonge's warehouse, where the door was on the jar, and called to the watchman who was sweeping the stairs: 'For God's sake, mate, come to my assistance.' From his appearance the watchman thought that he was ill. As he was an ex-policeman himself, and knew what to do, he ran into the square and blew his whistle for help as this was more likely to attract attention than the old fashioned rattle that the policeman was still carrying.

If his times were correct—and Watkins said that he checked his watch immediately after speaking to the watchman—then, allowing for the constable's time in entering and leaving the square and getting out of earshot, the Ripper could have had only between seven and eight minutes in which to kill the woman and do his work. This would apparently have been enough. The doctors said that he would have needed a minimum of five minutes. (This was always assuming that Eddowes was murdered where she was found. A more probable explanation is that he had taken her into one of the empty houses on the south side of the square, just a few feet away from where she was found, killed her there, and done the mutilations after dragging her body outside.) A search was made at the back of the empty houses but apparently not inside them. According to the medical evidence her throat was not cut until she was lying down. Thus, if the murderer had first strangled her, there would have been no risk of her screaming or calling out, and this would have given him more chance of getting safely away.

Nobody had seen them go into the square. But a couple of witnesses who had left the Imperial Club in Duke Street, close by, just after 1.30 a.m., had seen a man and a woman standing together at the corner of Church Passage leading into Mitre Square. The woman was wearing a black jacket and bonnet, and one of the witnesses thought that clothes he later saw in the mortuary were the same. The woman was about three or four inches shorter than the man, and the witness saw her put her hand on his chest, though not apparently to push him away. She was facing him and they were talking together quietly. When the witness was asked to describe him, the prosecution asked that the description should not be given as, it was claimed, the publicity might hinder police inquiries. Later, this description was published in the *Police Gazette:*

At 1.35 a.m., 30 September, with Catherine Eddowes, in Church Passage, leading to Mitre Square, where she was found murdered at 1.45 a.m., same date, a man, age 30, height 5 feet 7 inches, or 8 inches; complexion fair, moustache fair, medium build; dress: pepper and salt colour loose jacket, grey cloth cap with peak of same material, reddish neckerchief tied in knot; appearance of a sailor. Information respecting this man to be forwarded to Inspector MacWilliam, 26 Old Jewry, London, E.4.

Dr Sequeira and Dr Brown, both of whom had been called to Mitre Square and been present at the post mortem, thought that the murderer had shown no evidence of any anatomical knowledge other than that which could be expected of a professional butcher or meat cutter. Dr Saunders, who had examined the contents of the stomach for poison, and who had also been present at the post mortem, agreed with them. Most of the relevant points of this examination were dealt with by Dr Brown, who was the surgeon of the City of London police force, in his long and detailed statement, followed by cross examination.

The throat was cut across to the extent of about 6 inches or 7 inches. The sterno cleido mastoid muscle was divided; the cricoid cartilage below the vocal cords was severed through the middle; the large vessels on the left side of the neck were severed to the bone, the knife marking the intervertebral cartilage. The sheath of the vessels on the right side was just open; the carotid artery had a pin-hole opening; the internal jugular vein was open to the extent of an inch and a half—not divided. All the injuries were caused by some very sharp instrument, like a knife, and pointed. The cause of death was haemorrhage from the left common carotid artery. The death was immediate. The mutilations were inflicted after death. They examined the injuries to the abdomen. The walls of the abdomen were laid open, from the breast downwards. The cut commenced opposite the ensiform cartilage, in the centre of the body. The incision went upwards, not penetrating the skin that was over the sternum; it then divided the ensiform cartilage, and being gristle they could tell how the knife had made the cut. It was held so that the point was towards the left side and the handle towards the right. The cut was made obliquely. The liver was stabbed as if by the point of a sharp knife. There was another incision in the liver, about 2½ in., and, below, the left lobe of the liver was slit through by a vertical cut. Two cuts were shown by a jag of the skin on the left side. The abdominal walls were divided vertically in the middle line to within a quarter of an inch of the navel; the cut then took a horizontal course for 2½ in. to the right side; it then divided the navel on the left side—round it—and made an incision parallel to the former horizontal incision, leaving the navel on a tongue of skin. Attached to the navel was 2½ in. of the lower part of the rectus musela of the left side of the abdomen. The incision then took an oblique course to the right. There was a stab of about an inch in the left groin, penetrating the skin in superficial fashion. Below that was a cut of 3 in., going through all tissues, wounding the peritoneum to about the same extent. There had not been any appreciable bleeding from the vessels.

MR CRAWFORD: What conclusion do you draw from that?

DR BROWN: That the cut in the abdomen was made after death, and that there would not be much blood left to escape on the hands of the murderer. The way in which the mutilation had been effected showed that the perpetrator of the crime possessed some anatomical knowledge.

MR CRAWFORD: I think I understood you to say that in your opinion the cause of death was the cut in the throat?

DR BROWN: Loss of blood from the throat, caused by the cut. That was the first wound inflicted.

MR CRAWFORD: Have you formed any opinion that the woman was standing when that wound was inflicted?

DR BROWN: My opinion is that she was on the ground.

MR CRAWFORD: Does the nature of the wounds lead you to any conclusion as to the kind of instrument with which they were inflicted?

DR BROWN: With a sharp knife, and it must have been pointed; and from the cut in the abdomen I should say the knife was at least six inches long.

MR CRAWFORD: Would you consider that the person who inflicted the wounds possessed great anatomical skill?

DR BROWN: A good deal of knowledge as to the position of the organs in the abdominal cavity and the way of removing them.

MR CRAWFORD: Could the organs removed be used for any professional purpose?

DR BROWN: They would be of no use for a professional purpose.

MR CRAWFORD: You have spoken of the extraction of the left kidney. Would it require great skill and knowledge to remove it?

DR BROWN: It would require a great deal of knowledge as to its position to remove it. It is easily overlooked. It is covered by a membrane.

MR CRAWFORD: Would not such a knowledge be likely to be possessed by one accustomed to cutting up animals?

DR BROWN: Yes.

MR CRAWFORD: Have you been able to form any opinion as to whether the perpetrator of this act was disturbed when performing it?

DR BROWN: I think he had sufficient time. My reason is that he would not have nicked the lower eyelids if he had been in a great hurry.

MR CRAWFORD: About how long do you think it would take to inflict all these wounds, and perpetrate such a deed?

DR BROWN: At least five minutes would be required.

MR CRAWFORD: Can you as a professional man assign any reason for the removal of certain organs from the body?

DR BROWN: I cannot.

MR CRAWFORD: Have you any doubt in your mind that there was no struggle?

DR BROWN: I feel sure that there was no struggle.

MR CRAWFORD: Are you equally of opinion that the act would be that of one man, one person, only?

DR BROWN: I think so; I see no reason for any other opinion.

MR CRAWFORD: Can you as a professional man account for the fact of no noise being heard by those in the immediate neighbourhood?

DR BROWN: The throat would be so instantaneously severed that I do not suppose there would be any time for the least sound being emitted.

MR CRAWFORD: Would you expect to find much blood on the person who inflicted the wounds?

DR BROWN: No, I should not.

At the conclusion of the hearing on 12th October the jury brought in a verdict of 'Wilful murder by some person unknown.'

4

MILLER'S COURT

Number 26 Dorset Street was less than a quarter of a mile away from Hanbury Street where Annie Chapman had been murdered. The rooms were let to anyone who wanted them by the lodging-house keeper, John M'Carthy, who kept a small chandler's shop close by. The original back parlour had been cut off from the rest of the house by the erection of a false partition and, according to the house numbering, this was now known as Room 13. Although it was only a single room, and as such was part of the house, it had its own entrance (the first door on the right) into Miller's Court; this was a narrow court about a yard and a half wide at the side of the house. Further up this court, which was approached through a narrow arch, there were six more houses with whitewashed fronts, three on each side, two of which were certainly occupied by prostitutes (and so, one suspects, were the rest). Most of the slum housing in the area had been converted into common lodging houses. One of them, directly opposite Miller's Court, had three hundred beds which were taken every night.

Earlier in the year, in February or March, Room 13 had been let for four shillings a week to an attractive 24-year-old, Mary Jane (or Mary Ann) Kelly. She shared the room with her common-law husband Joseph Barnett until 30 October when they had a violent quarrel, breaking a window in the process. According to Barnett, who left her and went to live in a lodging house in Bishopsgate, they broke up because Kelly brought home another prostitute and insisted on their sharing the room with her. After two or three nights he had refused to do so any longer and this had led to the violent quarrel and break up. He apparently made no attempt to move back, not even when this prostitute, Mrs Harvey, moved out to lodgings in nearby New Court. At this time Kelly was three months pregnant, although the few facts we have indicate that Barnett probably wasn't the father.

Kelly was desperately short of money and went back to soliciting in the Aldgate and Leman Street areas. She owed over three months' rent and was drinking more heavily than usual. On the last night she was seen alive she spent part of it in the public houses in Commercial Street. It was probably in one of these that she picked up a client and took him back home. Mrs Cox, one of the Miller's Court prostitutes, followed them into the court at about 11.45 p.m. Kelly was very drunk. She was with a short stout man, shabbily dressed, with a billycock hat on his head; he had a blotchy face and heavy carrotty moustache and a quart can of beer in his hand. Mrs Cox said 'Goodnight Mary,' and as the man banged the door behind them Kelly called out 'Goodnight, I'm going to have a song'. She began to sing 'Only a violet I plucked from my Mother's Grave when a Boy'. She was still singing when Mrs Cox went out again about a quarter of an hour later and when she returned home at 1 a.m. At about 3.10 a.m., when Mrs Cox returned home for the last time, wet through from the rain, the light was out in Room 13 and the court was quiet.

Directly above Mary Kelly's room was No. 20, occupied by Mrs Elizabeth Praten. She was separated from her husband and almost certainly a prostitute like the others in the court. She went wearily to bed about 1.30 a.m. and fell asleep still wearing her clothes. About 3.30 or 4 a.m., she wasn't sure which, she was woken up by her cat. At the same time she heard a low cry of 'Oh! murder' coming from somewhere close by. The voice was a woman's but she wasn't sure whether it came from the court or one of the houses. She said later that Kelly had had only to move about in her room and she could hear her. As she didn't hear it again she dropped off to sleep once more. This wasn't callousness on her part. She didn't pay any attention because such shouts were a normal occurrence in the neighbourhood. She slept on until 5 a.m. when she got up and went to the Five Bells public house for her morning tot of rum and to solicit for custom among the market porters.

At 10.45 a.m. the lodging-house keeper sent his shop assistant, Thomas Bowyer, to ask Kelly if she could pay the rent as she was thirty-five shillings in arrears. Bowyer knocked on the door. When he couldn't get an answer, he went to the side and poked his hand through the broken pane of glass (which he knew had been stuffed with rags ever since the final quarrel with Barnett) and pulled back the muslin curtain inside. He was horrified by what he saw. The first thing he observed was that there appeared to be two pieces of flesh lying on the table in front of the bed. When he could steel himself to look again he saw the body, which was lying on the bed, and a pool of blood on the floor. He went back to the shop and told M'Carthy what he had seen.

'Good God, do you mean that Harry?' M'Carthy said. They ran back together to Miller's Court and he peered through the jagged glass. The sight was even more ghastly than M'Carthy had expected. He sent Bowyer to the police station for help while he waited outside for the police to arrive. Inspector Beck soon arrived and after he had looked through the window and confirmed the accuracy of the report he sent a telegram to Divisional Superintendent Arnold telling him what had happened. Shortly afterwards Inspector Abberline arrived and gave orders to seal off the Court. Nobody was to enter or leave without his permission. At Dr Phillips' suggestion he refused to let anyone enter the house until the bloodhounds had been given a chance to show what they could do. He cabled a telegram to Warren requesting that they be brought immediately.

Unfortunately none of them knew that Warren had resigned the day before.

Monro's resignation in the summer as head of the C.I.D. had only added to the Commissioner's troubles. Monro had transferred to the Home Office but, even though no longer at Scotland Yard, he still retained his hold over the C.I.D. He was only able to maintain his grip on the plain-clothes department with the support of the Home Secretary, Sir Charles Matthews, who was just as much of a square peg in a round hole as was Warren himself. Warren had vigorously campaigned against this twin-pronged attack, and against the constant undermining of his authority, but his complaints had been ignored and for the past few weeks he had been given only the scantiest details of the conferences which were held at the Home Office every day between Monro, Anderson and the heads of the C.I.D. In November Warren forced a crisis by writing an article for *Murray's Magazine* on 'The Police of the Metropolis'. In it he stressed that the head of C.I.D. should be subordinate to the Commissioner of Police, and that it was impracticable for police work to be done efficiently when one was independent of the other.

Matthews angrily drew his attention to a Home Office circular forbidding police to discuss internal matters in the press and Warren replied by tendering his resignation for the second time on 8 November, the day before Kelly's murder. This time his resignation was accepted. The pill was made even more unpalatable for him by Matthews then appointing Monro as Commissioner in his place.

His resignation momentarily paralysed the police machine and was the reason for the hesitation and indecision next morning after Kelly's body had been found. Nobody in Miller's Court knew, as they waited, that Warren, even then, was still undecided about the merits of buying Burgho and Barnaby, and in spite of several promptings from their owner had not come to any firm conclusions about them. Burgho had been sent back, at the owner's request, to compete in some dog shows, while Barnaby stayed in London at a house in Doughty Street. After the Mitre Square murder, his temporary keeper was asked to take him to a shop that had been burgled close by that same night, just in case the two incidents were linked and that the dog might be able to pick a scent. This was an impossibility as any scent that might have existed had been scoured from the ground by the large number of curious policemen blundering in and out of the shop that night in the hopeless quest for clues. Barnaby's owner was furious when he heard that his dog had been used for such a purpose and demanded its return at once. His greatest fear was that, if it became known that his dogs were being used to track burglars, certain 'ruffians of the night' might try to kill them by putting down traps of poisoned meat. As the police hadn't bought his dogs it was unlikely that in this event they would compensate him for their loss.

Throughout the morning the crowds steadily gathered in Dorset Street. It was Lord Mayor's Day but Jack the Ripper had stolen the show. When the procession had turned into Ludgate Hill in front of St Paul's Cathedral, the newsboys burst through the crowds with their newspapers and placards screaming MURDER—HORRIBLE MURDER. At the same time scores of medical students dashed along the street and the wet, greasy pavements knocking off hats in their high exuberance of animal spirits. One policeman was knocked to the ground by a student who jumped on his back and bit his thumb. All the 'circus element was let loose' and for the Lord Mayor, Sir James Whitehead, the day was ruined. If, as *The Star* thought, the Ripper was craving notoriety and wanted to 'be the sensation of the hour' then he had chosen his time well. 'He got his sensation. While the well-stuffed calves of the City footmen were being paraded for the laughter of London his victim was lying cold in a foul, dimly-lit court in Whitechapel'.

At 1.30 p.m. Superintendent Arnold decided that they could wait for Warren no longer and ordered one of the windows to be taken out. The investigators were appalled by what they saw. The *Illustrated Police News* reported, 'The throat had been cut right across with a knife, nearly severing the head from the body. The abdomen had been partially ripped open, and both of the breasts had been cut from the body, the left arm, like the head, hung to body by the skin only. The nose had been cut off, the forehead skinned, and the thighs, down to the feet, stripped of the flesh. The abdomen had been slashed with a knife across downwards, and the liver and entrails wrenched away. The entrails and other portions of the frame were missing, but the liver etc., it is said, were found placed between the feet of this poor victim. The flesh from the thighs and legs, together with the breasts and nose, had been placed by the murderer on the table, and one of the hands of the dead woman had been pushed into her stomach.'

A photographer arrived and took pictures of this butcher's shambles. There was a popular theory that in cases of violent death the last images were permanently fixed on the retina of the eye and, that by photographing them, the killer could be thus identified. This was the basis of Jules Verne's story 'Les Frères Knap'. Surprisingly, the killer had not mangled the eyes at all. Possibly he had left them alone as some sort of unspoken challenge to the police to do their best— or worst. According to a German correspondent there were three ways of photographing the retina. The eye had to be drawn a little way out of its socket and a small incandescent lamp placed behind the eye. Three photographs had to be taken: (1) of the illuminated pupils; (2) of the illuminated pupils with the nerves of the eye excited by electricity; and (3) the eye not illuminated but again with the nerves electrically excited. Other than the official statement that the eyes were photographed, nothing more is known.

After the photographs had been taken, M'Carthy broke open the door with a pickaxe. This again is a so far unexplained mystery. According to Inspector Abberline, giving evidence at the subsequent inquest, the murderer had not locked the door and walked off with the key as some newspapers supposed. The key, he said, had been missing for some time. Barnett confirmed this. He said that he and Kelly used to open the door by reaching through the broken window at the side and pulling back the bolt. Yet this window was not broken until their quarrel on 30 October. After that, Barnett had visited Kelly several times, on friendly terms—indeed he brought her money— and it is only on these subsequent visits that he could have used this means of entrance. It also means that the key was only lost within the last ten days. Yet *someone* had a key, and used it, which is why the door had to be forced.

As Dr Phillips pushed the door back it knocked against a table by the bed. The first thing he noticed was how sparsely the room was furnished. It was about twelve foot square, and apart from the bed the only furniture was a chair and two tables. The body was wearing a chemise or some linen undergarment and was lying on the edge of the bed nearest to the door. The other side of the bed was touching the wooden partition. From the amount of blood on the floor and on the sheets nearest to the partition Phillips was sure that the body had been moved after the carotid artery had been cut (this having been the immediate cause of death). The bedclothes had been rolled back, presumably by the murderer, but the dead woman's clothes were still neatly folded up on one of the chairs. There were no signs of a struggle, and there was no knife.

A large fire had been burning in the grate. The ashes were still warm, even seven hours after the estimated time that the Ripper had probably left the house. When they were sifted it was evident that he had burnt some woman's clothing, and it was presumed that he had done this to enable him to see what he was about. There were parts of a woman's skirt and the rim of a hat in the grate.

Phillips ordered the body to be taken away to Shoreditch mortuary for a detailed post mortem and inquest. A one-horse carrier's cart trundled into Dorset Street at 3.45 p.m. and the crowds of horrified but interested bystanders watched as a scratched and dirty coffin which had seen a lot of use was carried into the court. When it was realised that the body was to be brought out there was an immediate rush of spectators into Dorset Street from the surrounding area, and a determined effort was made to break through the police lines. 'Ragged caps were doffed and slatternly-looking women shed tears as the shell, covered with a ragged-looking cloth, was placed in the van' and taken away.

After it had gone, the windows of Room 13 were boarded up, a padlock was put on the door and policemen had to be stationed temporarily by the court to keep sightseers away.

Dr McDonald, who was the coroner for the district, fixed the following Monday morning for an inquest to be held at Shoreditch Town Hall.

From the police inquiries, it transpired that only Mrs Prater and Sara Lewis, a laundress, who was visiting a friend's house in Miller's Court, had heard a cry for help. Barnett, who was the main suspect until he had satisfied the police about his quarrel with Kelly, was soon eliminated from the inquiry. His story of the quarrel was confirmed by Mrs Maria Harvey, the prostitute who was the cause of the quarrel. She told the police that Kelly was a better educated woman than most of her class, and that she had last seen her alive on the Thursday night. In spite of a few drinks Kelly had been quite sober when they had split up, and she had gone on to her beat in the Leman Street area. That was the last time that Mrs Harvey had seen her alive.

Already there was a flood of new rumours and scare stories in the newspapers. The latest was that the murderer might be a butcher or drover on one of the cattle boats that usually docked in the Thames on a Thursday or Friday night and left again for the continent on Saturday or Sunday. This schedule explained why the murders had been committed at weekends, and also how the murderer had made his escape. This theory had a lot of support, including that of Queen Victoria who mentioned it in one of her letters and asked if the cattle boats had been searched. Another argument in its favour was that it fitted in with the assertion made at some of the inquests that a butcher might have sufficient knowledge of anatomy as well as the skill to perform the mutilations.

The Whitechapel Vigilance Committee called a special meeting for the following Tuesday at the Paul's Head tavern to discuss further ways in which they could help the police. Certainly people were not slow in coming forward to say that they had been accosted by or had seen the Ripper. Mrs Paumier, who sold roasted chestnuts at the corner of Widegate Street, only two minutes' walk away from Miller's Court, said that on the day the body was found a man, dressed like a gentleman but clearly not one, asked her if she had heard that there had been another murder. When she replied that she had he had grinned and said that he knew more about it than she did. From her description—black moustache, black silk hat, black coat, and speckled trousers, carrying a black shiny bag—he was the same man that had accosted three friends of Mrs Paumier on the night that Kelly was murdered. When one of them had asked him what was in his bag he told her 'Something the ladies don't like', and walked away. A man carrying a similar bag was arrested and taken to Leman Street police station. Another, arrested near Dorset Street, was followed by a howling mob to the police station in Commercial Street.

There were more sensations when the inquest opened on the following Monday morning at Shoreditch Hall. The hearing, to everyone's astonishment, lasted less than half a day. Several newspapers commented unfavourably on the unnatural brevity of the proceedings and on the behaviour of the coroner, Dr Roderick McDonald, M.P., who told the jury that he was only going to take the preliminary part of Dr Phillips's evidence, which was otherwise omitted, and which would be heard in full at an adjourned date. His abrupt termination of the hearing thus allowed for only a minimum of evidence to be given, and he went out of his way to stifle the criticisms of the inquest jury.

The jurors' main objection to the hearing was that it should have been held in Shoreditch at all. The murders had happened in White-chapel and came within Mr Wynne E. Baxter's district. Some of them resented having to hear cases which didn't properly belong to their district, and others to the hearing being presided over by Dr Mc-Donald instead of Mr Baxter. Dr McDonald was a former police surgeon for K Division and was clearly determined to have his own way from the beginning:

> JUROR: I do not see why we should have the inquest thrown on our shoulders when the murder did not happen in our district, but in Whitechapel.
> CORONER'S OFFICER (severely): It did not happen in Whitechapel.
> CORONER (severely): Do you think that we do not know what we are doing here? The jury are summoned in the ordinary way, and they have no business to object. If they persist in their objection I shall know how to deal with them. Does any juror persist in objecting?
> JUROR: We are summoned for the Shoreditch district. This happened in Spitalfields.
> CORONER: It happened within my district.
> ANOTHER JURYMAN: This is not my district. I come from White-chapel, and Mr Baxter is my coroner.
> CORONER: I am not going to discuss the subject with the jurymen at all. If any juryman says he distinctly objects, let him say so. (After a pause.) I may tell the jurymen that jurisdiction lies where the body lies, not where it was found.

He stressed this point a little later by saying that he hadn't been in touch with Mr Baxter, as some newspapers had suggested. 'The body is in my jurisdiction, it was taken to my mortuary, and that is the end of the matter,' he said stiffly.

Before the evidence was given, the jury were taken to the mortuary to see the body which was still lying in the scratched and much-used shell. A dirty grey sheet covered the body up to the neck, so that the mutilations mercifully couldn't be seen. The face itself was slashed and disfigured beyond recognition. Only the eyes showed any signs of humanity. It resembled, according to the *Pall Mall Gazette,* 'one of those horrible wax anatomical specimens.'

After viewing the body, the jurors were taken to Miller's Court and then back to the town hall to hear the first witness, Joseph Barnett. He told the court that he had last seen Kelly alive between 7.30 and 7.45 p.m. on the Thursday evening when she was talking to Maria Harvey. He was questioned in some detail about her background. He said she had told him several times that she had been born in Limerick but had been taken when she was quite young to Wales, where her father had been employed at an ironworks in Carmarthenshire. She had also mentioned that she had six brothers and sisters; one of these brothers was in the army. When she was sixteen she had married a collier named Davis but a year or two later he had been killed in an explosion. Apparently it was the delay in paying her compensation which first drove her onto the streets. This is unconvincing, as she had no children of her own to look after, she wasn't quite eighteen and was capable of earning a living other than as a prostitute. She was twenty when she moved to London in 1884. It's difficult to separate fact from fancy, at this point, but she allegedly lived in a gay house in the West End and then for a short time with a gentleman in France but she didn't like the life and returned to England. Hard facts creep into her story once again with Barnett's disclosures that she had subsequently lived with a man named Morganstone in the Ratcliffe Highway, somewhere near the gasworks, and in Bethnal Green with a mason named Joseph Fleming.

From the medical and other evidence, the time of death had been established as being between 3.30 and 4 a.m. Sara Lewis was one of the witnesses who confirmed this timing. She was a laundress living at 24 Great Pearl Street but had gone to Miller's Court at 2.30 a.m. on Friday morning to visit Mrs Keyler, who lived in the house opposite Room 13. One strongly suspects that she was a prostitute and that possibly she had gone there to shelter from the rain or, like Mrs Harvey, who had shared Kelly's room for a while, had nowhere else to sleep. She said that she had seen a man standing outside the lodging-house door. He was stout, not very tall and had on a black wide-awake hat. She didn't hear any noise as she went down the court, but she heard a woman's scream later on. At the time she

was sitting in a chair in Mrs Keyler's house, having been unable to
sleep, and it was just before 4 a.m., when she heard a woman's voice
shout 'Murder' quite loudly. Her impression was that it was a young
woman's voice and that it came from just outside the door.

There was only the one scream.

She was asked if she was frightened or if she woke anyone up.
Mrs Lewis shrugged her shoulders. 'No,' she said. She had taken no
notice as the woman only screamed once.

Mrs Prater confirmed that she had heard the scream at about that
time.

Yet the evidence of another witness, Mrs Maxwell, contradicted
them both. According to her, she had spoken to Kelly at 8 a.m. *the
next morning*. This was in such direct conflict with all the evidence
that had already been given—including the medical—that the coroner
warned her to be careful about what she said. She told him that she
was the wife of the lodging-house keeper at 14 Dorset Street and
had known Kelly for about four months although she had only spoken
to her about twice. She was positive that she had seen Kelly between
8 and 8.30 a.m. at the corner of Miller's Court, less than three hours
before her body was found, as this was the time that her husband
normally left off work. It was so unusual to see her at such an hour
that Mrs Maxwell had asked her to have a drink. Kelly explained
that the reason why she was up so early was because she felt so bad.
She had drunk a glass of beer and brought it up again. Mrs Maxwell
sympathised and said she could pity her feelings. From this conversation, it is a reasonable inference that she knew that Kelly was pregnant and was referring to her morning sickness. Half an hour later
she saw her outside the Britannia public house talking to a man. She
could see that Kelly was wearing a dark skirt, velvet bodice, maroon
shawl and no hat. The man she was with was wearing dark clothes
and seemed to have a plaid coat on. He was little taller than Mrs
Maxwell herself, and stout.

Almost the last witness was Dr George Bagster Phillips. The Coroner said that he would not go into all the medical details at this
stage and that his more detailed evidence could be given at a later
date. Dr Phillips complied with this directive and said that the immediate cause of death was due to the severing of the carotid artery.

Shortly after Phillips finished giving his evidence, the Coroner, to
the astonishment of his listeners, said that he did not propose to take
any more evidence that day and, turning to the jury, asked if they
had enough evidence to reach their verdict! He said that if they were

satisfied that Mary Kelly had died as the doctor said, by having the carotid artery cut, then they could bring in a verdict to this effect and leave the rest of the investigation in the hands of the police. Of course, if they disagreed with this he would adjourn the inquest for a week or fortnight, when they could hear the evidence they wanted.

The foreman stood up and said that the jury considered that they had heard enough evidence to return a verdict of wilful murder against some person or persons unknown.

This abrupt termination of the inquest was instantly criticised by several newspapers including the *Daily Telegraph,* which gave a plain hint that the Home Secretary should order a new inquiry. By hurriedly closing the hearing, it pointed out, the opportunity had been lost to take statements while the evidence of witnesses was still fresh in their minds. Such mishandling of the most sensational murder of all might, if the killer was ever caught, materially affect the outcome of any future trial and might possibly be the flaw in the case which could lead to his acquittal.

Incredibly there was one witness who didn't come forward until after the inquest. His name was George Hutchinson and he had been out of work for several weeks. He had known Mary Kelly for about three years, and was occasionally able to give her a few shillings. Whether this was meant to imply that he was a casual client is not clear. His statement to the police was the most important one to date as he said that he had met Kelly at 2 a.m. in Thrawl Street, about an hour and a half to two hours before she was murdered. If true, he was the last man to see her alive apart from the killer.

He said that at 2 a.m. he was walking down Thrawl Street, without the money for a bed, and just before he reached Flower and Dean Street he met Kelly who asked him, 'Hutchinson, will you lend me sixpence?' He told her, 'I can't. I have spent all my money going down to Romford.'

She shrugged and said, 'Good morning. I must go and find some money.'

She walked away towards Thrawl Street. As she did so a man coming in the opposite direction tapped her on the shoulder and said something, and they both burst out laughing. Hutchinson was surprised to see her with such a well-dressed man and he stared curiously at them. The man was about 34 or 35 years old, 5 ft. 6 in. tall, with a pale complexion, dark hair and a slight moustache which was curled up at each end. He wore a long dark coat, with collar and cuffs of trimmed astrakhan and a dark-coloured jacket underneath; this was worn over a light-coloured waistcoat holding a very thick gold chain, dark trousers and button boots and gaiters with white buttons. His white shirt and black tie were fastened with a horseshoe pin. In appearance he was Jewish and quite respectable.

He also had a kind of parcel in his left hand with a strap around it.

Hutchinson heard her say 'All right,' and the man reply 'You will be all right for what I have told you.' He then placed his right hand around her shoulders and Hutchinson, who was standing against the lamp outside the Queen's Head public house, watched them as they walked back towards him. The man kept his head down and his dark felt hat over his eyes. Hutchinson was so curious to know what he looked like that he bent down and looked him in the face. This would explain the 'surly face' in his description.

He followed them into Dorset Street and watched them as they stood talking at the corner of Miller's Court for about three minutes. He said something in a low voice and Hutchinson heard Kelly say, quite clearly, 'Alright, my dear. Come along, you will be comfortable.' He then placed his hand on her shoulder and gave her a kiss. She said that she had lost her handkerchief, whereupon the man pulled out his, a red one, and gave it to her before they went up the court together. Hutchinson was curious enough to follow them to see if he could see them—but he couldn't. He waited for about three-quarters of an hour to see if they came out again—but they didn't. And so he went away.

There isn't any description of Hutchinson, unfortunately, but it is probable that he was the man that the laundress saw waiting outside the court when she went into Mrs Keyler's at 2.30 a.m. The probable sequence of events that night was that Kelly took the man home with the pail of beer and got rid of him pretty quickly. This would be sometime between 12 midnight and 2 a.m. when she met Hutchinson. Now she told Hutchinson that she hadn't got any money and so we can assume from this that either this first client didn't pay her, which is unlikely, or that she was pretending poverty and had some reason for doing so. At this point it is worth referring back to M'Carthy and his behaviour the next day. Both he and Barnett tried to pretend ignorance of the fact that Kelly was a prostitute or, in M'Carthy's case, that he had only just learned that she walked the streets in Aldgate. As almost every woman in Miller's Court was a known prostitute this is hard to believe, especially as he rented them their rooms and houses, which were locally known as M'Carthy's Rents, which was probably a local phrase referring to the prostitutes in Miller's Court that were controlled by M'Carthy and not the houses that he owned as has been often assumed.

This interpretation might explain certain other puzzling facts about the Kelly case. All the sources agree that she was owing three months rent to M'Carthy, amounting to thirty-five shillings. However, according to the *Illustrated Police News,* Mrs M'Carthy adhered very 'strictly to the principle of "ready" cash in dealing with lodgers. It is usually her practice to wait on them in the course of the morning, and receive each day's rent in advance.' This was normal practice throughout the area. Why then was Kelly privileged? According to neighbours, Barnett had kept her off the streets—presumably because of her condition. Although there may have been a certain amount of casual prostitution this was probably minimal, and her earnings would have been very little. Barnett could scarcely have earned much more from his casual earnings in the markets. Probably they were just managing to eke out a living, with Kelly's heavy drinking making matters even more difficult.

The room was in her name and probably she was drinking the money that Barnett gave her for the rent. M'Carthy probably allowed her to run up the debt so that he could make even more out of her when he chose. From the facts it seems likely that at the end of October, to get her back to work, he told her that she had to share her room with Mrs Harvey, knowing that this must force Barnett to leave until the debt was paid. This was probably what the real quarrel with Kelly was about, the discovery that they were thirty-five shillings in debt to M'Carthy and that Kelly, in spite of her condition, had to pay it off in the only way that she could. This would also explain why, even after Mrs Harvey had moved out, he did not move back into Room 13 and why he continued to visit Kelly almost daily to give her money and even, the last time that he saw her alive, just to tell her that he had not got any.

Kelly, not quite three months pregnant and probably feeling the effects of morning sickness, was generally too unwell to solicit for much custom. Mrs Maxwell's evidence that Kelly had told her that she felt unwell and had just thrown up had the ring of truth about it and Mrs Maxwell might, just might, have confused the dates when she saw her. Possibly Kelly had been given an ultimatum that she had to earn more money or get out of her room. This would explain why she was so desperate for money on the night she was murdered and why she was ready to pound the streets on a rainy night long after everyone else had gone to bed. It might also offer an explanation for the behaviour of M'Carthy's other 'rents' who felt equally impelled to stagger about the streets until after 3 a.m. in the morning and get up to go to work only two hours later.

In fact, with thirty-five shillings owing in rent, Kelly needed quite a lot of customers to raise the money. Barnett had not given her all the money that he could, and she might have been paid something by the man she took home from the pub, but Hutchinson could give her nothing. And then she meets the stranger. There is some haggling, which Hutchinson witnesses. Probably it was about how much he was willing to pay for spending what was left of the night with her. This might explain the remark that Hutchinson overheard him make 'You will be all right for what I have told you.'

After they had entered the house, Hutchinson waited outside to see if they came out again. (It is almost certain that he was the man whom Mrs Lewis saw standing outside the lodging-house door when she walked up Miller's Court at 2.30 a.m.) Shortly after 2.30 a.m. he went away.

Between 3.30 and 4 a.m., according to an independent medical report, Mary Kelly's killer partly smothered her with a sheet as he killed her, probably by stabbing. Because of the extensive mutilations it was not possible to say how the first blow was struck.

At 6.15 a.m. Mrs Cox heard someone walking down the court. As she didn't hear a door bang it might have been the local policeman but she couldn't be sure. It might just as easily have been Jack the Ripper. This, like so much else, is only conjecture.

One of the things that the police found when they broke down the door was the remains of a large fire in the grate. According to Inspector Abberline the heat had been so intense that it had burnt off the handle and spout of a tin kettle. The ashes were still warm when they entered the house at 1.30 p.m. Assuming 6 a.m. to be roughly the time that the killer left Miller's Court, this means that the ashes had been cooling for over seven hours. When the ashes were sifted they found some pieces of skirt and the brim of a woman's hat. This, it is not unreasonable to assume, was the clothing that Maria Harvey had left behind her. At the inquest she said that it consisted of two men's dirty shirts, a boy's shirt, a black overcoat (which was all the police could find) a black crape bonnet with black satin strings and a girl's white petticoat. Yet this would not have created a great blaze. Mary Kelly's own clothes were lying folded up on the bedside chair and so the unanswered question is: what had been burnt in that grate?

There have been various suggestions. It might have been clothing that the killer himself wore. But the only reason he could have for burning it would have been if it was bloodstained; and as such it is only likely that it would smoulder, and not flare—certainly it would not throw out enough heat to burn the handle and spout off a tin kettle that was designed to withstand intense heat. Even ordinary combustibles such as coal and coke would have to have the help of a bellows to throw out the sort of heat that would do this. Another suggestion is that these things were burnt to give him light. If light was what he needed, why had he not used the candle which stood there. Surely the risks were much smaller with one small flickering flame than with a roaring fire?

While Inspector Abberline was busily following up these clues, the newspapers and public at large were rejoicing over the downfall of Sir Charles Warren. *Punch* jeeringly published a parody of the nursery rhyme which they called 'Who Killed Cock Warren?'

Who chased COCK WARREN?
'I,' said the Home Sparrow,
'With my views cramped and narrow,
I chased COCK WARREN.'

And who'll fill his place?
'I,' said Monro,
'I'm the right man, I know,
And I'll fill his place.'

And who'll tie your hands?
'I,' said Routine,
'That my business has been,
So I'll tie his hands.'

Who'll see fair play?
'I,' said John Bull,
'For I'm quite a fool;
I'll see fair play!'

Warren had tendered his resignation on 8 November but he didn't remove his papers from his office until 12 November when it was officially announced in the House of Commons to the cheers of the Opposition.

One of his last acts had been to put his name to a document that was nothing more or less than a confession of failure. It was an official pardon and read:

MURDER–PARDON. Whereas, on November 8 or 9 in Miller's Court, Dorset Street, Spitalfields, Mary Jane Kelly was murdered by some person or persons unknown, the Secretary of State will advise the grant of Her Majesty's pardon to any accomplice not being a person who contrived or actually committed the murder who shall give such information and evidence as shall lead to the discovery and conviction of the person or persons who committed the murder.

Ironically, within a few months it was evident that the murders had come to an end, and it was widely assumed that the Ripper was dead.

5

FROM HELL

At the peak of the murders, the police were being bombarded with an estimated one thousand letters per week. The Lord Mayor, bishops, spiritualists and the newspapers were similarly deluged with letters. Few of them were of any genuine help. Many were from cranks. All of them had to be bundled up and passed on to the hard-pressed police, who had to sift through them and decide which were worth following up. Occasionally one gets more than a hint of the exasperation they felt at this correspondence. Scribbled across many of them in red ink are such remarks as 'Take no notice of this', 'The man must be a lunatic!' and 'Not acknowledged'. Letters were still coming in at such a rate the following July that the Yard was forced to go to the unusual length of having acknowledgment slips, headed 'Whitechapel Murders', specially printed. The newspapers also suffered from the collective madness only slightly less. After *The Star* published a leader on the murders, it was inundated with letters and for several days it overflowed with correspondence on the question 'Is Christianity a Failure?' Two of the many letters not accepted for publication were signed respectively 'J.C.' and 'Shendar Brwa'—the latter being an anagram of Bernard Shaw. The Shavian wit is evident throughout the first letter, too, blasphemously signed 'J.C.' (Jesus Christ):

Sir,

Why do you try to put the Whitechapel murders on me? Sir Charles Warren is quite right not to catch the unfortunate murderer, whose conviction and punishment would be conducted on my father's old lines of an eye for an eye, which I have always consistently repudiated. As to the eighteen centuries of what you call Christianity, I have nothing to do with it. It was invented by an aristocrat of the Roman set [St Paul], a university man whose epistles are the silliest middle class stuff on record. When I see my name mixed up with it in your excellent paper, I feel as if nails were going into me—and I know what the sensation is like better than you do. Trusting that you will excuse this intrusion on your valuable space.

I am, Sir &c., J.C.

Most readers could not grasp that the murders were being committed by an individual such as themselves. There had to be something extraordinary about such a man. One woman, writing 'In confidence' from the Isle of Wight, thought that he might be a large ape belonging to some wild beast show. Clearly she had been reading Poe's *The Murders in the Rue Morgue,* for she continues, 'This animal would be swift, cunning, noiseless and strong, standing over its work until a footstep was heard and then vaulting over a fence or wall, disappearing in a moment, hiding its weapon high up in a tree [in Whitechapel?] or other safe place, and returning home to lock itself up in its cage.'

A 46-year-old widow, however, believed that respectable women such as she had nothing to fear from the Whitechapel murderer as she thought it was true that he 'respects and protects respectable females.' His manners were none too gentlemanly, it seems, for she continues, 'I feel certain it was him whom I saw one night in the Devonshire Street end of Cavendish Court on or about the 30th of August. Although conducting himself in a disgusting manner he allowed one to pass without a murmur.' Piously she hopes that, 'when in the agony of his own death he takes the last look for mercy, may the sigh of his soul be Jesus, sweet Jesus.'

One popular theory for the killings was that the criminal had been 'badly disfigured by disease—*possibly had his privy member destroyed* —and he is now revenging himself on the sex by these atrocities.' Somebody else, who had reached the same conclusion, thought that he might be 'suffering from syphilis and is using the part cut off from the woman as a kind of poultice to suck off the virus from his ulcers. This is a vile superstition of the Chinese and Malays who commit this kind of crime for this very purpose.' If true, it pointed to a man who had travelled in the China seas.

The alternative, which another correspondent suggested, was that he was a Hill tribesman. 'In the sanscrit mythology, particular reverence is paid to the male and female generative organs. I have been informed by old soldiers who had been admitted to the home life of the *Hill Tribes,* the very organs themselves, preserved are hung

up as *Amulets* &c.' Warming to his theme he asks, 'Has a gang of
these Hill tribes started to work? They would be scarcely distinguished from Europeans in a dimly lighted street. Murder for ob-
taining the female organ among them is a sacred action.' The other
possibility—too dreadful to contemplate—was that it might be a white
man who had adopted their customs while on civil or military duties:
'Sunstroke would then loose all civilized restraints on such matters.'
The same correspondent, in further conversations with his old soldier,
had been told by him that it was quite common for the East Indian
tribes to carry a concealed weapon with a fine point like a needle,
dipped in poison, of which one prick on the vein would mean instantaneous death. A man armed with such a weapon could, while caress-
ing a woman, deliver 'the fatal prick on the spine or veins of the neck,'
and she would fall to the pavement with very little noise. 'The cutting
of the throat, diverts suspicion and complies with the savage ritual.'
He forwarded with his second letter thirty copies of his pamphlet 'The
Apocalypse Unveiled and a Fight with Death and Slander', which
was his own translation of the Book of Revelations into plain every-
day speech; he didn't guarantee the correctness of his explanations
of the symbols but had simply thrown the pamphlet out as a challenge
in order that a fuller understanding could be attempted.

An English teacher who had been in Turin for the past twenty-
two years thought that a follower of Buddha might be the killer—
perhaps one of the Thugs, who were practised killers and 'bound to
offer human victims to their deity. . . . The murders taking place
at given periods in the month may be some indication as to the time
such human sacrifices are offered—perhaps at different phases of the
moon. . . .'

Dreams often suggested ways of tracking down the killer. A clergy-
man at Newmarket dreamed that the two murderers were two men
named Pat Murphy and Jim Slaney, and that they would walk past
22 Gresham Street at 4.10 p.m. on Wednesday 28 November. As
he couldn't leave Newmarket on that day would the police kindly
send a couple of detectives to watch for two young men passing No.
22 about that time? As proof that his letter wasn't a hoax he had
asked his churchwarden to countersign his letter, which was politely
acknowledged as was another from B. Barraclough, of York, who
said that he had sent a telegram two days before that read: 'Watch
the house 20 Wurt Street, W.C.' He explained why in the letter that
followed. His children had been experimenting with the table to see
if it would rap out a message, as it was supposed to do in a seance.

It did, in fact, rap out, 'More murders tonight in London.' In reply to further questioning it said that another woman would be killed by the same man, whose name and address were 'Tom Totson, 20 Wurt Street, W.C.' Furthermore, the spirit had told the sender to warn the police by telegram, which he had done, partly to relieve himself of the heavy responsibility lying on him and partly from a belief that there may be 'more things on heaven and earth . . . Than are dreamt of in your philosophy.'

Equally receptive to these unseen influences was Josiah E. Boys, late Private King's Own Scottish Borderers, who wrote a warning to Sir James Fraser, the City Police Commissioner, that he had seen a message scrawled on one of the walls of a water closet in Guild-hall and reading: 'I am Jack the Ripper and Intend to do another murder at Adelphi Arches, at 2 a.m.' Mr Boys thought that this warning might be a hoax but as the writer had added 'I will send the ears to Colonel Frazer' he thought that he had better communicate these facts at once, as he thought the handwriting bore a striking similarity to the letters which had been published in the newspapers. The message, he concluded lamely, had been scrawled on the wall in lead pencil.

The commonest suggestion of all was that the killer could be trapped by disguising policemen as women. These letters nearly all stress that the men must be clean shaven and armed with snaps (handcuffs) and revolvers. Richard Taylor, who gives his address as the Public Baths, Endell Street, Long Acre, asked for the following suggestion to be forwarded to the Vigilance Committee as he couldn't find out their address: '. . . in addition to the ordinary costume, I would suggest that a kind of corset of metal (ring mail would be most efficient) should enclose the trunk and that, as broad a band as possible of thin flexible steel be worn round the throat, this being light could be made with a suitable covering to represent an ordinary collar, and if a broad tapering piece were attached to that and bent up under the jaw, it would shield the throat from anything like serious injury. This collar would be further utilized as the terminal of a powerful storage battery, to be varied *à la* dress improver—the ter-minals could be on either side of the collar, or assuming the victim is (as is most probable) grasped from the rear, a pair might be led up the headgear and discharged if grasped from that position. The shock would possibly so seriously disconcert the assassin, that it would be a comparatively easy matter to secure him.'

A gentleman in Cheshire, not quite so vicious, suggested that women should carry a piece of paper liberally pasted with bird lime which they could slap upon the Ripper's rear shoulder or back and which he would not observe but which would identify him to the police. Precisely at what stage of the attack they were to get this out of their handbag he does not make plain. An extra precaution, wrote an ex-patriate Yorkshireman from Cleveland, Ohio, would be an alarm wire fixed to the pavement kerbs with electric warning buttons about thirty feet apart; these would lead to a shop or store, 'where the police have got to warm themselves in winter nights,' where there would be a panel of alarm bells, each of which would indicate the street that they were connected to. Prostitutes would be additionally armed with revolvers so that, when attacked, they could keep the Ripper at bay and ring one of these bells for help. A policeman on horseback, so the same writer calculated, should be capable of galloping to any one of these points within half a minute. He stressed that on no account must you (the Lord Mayor) let an Irish detective peep at it (his plan). He must be an Englishman. Should the police wish to make him an offer . . .

A more practical suggestion was that there should be better street lighting and that the police, by means of their whistles, should innovate a rapid warning system to alert colleagues on other beats.

Of course, some of the letters were decidedly odd. The instructions in the following letter are so explicit that it is a reasonable assumption that the writer was himself some kind of fetishist. He asks for locks of hair from the last two victims to give to a friend of his who, so he says, by similar means had brought to justice persons who were guilty of cruelty to animals when there was no other evidence to convict them. (Did he use hair from these animals?). He instructs: 'cut the hair with any human hand and send it to me. . . . If the hair cannot be procured send on something belonging (to) the victims (that) they were wearing at the time and worn close to the skin.'

Some letters had quite hilarious origins. A telegram from Dublin warned, 'Arrest Palermo Nagro, Alias Wilmo, ht 5 feet to 5 feet 9, as Whitechapel Murderer.' It was signed 'I. Fogarty, 47 North Strand Road'. The report which followed from the Dublin C.I.D., who interviewed the sender, was that 'Fogarty is and was for some days suffering from Delirium Tremens. He is aware that he sent a telegram to London, but respecting what he cannot say.' Apparently his friends had telegraphed his wife in Cork to come and fetch him home, which she did, but she had only managed to get him as far as Dublin when he gave her the slip. He only got away for just a few minutes but this was long enough for him to send the telegram. He was horribly frightened when he was questioned about it and thought that he was going to be prosecuted for causing a public mischief. The officer charitably concluded that, 'There is no doubt that the fellow was mad when sending the telegram' and presumably recommended no further action.

Some writers thought that the Ripper was a foreigner and that he should be kicked out of the country with other political refugees and into the sea: 'If the government don't act plucky . . . the City is doomed to destruction,' said one. He added that the murders were committed from anti-police motives and that they were calculated to overthrow the Empire. He explained:

> A week or two ago I noticed a poster of *The Star* saying 'War on Warren'. I have been daily looking for the outbreak in any form and I admit it is apparent [that] in the Horrors they thought [that] by demoralising the Police force [that] they would make government impossible [and] that Lord Salisbury would resign and Gladstone come in and the ruin of the Empire certain—and their distinguished object gained—A Republic—*God Forbid*.
>
> The safety of the public has depended very much upon the Salvation Army who have been going about the country, amongst the labouring classes especially making good citizens and antagonistic to the Socialists who hates them and would like to destroy them.

Another writer took the opposite view. He thought that, because the victims were working class, the Ripper must be of the 'upper or wealthy sort' who think that the world and its inhabitants exist 'for their pleasures—that of revenge being included—as a life business; without regard to any law but their own will.'

Yet another thought that the Ripper might be one of the socialist pedagogues who nearly every day hoisted the red flag in Hyde Park. He had overheard one of them say, 'Wait till we get a few murders done up here in the West End and then you'll see what a howl there'll be.'

A number of the many suspects were named. They included the lunatic living at Fulham who used to recite and sing tragical stories, accompanying his gestures with an ivory-handled knife which he used to keep in a black shiny leather Gladstone bag; Herbert Freund, who used to create disturbances in St Paul's Cathedral; the Germans who worked in the Sugar House in Hanbury Street (and seldom leaving it), who had come to England to avoid army conscription in their own country; Richard Mansfield, the star of a successful stage production of *Dr Jekyll and Mr Hyde* (the writer accusing Mansfield had not been able to rest for a day and a night after seeing the performance, claiming that no man could disguise himself so well and that, since Mansfield worked himself up into such a frenzy on stage, he probably did the real life murders too); William Onion, who had been released from Colney Hatch lunatic asylum and who had 'ginger wiskers' and 'a Crucked flatish nose' with a faint scar, the result of being hit by a pepper box. One correspondent was positive that the Ripper could be identified by procuring *Davidson's Illustrated Comprehensive Bible*. This, if it were to be opened at the Lord's Supper, would show a 'knife clearly visible, but who is the holder of that knife, I seem to think he will be found out. I may be saucy when I am irritated but I would shrink from those deeds. Yours respectfully John Legg Bagg Junior. P.S. I do not think it is my Father because I know he would not do it neither do I think he been to London.' Another anonymous correspondent signed himself 'Richard Whittington the Second', another forwarded his suggestions on Home Office notepaper! A popular suspect was the watchman in Mitre Square: one writer said she had dreamt she had seen him peeping out of the warehouse door and laughing at the policemen as they turned the corner. A writer from Australia thought the murders were the work of Germans who skinned people and wore these second skins as disguises which they pasted on with American glue; their motives were that they were working in league with their men in the Colonial office, and in time hoped to get the Crown of England, the Colonies and India and the New World! (The Commissioner, not surprisingly, scribbled across the letter: 'This appears to be the work of a lunatic.')

There was no lack of volunteer detectives ready to help the police. Ladies offered to take the place of the prostitutes and were quite willing to be martyred for the sake of their country. A father of five daughters, four of them living with him, asked that, should his help be needed, advertisements be placed as follows in the *Evening Standard:*

Nemo Come—I should then present myself in Old Jewry
Nemo Go—I should then present myself at Scotland Yard
Nemo Remain—In this latter case I should present myself at Leman Street Station at 7 o'clock in the evening of the day on which the advertisement appears.

One of the Ripper's hiding places, it was suggested, might have been an old vault in the Jews' Cemetery. Alternatively, he could have escaped through the underground sewers which would account for his sudden disappearances; at the same time he could tear into shreds the dark woollen serge coat which he would have been wearing and scatter its bloodstained pieces underground. Other letter writers were obviously having a good laugh at the expense of the police, including Andy Handy who, 'saw A man go into Mr Barclay & Son he had A bag in his hand and it snap open and I saw to feet and A head of A human Person he had A large knife in his pocket'. Another prayed that God would show him the murderer. Apparently He did better than usual: He showed him the Ripper in his three disguises, one of them involving a black turban cap of Scotch pattern, which led the writer to conclude that the Ripper might be a Frenchman, a German, or an Italian, a soldier or a Lord; a final bonus, granted to this same visionary, was the vision of an unknown woman who could be identified by her missing nose—and who was the missing link in the case (she was apparently the woman that the Ripper had been searching for and now that he had killed her there would not be any further killings). Of course, if the police have no faith and didn't believe him . . .

There were many suggested ways of trapping Jack. One nineteenth-century Emmett suggested that female dummies should be placed in the darkest and loneliest spots; their arms and legs would be powerful springs 'capable of being released by moderate force, such as raising the chin or pressing the throat. Once released these springs would act like the arm of an "Octopus" and hold the person entrapped, while a sound resembling a police whistle might proceed from the machine.'

Another was that women should wear velvet-covered steel collars and, something far nastier, a soft-covered collar with 'fine, sharp pointed stings (thorns), that the infernal assassin will be thus hardly wounded. . . . At the same moment the officer will turn round and take hold of the murderer *above the hand, turning it with all the power of his two hands against the breast* of the scoundrel; thus, that this monster must *bore his own knife into his own breast* or *must let fall it* . . . and don't give this *Idea* to any one except the *Chief of Police* (as your Lordship would warn unconscious that way the blood-hound). *For—who can say, that this criminal don't belong to a rich family*. The officer or officers should look at every suspicious

women or all women in general. . . . The *D—* may know what
is often in such a *petticoat!!!!*'.

This was as about as sensible as the suggestion that suspicious-
looking couples should have corrosive matter discharged onto their
clothes by means of glass syringes, so that there would be a distinc-
tive mark by which to identify them. When the next victim was found
her killer could be then traced (1) through the description of him
that the police would already have; and (2) by matching up the stains
on his clothes!

The three hundred to five hundred detectives that would be needed
for this manhunt could be recruited, one writer felt sure, from the
young Emperor of Germany who was known to be very fond of his
Royal Grandmother Queen Victoria and who would willingly loan
her a thousand detectives from Berlin. The Emperor of Russia and
the French President would, he felt sure, be equally agreeable to loan-
ing her a similar number of men.

Another writer warned that the policemen must be constantly on
their guard as he felt sure the Ripper was stupefying his victims with
a chloroform-soaked handkerchief before killing them; therefore, as
an urgent precaution, they were to arrest anyone who came near them
and tried to blow his nose! As a final precaution, all detectives were
to act drunk, and wear iron collars and body armour.

Of course, there was always the possibility that the killer's vanity
might lead to his downfall. Why could not he be traced through the
newsagents and newsboys when he bought the newspaper accounts
on the mornings after his murders. This was assuming that it was
only at such times that he bought newspapers. No doubt the newsagents could identify such a monster. Every one of them should keep
a list of clients and against the ones that they most suspected they
should scribble the word 'horrible'.

With so much activity in Whitechapel it was clear that the police,
as well as the Ripper, were going to be stumbling over each other
every few yards. This led to a suggestion that Whitechapel should
be cleared of policemen, except for one hundred pairs of detectives
and the prostitutes they could hire for two shillings a night as decoys.
Otherwise, too much activity was only going to frighten the Ripper
away. Alternatively, since he took such an interest in the efforts that
were being made to catch him, why not call a public meeting in a
hotel, to discuss these ways, and as he was bound to attend, lock
him in once the meeting had started!

The final suggestion was perhaps the best of all. The following advertisement was to be inserted in the newspapers to trap the medical man that the Ripper was thought to be:

> Medical Man or Assistant Wanted in London, aged between 25 and 40. Must not object to assist in occasional post mortem. Liberal terms. Address stating antecedents. PTR [Please to reply]
> NAME   STREET

If only he had!

Few of the letters signed 'Jack the Ripper', or purporting to come from him, are of any real value—in fact, a ruthless weeding-out process leaves only two. Of interest, however, is the first letter to use the name. It was posted on 28 September 1888, and had a London East Central postmark. It read:

25 Sept. 1888

Dear Boss,

    I keep on hearing the police have caught me but they won't fix me just yet. I have laughed when they look so clever and talk about being on the right track. That joke about Leather Apron gave me real fits. I am down on whores and I shan't quit ripping them till I do get buckled. Grand work the last job was. I gave the lady no time to squeal. How can they catch me now. I love my work and want to start again. You will soon hear of me with my funny little games. I saved some of the proper red stuff in a ginger beer bottle over the last job to write with but it went thick like glue and I can't use it. Red ink is fit enough I hope *ha ha*. The next job I do I shall clip the lady's ears off and send to the police officers just for jolly wouldn't you. Keep this letter back till I do a bit more work, then give it out straight. My knife is nice and sharp I want to get to work right away if I get a chance. Good luck.

Yours truly
JACK THE RIPPER

Don't mind me giving the trade name.
wasn't good enough to post this before I got all the red ink off my hands curse it.
No luck yet they say I am a doctor now *ha ha*.

As it was posted two days before the 'double event', he was clearly referring to the Hanbury Street murder when he says 'Grand work

the last job was. I gave the lady no time to squeal.' Did he mean
that he took her by surprise or—recalling the witness who remembered
hearing a woman call out 'No!' and then heard something fall against
the fence—did he mean that he killed her before she could call out
again? Unfortunately the wording is too ambiguous to decide one way
or another. However, the threat to 'clip the lady's ears off' meant
that the letter had to be taken seriously, as the killer tried to do precisely that with both Eddowes and Stride. The ugly slash that can
still be seen on the post-mortem photographs of Eddowes is apparently where he drew his knife across her face with the apparent intention of cutting off her right ear. Yet, if this letter was genuine, and
he really wanted to send the ears to the police as he had threatened,
why didn't he? It could hardly have been for lack of time, since he
had enough to disembowel the unfortunate woman—it would have
required but a second's further work to cut off an ear.

The second letter was posted on 30 September, the day of the
'double event'. This time his communication was written on a postcard and, like the first, was sent to the Central News Agency. It read:

> I was not codding dear old Boss when I gave you the tip. You'll
> hear about Saucy Jack's work tomorrow. Double event this time.
> Number one squealed a bit. Couldn't finish straight off. Had not
> time to get ears for police. Thanks for keeping last letter back till
> I got to work again.
>
> JACK THE RIPPER.

Details of the 'double event' were not known until they were published in the newspaper on the following day, Monday 1 October,
and for twenty-four hours at least they would have been confined
to Whitechapel and some of central London. Only the murderer could
have known that he had not been able to finish the first victim off
and had not had time enough to 'clip her ears'. In conjunction with
the first letter which he thanked the police for keeping back—a cir-
cumstance that only the killer could have known about—both letters
unless proved otherwise, must be considered as having a common
source. The police tried to trace the writer by publishing a facsimile
poster of both the letter and the postcard and circulating it within
three days of the double killing asking for anyone who recognised
the handwriting to communicate with the nearest police station.

The most apparently genuine letter of all was not received until
16 October. It was sent to George Lusk, who was head of the White-

chapel Vigilance Committee, and was enclosed within a small parcel containing part of a kidney! The note was addressed 'From Hell' and read

> Mr Lusk
>
> Sir I send you half the Kidne I took from one woman prasarved it for you tother piece I fried and ate it was very nise I may send you the bloody knif that took it out if you only wate a whil longer
>
> signed   Catch me when you can Mishter Lusk

When Eddowes' body had been examined by the police surgeon one of the kidneys had indeed been found to be missing. This letter and the kidney were sent to Major Smith of the City Police who asked the police surgeon to consult with the most eminent specialists in the medical profession about it and get a report to him without delay. Unfortunately, as he later wrote, 'some clerk or assistant in the office was got at, and the whole affair was public property next morning. Right royally did the Solons of the metropolis enjoy themselves at the expense of my humble self and the City police force. "The kidney was the kidney of a dog, anyone could see that," wrote one. "Evidently from the dissecting room," wrote another. "Taken out of a corpse after a post-mortem," wrote a third. "A transparent hoax," wrote a fourth.'

The kidney was examined by Dr Openshaw, the Pathological Curator of the London Hospital Museum. He said that it was a 'ginny' kidney of the sort found in an alcoholic, that it belonged to a woman of about forty-five, and that it had been removed within the last three weeks. The kidney was in an advanced state of Bright's disease, and the one that had been left in the body was in an exactly similar state. As final proof that it did indeed come from the same body, Smith added that of the renal artery (which is about three inches long) two inches remained in the body and one inch was still attached to the kidney. Mr Sutton, one of the senior surgeons at the London Hospital, who examined the kidney with Dr Openshaw, said that he would pledge his reputation that it had been put in spirits within a few hours of removal from the body.

After the inquest a jeering letter, postmarked 29 October, was sent to Dr Openshaw. This he handed to Major Smith. It said:

> Old boss you was rite it was the left kidny i was goin to hoperate agin close to your ospitle just as i was going to dror mi nife along

of er bloomin throte them cusses of coppers spoilt the game but
i guess i wil be on the job soon and will send you another bit
of innerds

Jack the ripper

O have you seen the devle with his mikerscope and scalpul a-lookin
at a kidney with a slide cocked up.

How authentic were these letters? Of which of them could it be said
that the writer was definitely 'Jack the Ripper'? Sir Robert Anderson
in his book *The Lighter Side of My Official Life* threw considerable
doubts on the first two by saying: 'So I will only add here that the
"Jack the Ripper" letter which is preserved in the Police Museum
at New Scotland Yard is the creation of an enterprising journalist.'
And Sir Melville Macnaghten confirmed that this was so by com-
menting in his own memoirs: 'In this ghastly production I have always thought I could discern the stained forefinger of the journalist—
indeed, a year later I had shrewd suspicions as to the actual author!
But whoever did pen the gruesome stuff, it is certain to my mind
that it was not the mad miscreant who had committed the murders.'

This being so, it does suggest that both the letter and the postcard
were a hoax. Until now, it has generally been assumed that the early
reference to the 'double event' before it had been published in the
newspapers was proof positive that it must have come from the Ripper. If, as both Anderson and Macnaghten say, they had strong suspicions as to the identity of the author and that he was a journalist
(and probably working on the case for Anderson, at least, to have
known him), then the case for their being genuine falls down. Certainly it would explain how the writer knew in advance of the 'double
event'.

Donald McCormick disputes this and offers the evidence of Dr
Thomas Dutton who, prior to the murders, had specialised in micro-
photography and who was a prominent figure in the Chichester and
West Sussex Microscopic Society. Apparently he had made a hundred
and twenty-eight specimens of the Jack the Ripper correspondence
and of these at least thirty-four were in the same handwriting.

'The writing was disguised to appear to be that of an uneducated
man on some occasions; on others it was that of a painstaking clerk.
The same with the phraseology. But even that was marked by 'lapses'

into literacy, especially in Jack's effective essays into verse. To quote
one example:

> Eight little whores, with no hope of heaven,
> Gladstone may save one, then there'll be seven.
> Seven little whores begging for a shilling,
> One stays in Henage Court, then there's a killing.
> Six little whores, glad to be alive,
> One sidles up to Jack, then there are five.
> Four and whore rhyme aright,
> So do three and me,
> I'll set the town alight
> Ere there are two.
> Two little whores, shivering with fright,
> Seek a cosy doorway in the middle of the night.
> Jack's knife flashes, then there's but one,
> And the last one's the ripest for Jack's idea of fun.

It may not be verse in the accepted sense, but this is certainly not
the composition of an illiterate. Jack would sometimes misspell words
deliberately, then forget later on and write a word correctly. It was
the same with his punctuation. He wrote 'Jewes' with an extra 'e'
when he scrawled his message in chalk on the wall, and which the
police so stupidly washed off. But he also spelt the word correctly
in some letters.

I was asked by the police to photograph the message on the wall
before it was washed off, but Sir Charles Warren was so insistent
that the message must not be preserved in any form that he ordered
the police to destroy the prints I sent them.'

This I find frankly incredible. Even if true, why did Dr Dutton never
keep copies and what, in fact, did he do with the originals? Did they
ever exist? As he had apparently had full police co-operation with
the other hundred and twenty-eight specimens, why should they then
jib at this particular message when, according to Dutton, he 'definitely
established that the writing was the same as that in some of the letters'? His microphotograph would have settled once and for all the
doubts that still exist about precisely what was written on that wall.
Even the police constable who found it in Goulston Street reported
it wrongly when he was giving evidence at the inquest. He said the
message was 'The Jews are the men that will not be blamed for noth-

ing', and it was only after persistent cross-examination that he revealed that 'Jews' should have read 'Juwes' and that the correct wording of the full message was 'The Juwes are not the men that will be blamed for nothing'. According to a B.B.C. television presentation of the case in 1973, this spelling of Jews has a Masonic connotation. The Biblical Solomon ordered the three Jews who had murdered the Grand Mason Hiram Abiff to be killed with 'due ceremony and *formal ritual*'. The wording is that '. . . for the murder of J-U-W-E-S . . . Let the breast be torn open and the heart and vitals be taken from thence and thrown over the shoulder'. This recalls the following cross-examination at the Eddowes inquest:

> DR BROWN: . . . The abdomen was all exposed; the intestines were drawn out to a large extent and placed over the right shoulder; a piece of the intestine was quite detached from the body and placed between the left arm and the body.
> MR CRAWFORD: By 'placed' do you mean put there by design?
> DR BROWN: Yes.
> MR CRAWFORD: Would that also apply to the intestines that were over the right shoulder?
> DR BROWN: Yes.

A similar sort of thing had happened to Annie Chapman. Dr Phillips had said, when he examined the body in the backyard at Hanbury Street, 'The intestines, severed from the mesenteric attachments had been lifted out of the body and placed on the shoulder of the corpse.'

At the time several newspapers had said that the Yiddish spelling of Jewes was 'Juwes', but in *The Times* of 15 October Warren asked the newspaper to report that he had made inquiries about this very point, his attention having been drawn to the newspaper reports, and that the Yiddish equivalent was 'Yidden'. The report concluded, 'It has not been ascertained that there is any dialect or language in which the words "Jews" is spelt "Juwes"'. However, there is a spelling which approximates to it so closely that one can't help feeling that, had Police constable Long taken a little more care in copying down the message, the investigation might have taken a slightly different turn. The spelling is the French word for Jews which is 'Juives'. On the black fascia on which the message was written, it is possible that he didn't see or else ignored the dot over the 'i'; and in an italic hand the 'i' and 'v' when they are joined together can quite easily be mistaken for a 'w'. If so, are we looking for a Frenchman or a linguist?

When the dust has cleared away there is only one letter which has any bottom and that is the letter addressed 'From Hell'. The others may or may not have been written by the Ripper. It is unlikely that we shall ever know. Most writers have made the mistake, when they have been comparing specimens, of looking for similarities between such normal signatures as Druitt's and J. K. Stephen's and the Ripper letters. This is a mistaken approach, as was thoroughly proved at the trial of Peter Kürten who deliberately modelled himself on the Ripper even to the extent of writing to the newspapers. Under stress his handwriting became unrecognisable—so much so that he showed the 'murderer's' letters to his wife, when they were published in facsimile in the newspapers, and although she looked at them carefully she saw no resemblance between them and her husband's handwriting.

In August 1968 a Canadian graphologist, C. M. Macleod, published in *The Criminologist* an article called 'A "Ripper" Handwriting Analysis'. This was prompted by Professor Camps's article 'More About "Jack the Ripper"' which had appeared in the February issue and which had reproduced in facsimile some of the letters. The specimens he chose for analysis were the letter addressed 'From Hell' and the one beginning 'Old boss you was rite . . .'.

In Macleod's opinion, 'they are the efforts of two persons having similar perversions but important personality differences. Both specimens reveal a propensity to cruelly perverted sexuality to a degree that even the most casual amateur graphologist could hardly mistake.' The most obvious thing about both letters is their untidiness. The blotting and smearing suggest that the writers were addicted to drink or possibly drugs. Both were certainly sadists, as indicated by the 'sharp angles and dagger strokes' which 'can only be produced by a violently jerky thrust of the hand, suggesting extreme tension finding a vent in anger.' Their age would have been somewhere between twenty and forty-five, and both were probably 'working class'. If he had had to pick one of them as being the real Jack the Ripper then he would go for the writer of the letter 'From Hell', who 'shows tremendous drive in the vicious forward thrust of his overall writing, and great cunning in his covering-up of strokes; that is, the retracing of one stroke of a letter over another, rendering it illegible while appearing to clarify. While Sample 1 appears to be written better than Sample 2, it is in fact extremely difficult to decipher; whereas Sample

2, except for the atrocious spelling, is fairly readable.' Macleod continues:

> I would say that this writer was capable of conceiving any atrocity, and of carrying it out in an organised way. I would say he had enough brains and control to hold down some steady job which would give him a cover for his crimes. He has imagination, as revealed in the upper-zone flourishes. Those hooks on the t-bars, among other signs, indicate tenacity to achieve a goal.
>
> I could have looked for this killer among men such as cab-drivers, who had a legitimate excuse to be anywhere at any time. I should have sought a hail-fellow-well-met who liked to eat and drink; who might attract women of the class he preyed on by an overwhelming animal charm. I would say he was in fact a latent homosexual (suggested by lower-zone strokes returning on the wrong side of the letter,) and passed as a 'man's man'; the roistering blade who made himself the life and soul of the pub and sneered at women as objects to be used and discarded. He would, of course, have had wits enough to stop short of explaining how he used them.

6
AFTERMATH

The following year new fears began to spread that Jack the Ripper was not dead and that another wave of killings was about to start.

On 17 July 1889 a woman was murdered in Whitechapel. In almost every respect the killing in Castle Alley was a Ripper event. Shortly before 1 a.m., P.c. 272H Walter Andrew met the duty sergeant on his nightly rounds and, after a few words of desultory greeting, continued his patrol. The sergeant had only gone about 150 yards when he heard Andrews blow his whistle for help. He ran back to see what was the matter and followed the constable as he ran up Castle Alley. Lying on the pavement, close to two vans, was the body of a woman. She was lying on her right side with her clothes half up to her waist. The constable pointed to the pool of blood under her head and said 'Another murder'. He had already knelt down and felt the body which, in spite of a slight drizzle, was still warm. Close by was a man whom the constable had seen walking along the street with a plate in his hand innocently going for his supper. As he had been the only person in the street the constable had made him wait with him until he could prove his innocence, which he soon did. As soon as police reinforcements arrived they were sent immediately to the lodging and coffee houses to make searches.

There was an old scar on the top of the woman's left thumb, which was missing, as was a tooth from the upper jaw. The stuff bodice dress was patched under the arms and sleeves and she had on odd stockings, one black and the other maroon. Her brown stuff skirt, kilted brown linsey petticoat, white chemise and apron, paisley shawl (which was still around her shoulders) and button boots were all old clothes. Her only possessions were a farthing and an old clay pipe, which were found under her body.

The woman was soon identified as 'Clay pipe Alice' McKenzie. Not much was known about her. She had been living with a labourer,

John McCormac, who for the past sixteen years had done casual work for Jewish tailors in Hanbury Street (where Annie Chapman had been murdered) and for other people in the neighbourhood. He had met McKenzie in Bishopsgate and they had been living together in lodging houses in the Whitechapel area for the past six or seven years and at 52 Gun Street for the past twelve months. According to the other lodgers they had lived comfortably together. Previously McKenzie had lived with a blind man. In spite of their intimacy McCormac could tell the police little else about her background except that she had said that she came from Peterborough and had sons who were living abroad.

McCormac told the police that he had come home from work at about 4 p.m. on 16 July and had given McKenzie some money (one shilling and eight pence) before he went to sleep. When he had woken up between 10 and 11 p.m., he found she had gone out. He did not see her again until he was taken to the mortuary to identify her body.

McKenzie often went out at night but whether she was a prostitute or not is doubtful, although the police certainly regarded her as such. Like the other women, she was a heavy drinker.

Dr Bagster Phillips carried out the initial post mortem but Robert Anderson, the head of C.I.D., for some unknown reason wanted a second opinion and asked Dr Bond of the Great Western Railway to confirm the findings. On 18 July Bond went to the mortuary with Dr Phillips, who explained to him that the wounds on the throat had been so disturbed that any examination he might make would convey no definite information as to the injuries. He pointed out the original wounds, their character and direction, and Bond formed an opinion, as far as he was able to, that the cuts were made from left to right. He also thought, as far as he could make out, that the knife had been plunged deeply into the left side of the neck, behind the sterno mastoid muscle, and brought out by a tailed incision above the larynx on the same side. There appeared to have been two stabs in the throat. The knife had been carried forward into the wound, leaving just a small tongue of skin between the two stabs. (If this was a Ripper killing, then the murderer had changed his methods from his customary practice of severing the throat with two deep cuts). There were several small superficial cuts on the throat but the two main thrusts were about two inches long and had been made by a knife which had been driven in from above, in a downward and forward motion.

The weapon, Bond thought, was a sharp-pointed knife and he believed that the cuts had been made while the woman's head was thrown back upon the ground. Phillips thought that the knife must have been a smaller one than any that had been used before. There were no bruises on her face and lips, nor on the back of her head, but there were two bruises high up on the chest which indicated that the killer had stabbed her with his right hand while he held her down with his left.

On the right side of the abdomen and extending from the chest to below the level of the umbilicus there was a jagged incision made up of several cuts; these extended through the skin and sub-cutaneous fat. At the bottom of this cut there were seven or eight superficial scratches each about two inches long and lying parallel to each other. There was a small stab wound, one eighth of an inch deep on the mons veneris.

The abdominal wounds had been inflicted afterwards. Death had been instantaneous from the stab wounds in the throat. There was some disagreement as to whether the killer had been left or right handed. Dr Phillips thought that the bruises on the left side of the stomach had been caused by the murderer pressing down with his right hand while he used the knife with his left; Dr Bond thought that they indicated the exact opposite. Bond concluded:

I see in this murder evidence of similar design to the former Whitechapel murders, viz. sudden onslaught on the prostrate woman, the throat skilfully and resolutely cut with subsequent mutilation, each mutilation indicating sexual thoughts and a desire to mutilate the abdomen and sexual organs.

I am of the opinion that the murder was performed by the same person who committed the former series of Whitechapel murders.

However, Dr Bagster Phillips disagreed with this conclusion. He did not believe that all the Whitechapel killings had been the work of one man. After long and careful deliberation he had arrived at this conclusion 'on purely anatomical and professional grounds'. He stressed this point by emphasising that he was not taking into consideration all the circumstantial evidence and the facts in favour of the one-man theory. He had ignored all evidence which he hadn't had at first hand.

As he had carried out himself or had assisted in five out of the seven post mortems under discussion (Chapman, Eddowes, Kelly, McKenzie and Coles) his evidence on this point must carry a lot of weight.

Yet another murder, two months later, was thought to be the Ripper's handiwork. Fortunately it can be proved to be otherwise. At 5.20 a.m. on September 1889 a patrolling policeman found the naked trunk of a female body in some railway arches in Pinchin Street, not far from Berners Street where Long Liz Stride had been murdered. The street was a lonely spot but was patrolled every half hour by the night duty constable.

From the post-mortem report, the time of death fixed the murder as probably happening thirty-six hours before on the Sunday night, 8 September, which was the anniversary of Annie Chapman's murder just one year before. If this was a Ripper killing, then the murderer had once more changed a by now well-established technique.

It would also mean that for the first time the murder had been committed in the murderer's house.

However there was (1) no evidence to show that death had been caused by cutting the throat; (2) no mutilation of the body although there was dismemberment; (3) no removal of organs or intestines; and (4) the murder had not been committed in the streets nor in the victim's house. There was none of the frenzied mutilation of the body, as there had been with Mary Kelly, and which might have been expected as the murder had happened indoors.

There was a gash on the trunk but according to the doctor this had been done after death, probably to confuse the police and make them think that this was another Ripper killing. In fact, it looked as if the knife had slipped. The whole of the wound looked as though the murderer had intended to make a cut preparatory to the removal of the intestines but had then changed his mind.

On medical grounds and the evidence of the modus operandi any suggestion that this unidentified woman was a Ripper victim can be dismissed.

7

SUSPECTS

The best known of all the Ripper documents are the legendary Macnaghten papers. These are not a large manuscript collection, as is often supposed, but a single document written by Sir Melville Macnaghten several years after he joined Scotland Yard as an assistant chief constable in 1889 and before he was appointed head of the C.I.D. in 1903. There are two versions of these notes. One forms part of the Ripper case papers which are deposited in the MEPOL (Metropolitan Police) papers in the Public Records Office. Access to these papers is restricted, and they do not become available to the public generally until 1992. The other set of papers is in the possession of Lady Aberconway, Sir Melville Macnaghten's daughter, who made them available to Dan Farson in 1959 and to Tom Cullen in 1965. The former quoted from them in a television documentary which he made at the time, although only the initials of the suspects were given. Tom Cullen was more fortunate, and was able to print the names in full. Farson was able to do the same thing eight years later when he published his own account of the same story.

Yet although both sets of papers are supposed to emanate from the same source, there are very important differences between them.

For example; Farson and Cullen say that the main suspect was:

No. 1 Mr M. J. DRUITT, a doctor of about 41 years of age and of fairly good family, who disappeared at the time of the Miller's Court murder, and whose body was found floating in the Thames on 3rd December, i.e. seven weeks after the said murder. The body was said to have been in the water for a month, or more—on it was found a season ticket between Blackheath and London. From private information I have little doubt but that his own family suspected this man of being the Whitechapel murderer; and it was alleged that he was sexually insane.

Whereas the Scotland Yard version is:

(1) A Mr M. J. Druitt, said to be a doctor and of good family —who disappeared at the time of the Miller's Court murder, and whose body (which was said to have been upwards of a month in the water) was found in the Thames on 31st December—or about seven weeks after that murder. He was sexually insane and from private information I have little doubt but that his own family believed him to have been the murderer.

Which, we have to ask ourselves, is the original?

Some light was shed on this problem by Philip Loftus when he reviewed Farson's book in *The Guardian* on 7 October 1972. His own interest in Druitt had started several years earlier, in fact in 1950 when he was staying with a friend, Gerald Melville Donner, who happened to be also the grandson of Sir Melville Macnaghten. Donner owned a Jack the Ripper letter, which Loftus thought was a copy, written in red ink, framed and hanging on the wall.

'Copy be damned,' Donner said, 'that's the original.' As proof that he owned some original documents he pulled out Sir Melville Macnaghten's private notes which Loftus described as being 'in Sir Melville's handwriting on official paper, rather untidy and in the nature of rough jottings.' Loftus thought that they mentioned three suspects: a Polish tanner or cobbler; a man who went around stabbing young girls in the bottom; and a 41-year-old doctor, Mr M. J. Druitt.

Donner died in 1968 and the notes then seemed to have disappeared. Loftus wrote to his family inquiring their whereabouts, but the family told him that they did not know. He also wrote to Lady Aberconway, who was Donner's aunt and Sir Melville's other daughter, asking her the same questions. She explained, 'My elder sister, ten years older than myself, took all my father's papers when my mother died—which is why Gerald has them: I have never seen them. But in my father's book "Days of My Years" he talks of "Jack the Ripper" . . . that is, all the information I can give.'

The notes that are still in her possession, which Farson and Cullen both quoted from, are *typewritten copies*. Farson says, 'she was kind enough to give me her father's private notes which she had copied out soon after his death.' Tom Cullen also told me, in conversation, that the notes he had seen were typewritten.

So, in addition to the two existing sets of notes, whose whereabouts are known, there must be added those untidy 'rough jottings' which disappeared after Donner's death. This immediately prompts one to ask how many other papers have disappeared. As most of them have been in the possession of the police for nearly a hundred years one might imagine the answer to be 'very few, if any'. Unfortunately this is not the case. But before anyone begins attributing sinister motives to the police for the destruction or disappearance of relevant papers, certain explanations must be made to put the problem in its proper perspective.

It sounds unbelievable, but it is only in the last twenty years that the police force generally has taken an interest in its own fascinating past. It was only then realised, however, that in many forces much of its early history had already been lost. My own experiences in this field might help to clarify this point.

Several years ago I wrote a social history of police and crime in the City of London from Elizabethan to Victorian times. Although the City police force is the oldest in the country, far older in fact than the Metropolitan (which serves Greater London), it has nothing in the way of early documentation. Had it not been for papers in the possession of the Corporation of the City of London it would have been nearly impossible to write a history of this force. The police themselves were not entirely to blame for this situation. Their stations had been badly blitzed in the last war (one was completely wiped out). Inevitably, quite a lot of documents were destroyed but, tragically, of the papers that remained, nearly all were scrapped as salvage. Only a few letters, such as those from the Governor of Newgate gaol written when hangings were still public, were snatched from the shredding machines and retained as curiosities. Much later, I was fortunate enough to salvage case papers relating to the famous Siege of Sidney Street and to use them in a book. The maps were so brittle that the binder who restored them thought that they had been baked!

The point that I am making is that these papers were destroyed, as others have been, through indifference or ignorance—not through a desire to conceal or to protect some great name.

This record of neglect is just as true of other police forces, including Scotland Yard. The late Mr Heron, its first archivist, told me that until 1959, when the Yard's files came under the control of the Public Records Office (being Home Office papers), it was quite customary when more space was needed for the porters to yank out handfuls of papers from old files to make way for new ones! Some, I imagine, were a bit selective about what they took, and hopefully one day some of these papers will be returned. A Superintendent who was lecturing to the Metropolitan Police History Society several years ago touched on this same point. He told us that most of the early papers of the Special Branch were thought to have been destroyed by a Fenian bomb in 1884 which was planted against the wall of their office. Yet some papers had recently come to light. The widow of a Special Branch pensioner asked them to buy the contents of a large suitcase which she brought into their office. It was full of Special Branch papers, which her husband had kept under the bed!

Therefore, anyone who is hoping for startling revelations from the Jack the Ripper file will be very disappointed with what they find— being one of the few people who has seen them, I know that they are incomplete. There are three bundles of loose-leaf papers in brown wrap-round files tied up with tapes. On the top of each file is stamped the date, 1992, which is the date when they can be thrown open to the general public. The file has been officially closed since 1892.

Normal practice is that once a case has been officially closed then it stays closed for a hundred years. This only applies to criminal cases. There is a thirty-year ruling on domestic papers. The reason for the hundred-year rule is that it is thought that anything less would not guarantee the anonymity of the many highly confidential statements that are made to the police during the course of an investigation and which would not have been given if it was thought that they would be made public within such a short period as thirty years and in the witnesses' lifetime. Some of these statements are damaging to the persons making them as well as to their friends and families; in some cases, if they were made public, there would always be the threat of criminal reprisals even after so long a period.

The hundred-year ruling, in fact, covers one man's lifetime. It also does more than that. It protects the families of men who were known to have committed serious crimes such as murder but who, possibly because they committed suicide, never stood trial and so their guilt was never publicly proved. And because they were never found guilty in open court, before a jury, it is normal police policy not to brand these men as killers, although there is evidence that they were; it is felt that there is always the chance that, if these men had stood trial, then they might have had an innocent and convincing explanation for their apparently guilty behaviour. Rather than distress their families, in these circumstances, and accuse them of crimes which they cannot deny, the papers are filed away. The case is never officially closed although the police have proved it to their own, if not to the public's satisfaction.

Two of the Ripper files contain letters from the general public offering advice on the best way to catch the Whitechapel murderer. They contain nothing of any real importance. The third file has a number of thin brown folders—some of them very thin—which relate not only to the five definite Ripper murders but to others such as Alice McKenzie and Frances Coles which some contemporaries attributed to him. Each of these folders has the victim's, or alleged victim's, name across the top. There are very few documents in each file. The Eddowes murder was investigated by the City of London Police and contains only a single newspaper cutting. Some of the other files contain very little more. Several years ago, through the permission of the Commissioner of the City Police, I was able to place in the Eddowes and Kelly file copies of the original photographs which were in their possession and to deposit similar sets with the Black Museum and Bow Street Historical Museum. One can only assume that the Kelly photograph was removed from the file at a much earlier date, since Sir Melville Macnaghten refers to it in his notes. Stranger still was the fact that the photograph was the work of the City Police, in spite of the dressing down they had received from Sir Charles Warren for being in Whitechapel. A story which explains this, although it is at variance with the newspaper accounts, is that although the Metropolitan Police didn't dare to disobey Warren's order and break down Kelly's doorway before the bloodhounds arrived, the City Police did so as they ran no such risks. Apparently as the morning dragged on, and nothing happened in Miller's Court, somebody quietly asked the City Police for their help which they gave by breaking into Kelly's room and taking the photograph of her body as their only justification for doing so. Certainly all the surviving photographs of Ripper victims were taken by the City of London Police. Curiously enough, they may have taken others. The photograph of Miller's Court is now a well-known one, but it was only by chance that I found it and published it in *Police Journal* in 1969. In 1967 the City Police photographic department were clearing out a lot of old negatives, including some glass ones, and by chance I happened to spot them. Two were of immediate interest. One was of some Metropolitan policemen, taken about 1870, and the other—which I instantly recognised—was of Miller's Court, of which no photograph was known to exist. When I tried to trace their source, I was told that they had come from a large album of photographs which disappeared when the force museum was broken up in 1959 and lost at the same time as the 'From Hell' letter, which vanished with it. I don't believe that they have been lost for ever. But their present whereabouts is still a mystery.

In general, the documents are a haphazard collection and their very haphazardness suggests that they have been well picked over in the past hundred years. The only recorded destruction of any part of them is attributed to Sir Melville Macnaghten who is alleged to have burned the most incriminating of the papers to protect the murderer's family. His daughter denies this story and says that her father probably said that he had done this to stop himself from being pestered by people at his club.

His notes are reproduced below in full for the first time anywhere. There are seven foolscap pages, in his handwriting, with hardly a blot or deletion throughout. Presumably this copy was written from those rough jottings that were in the possession of his grandson. As such, and as it is dated, it must be regarded as the prima facie document. By the same token, the typewritten Macnaghten papers, which are in the possession of Lady Aberconway, must be regarded with some doubt—although emanating from the same source—until it is known with any certainty who revised them and why.

Confidential

The case referred to in the sensational story told in 'The Sun' in its issue of 13th inst, & following dates, is that of Thomas Cutbush who was arraigned at the London County Sessions in April 1891 on a charge of maliciously wounding Florence Grace Johnson, and attempting to wound Isabella Fraser Anderson in Kennington. He was found to be insane, and sentenced to be detained during Her Majesty's Pleasure.

This Cutbush, who lived with his mother and aunt at 14 Albert Street, Kennington, escaped from the Lambeth Infirmary, (after he had been detained only a few hours, as a lunatic) at noon on 5th March 1891. He was rearrested on 9th idem. A few weeks before this, several cases of stabbing, or jabbing, from behind had occurred in the vicinity, and a man named Colicott was arrested, but subsequently discharged owing to faulty identification. The cuts in the girl's dresses made by Colicott were quite different to the cut(s) made by Cutbush (when he wounded Miss Johnson) who was no doubt influenced by a wild desire of morbid imitation. Cutbush's antecedents were enquired into by C.Insp. (now Supt.) Chis(?) by Inspector Hale, and by P. S. McCarthy C.I.D.—(the last named officer had been specially employed in Whitechapel at the time of the

murders there,)—and it was ascertained that he was born, and had
lived, in Kennington all his life. His father died when he was quite
young and he was always a 'spoilt' child. He had been employed as a
clerk and traveller in the Tea trade at the Minories, and subsequently
canvassed for a Directory in the East End, during which time he
bore a good character. He apparently contracted syphilis about 1888,
and,—since that time,—led an idle and useless life. His brain seems
to have become affected, and he believed that people were trying to
poison him. He wrote to Lord Grimthorpe, and others,—and also to
the Treasury,—complaining of Dr Brooks, of Westminster Bridge
Road, whom he threatened to shoot for having supplied him with
bad medicines. He is said to have studied medical books by day, and
to have rambled about at night, returning frequently with his clothes
covered with mud; but little reliance could be placed on the statements made by his mother or his aunt, who both appear to have been
of a very excitable disposition. It was found impossible to ascertain
his movements on the nights of the Whitechapel murders. The knife
found on him was bought in Houndsditch about a week before he
was detained in the Infirmary. Cutbush was the nephew of the
late Supt. Executive.

Now the Whitechapel murderer had 5 victims—& 5 victims only,—
his murders were

(1) 31st August '88. Mary Ann Nichols—at Buck's Row—who
was found with her throat cut—& with (slight) stomach mutilation.

(2) 8th Sept. '88 Annie Chapman—Hanbury St;—throat cut—stomach & private parts badly mutilated & some of the entrails placed
round the neck.

(3) 30th Sept. '88. Elizabeth Stride—Berner's Street—throat cut,
but nothing in shape of mutilation attempted, & *on same date*

Catherine Eddowes—Mitre Square, throat cut & very bad mutilation, both of face & stomach.

9th November. Mary Jane Kelly—Miller's Court, throat cut, and
the whole of the body mutilated in the most ghastly manner—

The last murder is the only one that took place in a *room,* and
the murderer must have been at least 2 hours engaged. A photo was
taken of the woman, as she was found lying on the bed, without seeing which it is impossible to imagine the awful mutilation.

With regard to the *double* murder which took place on 30th September, there is no doubt but that the man was disturbed by some
Jews who drove up to a Club, (close to which the body of Elizabeth

Outside a Spitalfields common lodging house.

CASUAL WARDS

and common lodging houses were the
only hope for the down and out.
Right, lines for the casual wards
started early in the day.
Below, men and women shared beds
in many common lodging houses.

IN A COMMON LODGING HOUSE
IN DORSET STREET E:

No. 1423.—Vol. 55

THE · PENNY
ILLUSTRATED · PAPER
AND · ILLUSTRATED TIMES

SEPTEMBER 8, 1888

REGISTERED AT THE GENERAL POST-OFFICE AS A NEWSPAPER.

London: Printed and Published at the Office, 10, Milford-lane, Strand, in the Parish of St. Clement Danes, in the County of Middlesex, by Thomas Fox, 10, Milford-lane, Strand, aforesaid.

P.C. NIEL J 97.

DR LLEWELLYN

INSP. HELSON

THE CORONER

SKETCHES AT THE INQUEST

r London has a
or that must be
ped out. We
strate on this page,
describe in
ther, Police-Con-
le Niel's discovery
urdered Mary Ann Nicholls in Buck's-row, Whitechapel,
he early morning of August the Thirty-first. This crime
so many points of similarity with the murders of the two
r women in the same neighbourhood—one, Martha Turner,
ecently as Aug. 7, and the other less than twelve months
iously—that the police admit their belief that the three crimes are the
k of one individual. All three women were of the same class, and each of
n was so poor that robbery could have formed no motive for the crime.
three murders were committed within a distance of 200 yards of each other

THE WHITECHAPEL MYSTERY.

SOME OF THE WORST SLUMS
in London lined Whitechapel Road, right. Below, a map of the murder sites as published in 'Pictorial World'. Contemporary newspapers favoured a count of seven murders, including Emma Smith and Martha Tabram among the Ripper's victims.

LOCALITY OF THE SEVEN · UNDISCOVERED MURDERS

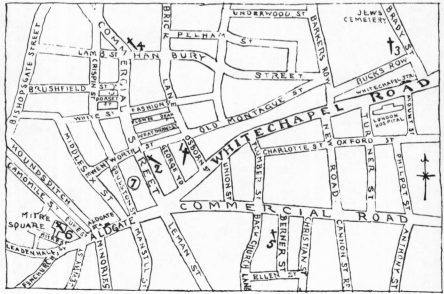

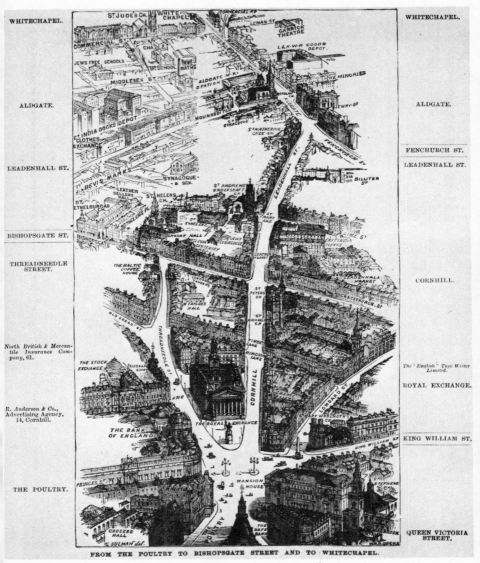

WHITECHAPEL.

ALDGATE.

LEADENHALL ST.

BISHOPSGATE ST.

THREADNEEDLE
STREET.

North British & Mercantile Insurance Company, 61.

R. Anderson & Co.,
Advertising Agency,
14, Cornhill.

THE POULTRY.

WHITECHAPEL.

ALDGATE.

FENCHURCH ST.
LEADENHALL ST.

CORNHILL.

The "English" Type Writer
Limited.

ROYAL EXCHANGE.

KING WILLIAM ST.

QUEEN VICTORIA
STREET.

FROM THE POULTRY TO BISHOPSGATE STREET AND TO WHITECHAPEL.

FROM THE WEALTH OF THE
BANK OF ENGLAND,
past Bishopsgate and the Leather Market, through Aldgate and
Houndsditch, to the appalling poverty of Whitechapel.

ANNIE CHAPMAN,
face slashed and body disembowelled, was found at the back of
a lodging house at 29 Hanbury Street.
She lay by the fence, her head almost touching the steps.

THE DOUBLE EVENT

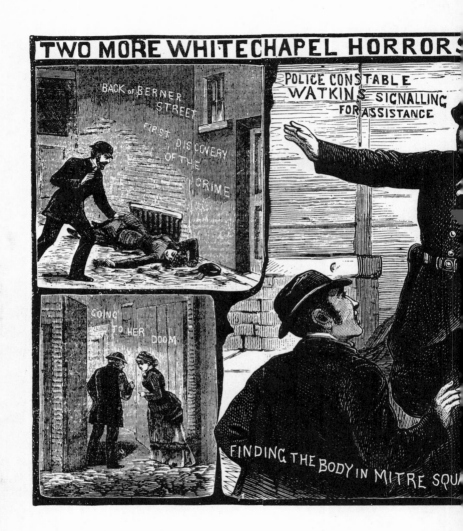

TERROR MOUNTED

after the news of the brutal double murder. Both victims were
seen talking with the murderer only minutes before their deaths.

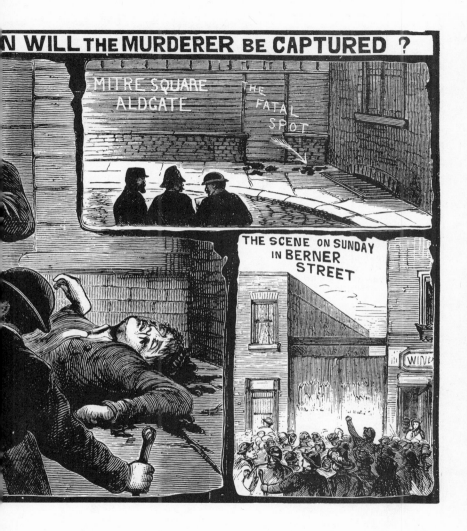

PANIC SPREAD
throughout the East End, leading to door-to-door searches,
lynch mobs, and petitions to the Queen.

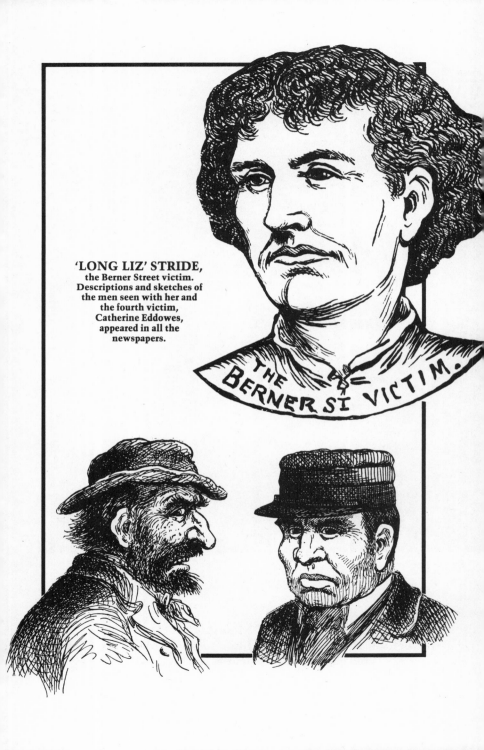

'LONG LIZ' STRIDE, the Berner Street victim. Descriptions and sketches of the men seen with her and the fourth victim, Catherine Eddowes, appeared in all the newspapers.

SKETCHES MADE 'IN SITU'

of Eddowes' body and Mitre Square. Doctors at the post mortem
thought the mutilations showed no evidence of special
anatomical knowledge. Probably the Ripper killed Eddowes
in one of the empty houses, then dragged the corpse
into the Square to mutilate it.

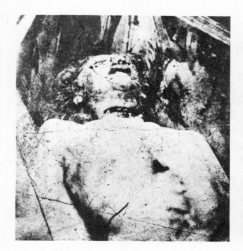

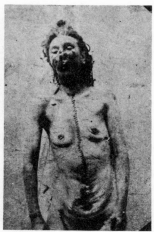

From a sketch taken at the Mortuary by Mr F.W. Foster 3.45. A.M. Sunday Sept 30th 1888.

Mortuary photographs of Catherine Eddowes. Note the nicks on the lower eyelids. After the post mortem, her body was sketched, placed in a coffin, then stitched up.

LOST WOMAN
MARY KELLY
MILLER'S COURT

THE SEVENTH HORRIBLE MURDE

MRS PRATER'S LAST LEAVE TAKING OF THE VICTIM.

MILLER'S COURT.
THE MURDERER'S CHOSEN SPOT.

A STRANGE MAN TRIED TO INDUCE GIRLS TO GO UP AN ENTRY WITH HIM

WINDOWS BOARDED UP.

THE SCENE OF THE MURDER, MILLER'S COURT.

THE SEVENTH V PICKED OUT FOR SLAUG FROM DESCRIPTIO

STARTLING STORY OF A MAN WITH A BLACK BAG

THE AWFUL DISCOVERY BY McCARTHY.

THE RIPPER'S FINAL VICTIM,
Mary Kelly, was twenty-four and pregnant.
The 'Illustrated Police News' of 17 November, 1888,

THE MONSTER OF THE EAST-END.

A WELL SCENE WITNESSED BY THE DOCTORS

LURED TO THE SLAUGHTER

PROPRIETOR OF THE ILLUSTRATED POLICE NEWS OFFERS £100 REWARD FOR THE CAPTURE OF THE WHITECHAPEL MURDERER

THE EAST-END FIEND.

BY HER TE FRIENDS.

THE MURDERER

GE STORY TOLD OF A MAN WITH A BLACK BAG

ESCAPING FROM THE WINDOW

sketched the whole story for its readers,
including the rumour that a mysterious man
with a black shiny bag was the Ripper.

THERE IS
STRONG EVIDENCE THAT
this contemporary post mortem knife may have belonged to
Jack the Ripper. Below, Mary Kelly as she was discovered
in Miller's Court. Her leg was slashed to the bone,
and her breasts and kidneys removed and
placed on the table.

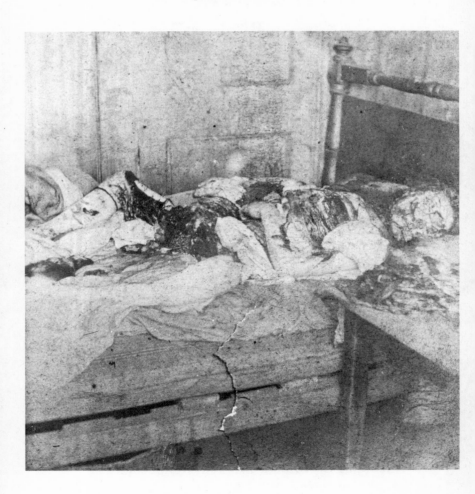

25 Sept. 1888.

Dear Boss

    I keep on hearing the police have caught me, but they wont fix me just yet. I have laughed when they look so clever and talk about being on the right track. That joke about Leather Apron gave me real fits. I am down on whores and I shant quit ripping them till I do get buckled. Grand work the last job was. I gave the lady no time to squeal. How can they catch me now. I love my work and want to start again. You will soon hear of me with my funny little games. I saved some of the proper red stuff in a ginger beer bottle over the last job to write with but it went thick like glue and I cant use it. Red ink is fit enough I hope ha. ha. The next job I do I shall clip the ladys ears off and send to the

police officers just for jolly wouldnt you. Keep this letter back till I do a bit more work. then give it out straight. My knifes so nice and sharp I want to get to work right away if I get a chance. Good luck

             yours truly

             Jack the Ripper

Dont mind me giving the trade name

wasnt good enough to post this before I got all the red ink off my hands curse it No luck yet. They say I'm a doctor now ha ha

THE FIRST LETTER to use the name 'Jack the Ripper' is dated 25 September, 1888, before the double murder. The writer threatened to 'clip the lady's ears off', and he tried to do just that with Eddowes and Stride.

I was codding
dear old Boss when
I gave you the tip
you'll hear about
saucy Jacky's work
tomorrow double
ev-ent this time
number one squeal
a bit couldn't
finish straight
off. had not time
to get ears for
police thanks for
keeping last letter
back till I got
to work again.
Jack the Ripper

The postcard sent on
30 September gave details of
the double event before
they were generally known.

From hell

Mr Lusk

Sor

I send you half the
Kidne I took from one women
prasarved it for you tother piece
I fried and ate it was very nise I
may send you the bloody knif that
took it out if you only wate a whil
longer

signed Catch me when
you Can
Mishter Lusk

The most convincingly
genuine of the letters
purportedly from the Ripper
was sent with part of a
human kidney to
George Lusk, head of the
Whitechapel Vigilance
Committee.

Old boss you was
rite it was the left Kidny i was goin
to hoperate agin close to you
ospitle just as i was going
to drop mi nife along of er
bloomin throte them
cusses of coppers spoilt
the game but i guess i will
be on the job soon and will
send you another bit of
innerds Jack the ripper

O have you seen the devle
with his mikerscope and scalpul
a lookin at a kidney
with a slide cocked up

A jeering letter, signed
'Jack the Ripper' and
postmarked 29 October,
was sent to Dr Openshaw,
who had examined the kidney.

HANDWRITING SAMPLES

25 September, the first 'Ripper' signature.

30 September, details of the double event.

6 October, 'From hell' to Mr Lusk.

29 October, 'Old boss' to Dr Openshaw.

METROPOLITAN POLICE.

Fac-simile of Letter and Post Card received by Central News Agency.

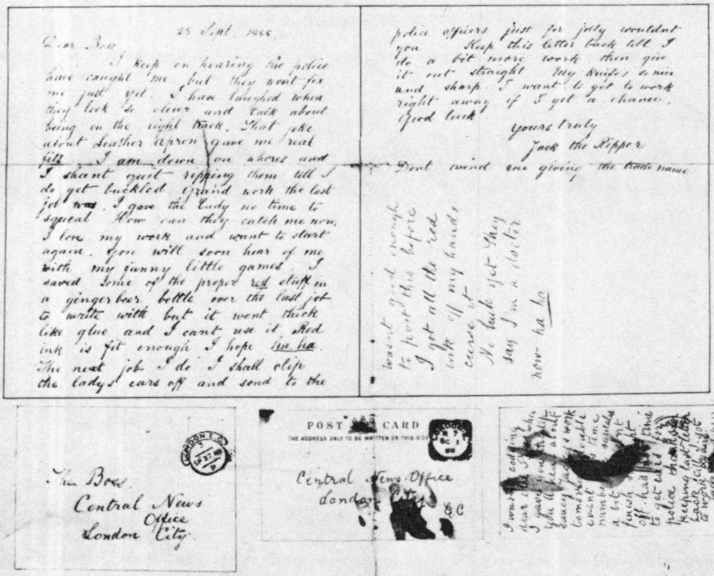

Any person recognising the handwriting is requested to communicate with the nearest Police Station.

Metropolitan Police Office,
3rd October, 1888.

Printed by M'Corquodale & Co. Limited, "The Armoury," Southwark.

THE INVESTIGATORS

Sir Robert Anderson,
Head of the C.I.D.

Sir James Fraser,
Commissioner of the City Police

Sir Charles Warren,
Metropolitan Police Commissioner

Lt. Colonel Sir Henry Smith,
Assistant Commissioner of the City Police

George Chapman

The Duke of Clarence

James K. Stephen

MOST OF THE MAJOR CANDIDATES
**for the shroud of Jack the Ripper were as
respectable-looking as the officials who investigated**

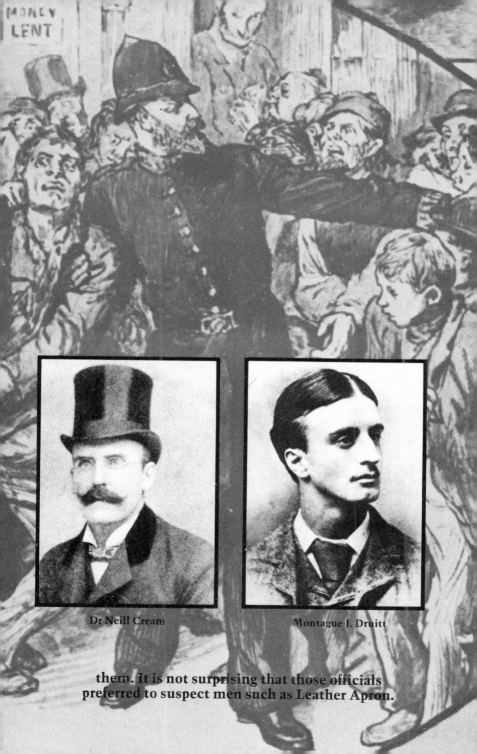

Dr Neill Cream

Montague J. Druitt

them. It is not surprising that those officials
preferred to suspect men such as Leather Apron.

INTERNAL SQUABBLES

beset the investigations, evidence was misfiled, and files were neglected. But the officials in charge did the best they could.

Sir Melville Macnaghten,
Assistant Chief Constable in 1889

Sir Charles Warren,
Metropolitan Police Commissioner

Dr Forbes Winslow

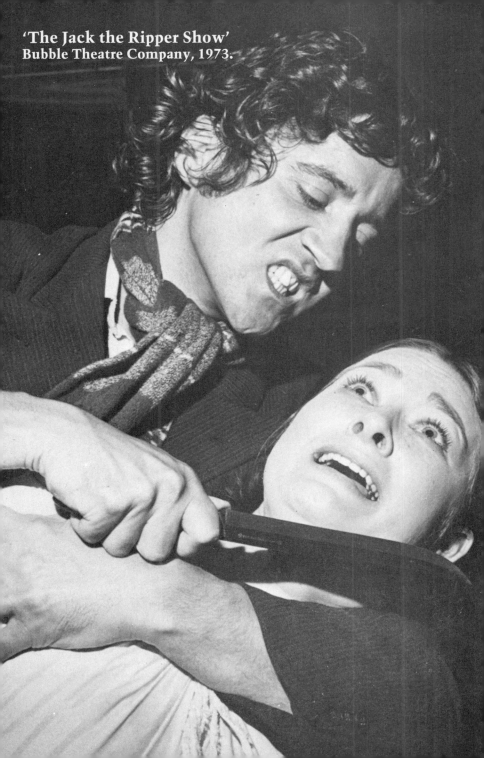

'The Jack the Ripper Show'
Bubble Theatre Company, 1973.

Alfred Hitchcock's version, made in 1926.
British Film Institute

'THE LODGER'
is the best-known adaptation
of the Ripper story.

Ivor Novello starred in Hitchcock's film.
British Film Institute

Charles Gray and Brenda Bruce in
ABC-TV's 'The Lodger'.
ABC-TV

Another film of 'The Lodger',
made in 1944 with Laird Cregar.
Twentieth Century-Fox Film Company Ltd

**RECENT VERSIONS
OF JACK THE RIPPER**
Left, the film 'A Study in Terror',
with John Neville as
Sherlock Holmes pitted against
Jack the Ripper.
Compton Cameo Films Ltd
Below, BBC-TV's 'Jack the Ripper'
series, with Stratford Johns and
Frank Windsor, was shown in the
United States.
BBC copyright

THE STORY OF
JACK THE RIPPER

'The Lodger', Pan Books Ltd; 'Yours Truly, Jack the Ripper',
Belmont Productions Inc; 'Jack the Ripper', Monarch Books Inc.

**JACK
THE STRIPPER,**
the Thames Nude Killer,
murdered six London prostitutes in
1964-65 and was never caught.

Bridie O'Hara

Mary Fleming

Irene Lockwood

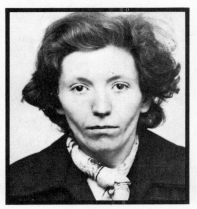

Hannah Tailford

Margaret McGowan

Kürten's apartment

THE DÜSSELDORF RIPPER,
Peter Kürten, terrorized the city in 1929-30.
The arrow in the background picture points to

Victim Luise Lenzen

Peter Kürten

**the corpse of five-year-old Gertrude Albermann,
whom he strangled and stabbed with a scissors.**

PETER KÜRTEN,
the picture of respectability in a pin-stripe suit,
was a pyromaniac, fetishist, masochist, sadist,
child molestor, and sex killer.

Stride was found) and that he then, 'mordum satiatus', went in search of a further victim who he found at Mitre Square.

It will be noticed that the fury of the mutilations *increased* in each case, and, seemingly, the appetite only became sharpened by indulgence. It seems, then, highly improbable that the murderer would have suddenly stopped in November '88, and been content to recommence operations by merely prodding a girl behind some 2 years and 4 months afterwards. A much more rational theory is that the murderer's brain gave way altogether after his awful glut in Miller's Court, and that he immediately committed suicide, or, as a possible alternative, was found to be so hopelessly mad by his relations, that he was by them confined in some asylum.

No one ever saw the Whitechapel murderer; many homicidal maniacs were suspected, but no shadow of proof could be thrown on any one. I may mention the cases of 3 men, any one of whom would have been more likely than Cutbush to have committed this series of murders:

(1) A Mr M. J. Druitt, said to be a doctor & of good family—who disappeared at the time of the Miller's Court murder, & whose body (which was said to have been upwards of a month in the water) was found in the Thames on 31st December—or about 7 weeks after that murder. He was sexually insane and from private information I have little doubt but that his own family believed him to have been the murderer.

(2) Kosminski—a Polish Jew—& resident in Whitechapel. This man became insane owing to many years indulgence in solitary vices. He had a great hatred of women, specially of the prostitute class, & had strong homicidal tendencies: he was removed to a lunatic asylum about March 1889. There were many circumstances connected with this man which made him a strong 'suspect'.

(3) Michael Ostrog, a Russian doctor, and a convict, who was subsequently detained in a lunatic asylum as a homicidal maniac. This man's antecedents were of the worst possible type, and his whereabouts at the time of the murders could never be ascertained.

And now with regard to a few of the other inaccuracies and misleading statements made by 'The Sun'. In its issue of 14th February, it is stated that the writer has in his possession a facsimile of the knife with which the murders were committed. This knife (which for some unexplained reason has, for the last 3 years, been kept by Inspector Hale, instead of being sent to Prisoner's Property Store) was traced, and it was found to have been purchased in Houndsditch in

February '91 or 2 years and 3 months *after* the Whitechapel murders ceased!

The statement, too, that Cutbush 'spent a portion of the day in making rough drawings of the bodies of women, and of their mutilations' is based solely on the fact that 2 *scribble* drawings of women in indecent postures were found torn up in Cutbush's room. The head and body of one of these had been cut from some fashion plate, and legs were added to shew a woman's naked thighs and pink stockings.

In the issue of 15th inst. it is said that a *light overcoat* was among the things found in Cutbush's house, and that a man in a *light* overcoat was seen talking to a woman at Backchurch Lane whose body with arms attached was found in Pinchin Street. This is hopelessly incorrect! On 10th Sept. '89 the naked body, with arms, of a woman was found wrapped in some sacking under a Railway arch in Pinchin Street: the head and legs were never found nor was the woman ever identified. She had been killed at least 24 hours before the remains which had seemingly been brought from a distance, were discovered. The stomach was split up by a cut, and the head and legs had been severed in a manner identical with that of the woman whose remains were discovered in the Thames, in Battersea Park, and on the Chelsea Embankment on 4th June of the same year; and these murders had no connection whatever with the Whitechapel horrors. The Rainham mystery in 1887 and the Whitehall mystery (when portions of a woman's body were found under what is now New Scotland Yard) in 1888 were of a similar type to the Thames and Pinchin Street crimes.

It is perfectly untrue to say that Cutbush stabbed 6 girls behind. This is confounding his case with that of Colicott. The theory that the Whitechapel murderer was left-handed, or, at any rate, 'ambidexter', had its origin in the remark made by a doctor who examined the corpse of one of the earliest victims; *other doctors did not agree with him.*

With regard to the 4 additional murders ascribed by the writer in the Sun to the Whitechapel fiend:

(1) The body of Martha Tabram, a prostitute was found on a common staircase in George Yard buildings on 7th August 1888; the body had been repeatedly *pierced,* probably with a *bayonet.* This woman had, with a fellow prostitute, been in company of 2 soldiers in the early part of the evening: these men were arrested, but the

second prostitute failed, or refused, to identify, and the soldiers were eventually discharged.

(2) Alice McKenzie was found with her throat cut (or rather *stabbed*) in Castle Alley on 17th July 1889; no evidence was forthcoming and no arrests were made in connection with this case. The *stab* in the throat was of the same nature as in the case of the murder of

(3) Frances Coles in Swallow Gardens, on 13th February 1891.— for which Thomas Saddler, a fireman, was arrested, and, after several remands, discharged. It was ascertained at the time that Saddler had sailed for the Baltic on 19th July '89 and was in Whitechapel on the nights of 17th idem. He was a man of ungovernable temper and entirely addicted to drink, and the company of the lowest prostitutes.

(4) The case of the unidentified woman whose trunk was found in Pinchin Street: on 10th September 1889—which has already been dealt with.

M.S. Macnaghten
23rd February 1894

The following document, which is also reproduced for the first time, was written by Dr Thomas Bond, who carried out the post mortems on both Alice McKenzie and Mary Kelly. Besides being a lecturer on Forensic Medicine and consulting surgeon to 'A' division and to the Great Western Railway, he was also the author of several publications including one on the 'Diagnosis and Treatment of Primary Syphilis'.

7 THE SANCTUARY,
WESTMINSTER ABBEY
November 10th '88.

Dear Sir,

Whitechapel Murders

I beg to report that I have read the notes of the four Whitechapel Murders viz:-

1. Buck's Row
2. Hanbury Street
3. Berners Street
4. Mitre Square.

I have also made a Post Mortem Examination of the mutilated remains of a woman found yesterday in a small room in Dorset Street:-

1. All five murders were no doubt committed by the same hand. In the first four the throats appear to have been cut from left to

right, in the last case owing to the extensive mutilation it is impossible to say in what direction the fatal cut was made, but arterial blood was found on the wall in splashes close to where the woman's head must have been lying.

2. All the circumstances surrounding the murders lead me to form the opinion that the women must have been lying down when murdered and in every case the throat was first cut.

3. In the four murders of which I have seen the notes only, I cannot form a very definite opinion as to the time that had elapsed between the murder and the discovery of the body. In one case, that of Berners Street the discovery appears to have been immediately after the deed. In Buck's Row, Hanbury St., and Mitre Square three or four hours only could have elapsed. In the Dorset Street case the body was lying on the bed at the time of my visit two o'clock quite naked and mutilated as in the annexed report. Rigor Mortis had set in but increased during the progress of the examination. From this it is difficult to say with any degree of certainty the exact time that had elapsed since death as the period varies from six to twelve hours before rigidity sets in. The body was comparatively cold at two o'clock and the remains of a recently taken meal were found in the stomach and scattered about over the intestines. It is therefore, pretty certain that the woman must have been dead about twelve hours and the partly digested food would indicate that death took place about three or four hours after food was taken, so one or two o'clock in the morning would be the probable time of the murder.

4. In all the cases there appears to be no evidence of struggling and the attacks were probably so sudden and made in such a position that the women could neither resist nor cry out. In the Dorset St case the corner of the sheet to the right of the woman's head was much cut and saturated with blood, indicating that the face may have been covered with the sheet at the time of the attack.

5. In the first four cases the murderer must have attacked from the right side of the victim. In the Dorset Street case, he must have attacked from in front or from the left, as there would be no room for him between the wall and the part of the bed on which the woman was lying. Again the blood had flowed down on the right side of the woman and spurted on to the wall.

6. The murderer would not necessarily be splashed or deluged with blood, but his hands and arms must have been covered and parts of his clothing must certainly have been smeared with blood.

7. The mutilations in each case excepting the Berners Street one

were all of the same character and showed clearly that in all the murders the object was mutilation.

8.   In each case the mutilation was implicated by a person who had no scientific nor anatomical knowledge. In my opinion he does not even possess the technical knowledge of a butcher or horse slaughterman or any person accustomed to cut up dead animals.

9.   The instrument must have been a strong knife at least six inches long, very sharp, pointed at the top and about an inch in width. It may have been a clasp knife, a butchers knife or a surgeons knife, I think it was no doubt a straight knife.

10.   The murderer must have been a man of physical strength and of great coolness and daring. There is no evidence that he had an accomplice. He must in my opinion be a man subject to periodical attacks of Homicidal and Erotic mania. The character of the mutilations indicate that the man may be in a condition sexually, that may be called Satyrcisis. It is of course possible that the Homicidal impulse may have developed from a revengeful or brooding condition of the mind, or that religious mania may have been the original disease but I do not think either hypothesis is likely. The murderer in external appearance is quite likely to be a quiet inoffensive looking man probably middle-aged and neatly and respectably dressed. I think he must be in the habit of wearing a cloak or overcoat or he could hardly have escaped notice in the streets if the blood on his hands or clothes were visible.

11.   Assuming the murderer to be such a person as I have just described, he would be solitary and eccentric in his habits, also he is most likely to be a man without regular occupation, but with some small income or pension. He is possibly living among respectable persons who have some knowledge of his character and habits and who may have grounds for suspicion that he isn't quite right in his mind at times. Such persons would probably be unwilling to communicate suspicions to the Police for fear of trouble or notoriety, whereas if there were prospect of reward it might overcome their scruples.

These are the two major documents, and most of the arguments for or against the respective theories hinge on them to some extent. The suspects that are now to be discussed are the main contenders for the shroud of Jack the Ripper. They will not be the only ones. In such a popular game as 'Hunt the Ripper' there will always be new contenders. If one is asked 'Is he among the following suspects?' one can only try to be objective and say that, without a lot more new evidence, the answer must always be 'Perhaps'. It can only remain conjecture. I have always had the feeling that on the Day of Judgment, when all things shall be known, when I and the other generations of 'Ripperologists' ask for Jack the Ripper to step forward and call out his true name, then we shall turn and look with blank astonishment at one another as he announces his name and say "Who?"

1. The Lodger

The Bible-spouting lodger with a 'down on whores' is probably the most popular image of the Ripper. The factual basis for Mrs Belloc Lowndes' fictional character 'The Lodger' began with the newspaper claims of Dr L. Forbes Winslow, who describes himself in his memoirs, *Recollections of Forty Years*, as a medical theorist and practical detective. His earliest theory, which was published in *The Times* after Chapman's death, was that the killer was a lunatic who had recently been released from an asylum or had escaped from one. He became so interested in the case that he soon found himself actively engaged in the hunt for the Ripper, pursuing clues and searching for facts to prove his deductions. 'Day after day,' he wrote, 'and night after night I spent in the Whitechapel slums. The detectives knew me, the lodging-house keepers knew me, and at last the poor creatures of the street came to know me. In terror they rushed to me with every scrap of information which might to my mind be of value. To me the frightened women looked for hope. In my presence they felt reassured, and welcomed me to their dens and obeyed my commands eagerly, and found the bits of information I wanted.'

It is not surprising that he subsequently went on to claim that it was he and not the detectives of Scotland Yard who had reasoned out an 'accurate scientific mental picture of the Whitechapel murderer'. He claimed that not only had he been able to prove beyond any doubt the identity of the murderer but also, by his revelations to the newspapers, he had been able to stop the Ripper killings!

Forbes Winslow soon abandoned his original theory of the escaped lunatic. He changed it to a more firmly held belief that the murders were committed by a homicidal lunatic who was goaded on by a religious monomania and a warped sense of duty, and that it was his mission in life to exterminate this class of woman from the face of the earth. One of Forbes Winslow's many suggestions was that the police should be replaced by warders from lunatic asylums, who would be stationed in Whitechapel to look for possible lunatics, since they were experienced in dealing with such persons while the police were not! Much to his annoyance, the only police reply was the usual printed acknowledgment from the Commissioner.

Pointing out that lunatics could be caught in their own traps if their ideas were humoured, he suggested that he might insert in the newspapers an advertisement reading: 'A gentleman who is strongly opposed to the presence of fallen women in the streets of London would like to co-operate with someone with a view to their suppression.'

He then proposed to have half a dozen detectives waiting at the prearranged meeting place to seize and question everyone who replied to the advertisement!

Forbes Winslow never doubted that if the police had acted on his suggestions then the police would have caught the Whitechapel killer. He was astonished that they did not appreciate their own incompetence and he was dismayed by their reluctance to allow others—himself—who were far more competent to handle the case, to take over the investigation.

He was not the only one obsessed with his own theories. Among the amateur detectives prowling Whitechapel was a director of the Bank of England who had disguised himself as a labourer. He roamed the lodging houses clad in heavy boots, a fustian jacket and with a red handkerchief around his head and a pick-axe in his hand!

Unfortunately, it wasn't until the following year, 1889, that Forbes Winslow was given the slender clues on which he built his shaky case. His theory rested on the initial acceptance that the Ripper had killed eight women, the earliest of his victims being an unknown woman who was murdered in Christmas week in 1887 and the last, Alice McKenzie, on 17 July 1889. In his book and in the interview he gave at the time, the facts of the case are very much the same.

He says that he was given the first clue on 30 August 1889 when a woman, with whom he was in communication, told him that she had been spoken to by a man in Worship Street. He had asked her to come down a court with him and had offered her £1 to do so. She had refused his offer but with some of her neighbours had followed him instead to a house in Finsbury out of which she had seen him coming some days before. Subsequently, after Alice McKenzie's murder on 17 July, she had seen him washing his hands in the yard of the house. He was in his shirt sleeves at the time and had a peculiar look on his face. This was about 4 a.m. in the morning. The inference was that he was washing off bloodstains.

The lodging-house keeper, where the man had lived, told Forbes Winslow that in April 1888 the man had rented a large bed sitting room in his house. The man had said that he was in England on business and that he might stay there for a few months or perhaps even a year. The lodging-house keeper and his wife noticed that each time he went out he wore a different suit of clothes, and would often change three or four times a day. He had eight or nine suits and the same number of hats. He used to stay out late and when he came home creep silently into the house. He had three pairs of rubber-soled shoes, one pair of which he always used to wear when he was going out. (Forbes Winslow subsequently showed a pair to a *New York Herald* reporter who tried them on: 'Here are Jack the Ripper's boots,' said the doctor, at the same time taking a large pair of boots from under his table. 'The tops of these boots are composed of ordinary cloth material, while the soles are made of india rubber. The tops have great bloodstains on them.')

On 7 August, the night that Martha Tabram was stabbed thirty-nine times, the landlord was sitting up late with his sister waiting for his wife to return home from the country. About 4 a.m. their lodger crept into the house and told them that he had had his watch stolen in Bishopsgate. This turned out to be false.

Next morning, when the maid went to make his bed she found a large bloodstain on the bedding. His shirt was found hanging up, with the cuffs recently washed. A few days later the lodger left, allegedly for Canada, but apparently he was seen getting into a tram car in London in September 1888.

He was thought by everyone who met him to be mad. He frequently expressed his disgust at the number of prostitutes in the streets and vented some of his spleen by scribbling over fifty or sixty pages of foolscap and filling them with his own blend of religion, morality and 'bitter hatred of dissolute women'. Sometimes he would read these diatribes to his landlord.

As soon as Forbes Winslow was in possession of this information he knew instantly: 'That's the man!' Had he constructed an imaginary man, he wrote, out of his experience 'of insane people suffering from homicidal religious mania, his habits would have corresponded almost exactly with those told me by the lodging-house keeper.'

At this point in the story, Forbes Winslow's published account begins to diverge from his contemporary statement of 23 September 1889 which he made to Chief Inspector Swanson and which is now filed away in the case papers in the Public Records Office.

In his book Forbes Winslow says that once he was in full possession of these facts he told the police and suggested to them a plan
to capture this lunatic on the steps of St Paul's Cathedral where he
went every morning at 8 a.m. To his dismay the police would not
co-operate with him. He finally warned them that, 'unless they assisted
me in the capture of Jack the Ripper on a certain Sunday morning,
and if they allowed the mysterious red tape-ism and jealousy surrounding Scotland Yard to interfere,' he would publish his clue to
the world. This is precisely what he was forced to do, he says, since,
according to his memoirs, the police ignored his threats, and so he
published his story in the *New York Herald*.

When the story was picked up by the British newspapers Chief
Inspector Swanson was sent from Scotland Yard to take a statement
from him. It is from this document, which is now quoted for the
first time, that the truth of Forbes Winslow's story emerges.

Forbes Winslow denied that the story was an accurate account of
his interview with the reporter. In fact, it was a misrepresentation
of the whole conversation. The original purpose of the reporter's visit
had not been to discuss Jack the Ripper but an autograph book that
Forbes Winslow possessed. Gradually the reporter had got him into
a discussion of the Whitechapel murders and Forbes Winslow had
not objected to this line of questioning as he had understood that
the conversation would not be published. In fact, he says that he
was much surprised and annoyed to see it in print, especially as it
so misrepresented what he had said. Frankly it is hard to believe that
Forbes Winslow was as naive as this.

Chief Inspector Swanson forcibly pointed out that Forbes Winslow
had not given any information to the police about any suspect bar
one (the escaped lunatic), yet there was a statement in the newspapers saying that he had. Forbes Winslow denied any responsibility
for this story. He had then produced a pair of Canadian felt galoshes
and an old boot. The felt boots were moth-eaten and the slough of
the moth worm remained on one of them. So much for the bloodstains.

He then related the previous story together with a few additional
particulars which he did not publish in his book. The entire story,
he said, had been told to him on 8 August 1889 by Mr E. Callaghan
of 20 Gainsborough Square, Victoria Park. In April 1888 Mr Callaghan and his wife had been living at 27 Sun Street, Finsbury Square,
and they had let a room to a Mr G. Wentworth Bell Smith, whose
business it was to raise money for the Toronto Trust Society. The

story about the writing, the suits, hats, late hours and the stolen watch are much the same as before. The household regarded him as a lunatic because of his delusions about 'Women of the Streets', who he frequently declared should be drowned.

His frequent complaint was that the prostitutes walked up and down the aisles of St Paul's during morning service. His other delusions were about his wealth and great brain power. Frequently he would talk and moan to himself. He kept in a chest of drawers in his room three loaded revolvers. If anyone knocked at his door he would stand with his back against this chest so that they were within easy reach of his hand. Because his lodger's behaviour was so erratic, the landlord had only given this information to the police after he had left!

He was described as about five feet and ten inches tall; he walked with his feet wide apart, and he was somewhat knock kneed. His hair and complexion were dark, his moustache and beard so closely cut that he appeared to be unshaven; his teeth were probably false. He could speak several languages, was well dressed and told the household that he had done some wonderful surgical operations!

This was the only information that Forbes Winslow possessed except for that relating to the woman who had been accosted by (apparently) the same man who carried the proverbial small black bag. All the withering scorn which he fires at the police in his book for their lack of inaction on his suggestions is only the mirror for his own incompetence. Certainly he was not the great detective he claimed to be. The only clues he possessed, and these are totally worthless, were given to him a year after the murders started. He did not even know the name of the woman who had seen the lodger washing in the yard (though in fairness he said that he could get the information from Mr Callaghan).

Chief Inspector Swanson reported to his superiors that he was unable to find a record of any information having been given to the police by Callaghan. Any such would have been given after the murder in George Yard and before 31 August when the investigation was still in the hands of 'H' division. Inspector Abberline had no record of any such information.

Happily for Forbes Winslow, the police made none of this public when he published his book.

2. M. J. Druitt

Montague John Druitt's parents had been married for three years when he was born on 15 August 1857, at Wimborne in Dorset. He was to be the second of their seven children. His mother, Anne Druitt, was twenty-seven years old, ten years younger than her husband, William, who was the town's leading surgeon just as his father had been before him. Medicine seems to have been a Druitt family tradition—William's brother Robert and his nephew Lionel were both doctors.

When Montague was thirteen years old he won a scholarship to Winchester College where he spent the next six years. From his school record it is clear that he enjoyed both sport and polemics. His only recorded failure was as Sir Toby Belch in a school production of *Twelfth Night*. He was not even damned with faint praise. His acidulous critic wrote in the college magazine: 'But of the inadequacy of Druitt as Sir Toby, what are we to say? It can be better imagined than described.' In November 1873 he defended the French Republic in debate, and it was presumably his post-Sedan sympathies which led him on another occasion to denounce the influence of Bismarck as 'morally and socially a curse to the world'. He championed Wordsworth as a bulwark of Protestantism. In a more light-hearted mood he defended the fashions of the 1870s as a graceful combination of beauty and utility, and not the social evil that his opponents represented them to be. In his final debate he defended his contemporaries against the older generation which had subjugated woman and tolerated slavery, by proclaiming 'The old theory of government was, man is made for States. Is it not a vast improvement that States should be made for man, as they are now?'

He was a good sportsman. He was the school Fives champion in 1875 and he played cricket for the school First Eleven at Lord's in 1876. In his final year he had the honour of being elected Prefect of the Chapel, and in 1876 he was awarded a scholarship to New College, Oxford.

He took a Second Class Honours degree in Classical Moderations in 1878 and scraped through his degree in 1878 with a Third Class Honours in Classics. He seems to have been popular with the other undergraduates and was elected Steward of the Junior Common Room. The same year, 1880, he graduated Bachelor of Arts. Three years later he could purchase, as is still the privilege with Oxford and Cambridge graduates, his Master's degree on payment of a small fee.

Two years passed before he enrolled his name at the Inns of Court. This delay seems to indicate some hesitation in deciding on a career in law, since it would have been more usual to enroll at one of the Inns before he left university. If this assumption is correct then it is possible that he studied medicine for one brief year before realising his mistake and switched back to the law. He applied for admittance to the Inner Temple on 17 May 1882. Because of the size of the fees he was called upon to pay over the next three years, he borrowed against a £500 legacy that his father was providing for in his will and which he was to have after his mother's death, or, if she was still alive, after his twenty-fourth birthday; this was done with his father's approval, who was still alive. William Druitt added in a codicil to his will that the money advanced to him was to be considered as part payment of this legacy, and that this sum was to be deducted accordingly. Actually the amount that Montague borrowed seems to have been quite small, as his father empowered the executor to make his son a further advance provided that it did not exceed half of what was left.

To supplement his income still further, he apparently began teaching at a school in Blackheath, where the records show that he was a master the following year, 1883, and where he remained until his death.

Montague was called to the bar on 29 April 1885. A few months later, in September, his father died of a heart attack. He left an estate worth £16,579. His will favoured his three daughters, the youngest aged fourteen, who were each left £6,000 on condition they did not marry before they were twenty-one. The eldest son, William, inherited a farm at Child Okeford, Dorset; and while she lived, Montague's mother was to benefit under the terms of the will 'from the use of all rents, income and all my wine, coal, corn and other articles of consumption.' Montague and his two other brothers had come into a very poor inheritance.

After his father's death he rented chambers at 9 King's Bench Walk, Temple and joined the Western Circuit and Winchester Sessions as a barrister. Without private income or an exceptional talent the failure rate of such fledgelings was very high: a contemporary wrote that, of eight thousand barristers, only one in eight could make a living.

In 1882 he began to earn some extra money by teaching at a crammer's school in Blackheath run by a Mr George Valentine. The school, at 9 Eliot Place, had forty-two boys as boarders. Montague's teaching career came to an abrupt end at the end of Michaelmas term 1888 when he was dismissed by his employer but for what reason is not known. It has been suggested that there was a homosexual explanation for his dismissal, but it is equally plausible that it was because of his own erratic behaviour, since he believed he was going insane. His mother was already confined in a private mental home at Chiswick, where she died on 15 December 1890 of 'melancholia' and 'brain disease'.

Montague himself was last seen alive on Monday 3 December 1888. Soon afterwards, and probably in a state of acute depression after visiting his mother, he weighted his pockets with stones and threw himself into the river. His body was found floating in the water at Thorneycrofts, near Chiswick, on Monday 31 December, exactly four weeks later. The body was fully clothed and in a state of decomposition when it was dragged ashore. Two days later the inquest was held at the Lamb and Tap in Chiswick.

His brother William, a solicitor living at Bournemouth, told the coroner that the last time he had seen his brother was when he stayed overnight at Bournemouth towards the end of October. It wasn't until the 11 December that he heard from a friend that his brother had been missing from his chambers for more than a week. He then went to London to make inquiries about his brother's disappearance and at the Blackheath school learned for the first time that his brother had got into some serious trouble and had been dismissed. He searched his things for clues and found a paper addressed to himself which read: 'Since Friday I felt I was going to be like mother and the best thing for me was to die.'

There were no other clues in his pockets. When he was searched he was in possession of £2 10s. in gold, seven shillings in silver, twopence in bronze and two cheques drawn on the London Provincial Bank, one for £50 and the other for £16; they could have been his wages from Mr Valentine but another alternative put forward is that they were drawn to pay off a blackmailer. There was also a first-class season ticket from Blackheath to London, a second half return from Hammersmith to Charing Cross (dated 1 December), a silver watch, a gold chain with a spade guinea attached, a pair of gloves and a white handkerchief. In his top coat were the four large stones with which he had weighted himself down.

The one obvious thing that is missing is any shred of evidence that Montague John Druitt was Jack the Ripper.

Among the Scotland Yard papers there is a letter that refers to some enquiries made about three medical students who were allegedly insane. The police had evidently managed to trace two, but the third had eluded them. The Home Secretary wanted to know what enquiries had been made about this third, and what they were. According to Chief Inspector Abberline's reply, which is dated 1 November 1888, searching enquiries had been made by an officer at Aberdeen Place, St John's Wood, which was the last known address of the medical student known as 'John Sanders'. The only information he had managed to glean was that a lady named Sanders had lived at No. 20 but had left and gone abroad about two years before. Unfortunately, the Scotland Yard papers contain no information other than this. The names of the other two students were not mentioned at all.

Sir Melville Macnaghten has been put in the unusual position of having given the vital clue that makes a slightly more than satisfactory solution possible. Whether he would have appreciated this position is a matter of doubt. One of his great disappointments in life was that he became 'a detective officer six months after Jack the Ripper committed suicide,' which deprived him of 'having a go at that fascinating individual.' (His other disappointment was at not playing cricket for Eton against Harrow.) No doubt he would be surprised that every one of his facts—precisely because they are so few—have been wrung dry of every possible shade of meaning. Even these can be wrong. He makes obvious mistakes, such as saying that Druitt's age was forty-one. Even this can be explained away if we remember that he was copying from the police file and notes about a case of which he knew nothing at first hand—as we may presume, from the rough jottings in the possession of his grandson, that he was—and that he might have been copying precisely this error as it was given in the *County of Middlesex Independent* of 2 January 1889, which reported the finding of Druitt's body and which would have been filed, as we have shown, along with the rest of the case papers:

FOUND IN THE RIVER

The body of a well-dressed man was discovered on Monday in the river off Thorneycroft's torpedo works, by a waterman named Winslow. The police were communicated with and the deceased was conveyed to the mortuary. The body, which is that of a man about 40 years of age, has been in the water about a month. From certain papers found on the body friends at Bournemouth have been telegraphed to. An inquest will be held today. (Wednesday.)

From this it seems perfectly reasonable to assume that Macnaghten was referring to Druitt, although he doesn't mention him by name, for he says, referring to his principal suspect, 'I have always held strong opinions regarding him, and the more I think the matter over, the stronger do these opinions become. The truth, however, will never be known, and did indeed, at one time lie at the bottom of the Thames, if my conjections be correct!'

This statement was made some years after his original notes, in which he was not quite so sure. In fact he hedged his bets: 'A much more rational theory is that the murderer's brain gave way altogether after his awful glut in Miller's Court, and that he immediately committed suicide, or, *as a possible alternative, was found to be so hopelessly mad by his relations, that he was by them confined in some asylum.*' (My italics.)

Major Arthur Griffiths, the author of *Mysteries of Police and Crime,* draws much the same conclusions. In fact, his wording is so similar that it is positively certain that he was quoting from Macnaghten's notes which, as an H.M. Inspector of Prisons, he would almost certainly have had access to. Other people have made much the same statements, but as they seem to be quoting from a common source—generally Macnaghten—it is fair to ask whether there is any independent evidence pointing to Druitt.

Strangely enough there is, although once again the original notes have disappeared. It is in a statement made by Albert Backert who, according to Donald McCormick, was a prominent member of the Whitechapel Vigilance Committee. After the Miller's Court murder, he became quite alarmed at the way that the police reduced the number of their patrols in the area and eventually, in March 1889, he complained to the senior officers 'that there seemed to be too much complacency in the force simply because there had been no more murders for some months.'

He was then asked if he would be sworn to secrecy on the understanding that he was given certain information. 'Foolishly, I agreed. It was then suggested to me that the Vigilance Committee and its patrols might be disbanded as the police were quite certain that the Ripper was dead. I protested that, as I had been sworn to secrecy, I really ought to be given more information than this. "It isn't necessary for you to know any more," I was told. "The man in question is dead. He was fished out of the Thames two months ago and it would only cause pain to relatives if we said any more than that."

'I again protested that I had been sworn to secrecy all for nothing, that I was really no wiser than before: "if there are no more murders,

I shall respect this confidence, but if there are any more I shall consider I am absolved from my pledge of secrecy."

'The police then got very tough. They told me a pledge was a solemn matter, that anyone who put out stories that the Ripper was still alive might be proceeded against for causing a public mischief. However, they agreed that if there were any other murders which the police were satisfied could be Ripper murders, that was another matter.'

If true, this means that the police had positively identified Druitt as the Ripper, soon after his body was found in January 1889.

But on what evidence?

Why should they pick on this cricket-playing barrister?

One theory, which has been developed, links him with the painter Walter Sickert who thought that he knew the identity of the murderer. According to him, some years after the murder he was living in a London suburb in lodgings which were looked after by an old couple. One day his landlady, as she was dusting, asked him if he knew the identity of the person previously occupying his room. When told that he didn't, she replied that it was 'Jack the Ripper'. He went on:

Her story was that his predecessor had been a veterinary student. After he had been a month or two in London, this delicate-looking young man—he was consumptive—took to occasionally staying out all night. His landlord and landlady would hear him come in about six in the morning and then walk about in his room for an hour or two, until the first edition of the morning paper was on sale, when he would creep lightly downstairs and run to the corner to buy one. Quietly he would return and go to bed. But an hour later, when the old man called him, he would notice, by the traces in the fireplace, that his lodger had burnt the suit he had been wearing the previous evening.

Gradually the old couple came to the reluctant conclusion that their lodger was none other than Jack the Ripper. But before they could make up their minds as to whether to warn the police or not about him, his health suddenly deteriorated and his mother, who was a widow, came and took him back to Bournemouth where she lived and where, according to Donald McCormick, he died three months later.

According to McCormick's source, Walter Sickert told this story to Sir Melville Macnaghten, who became convinced that the young man in question must have been Druitt because 'he had a widowed mother living at Bournemouth, the same as Druitt'. This is clearly nonsense. Druitt's brother William certainly lived in Bournemouth, but their widowed mother had been confined in a mental asylum since July 1888 and was clearly incapable of fetching home her son who, by the by, was not a veterinary surgeon.

The same anonymous source says that Druitt was being black-mailed and that he confided this to his mother whom he told 'about the whole affair and she presumably told the police when he was reported missing some time during December 1888. Anyhow, my father was emphatic that Druitt was living at Bournemouth when the first two Ripper crimes were committed.'

And, says McCormick, 'this seems finally to dispose of the case that Druitt had any connection with the crimes.'

Unfortunately it does not.

Even if we assume that Druitt was living in Bournemouth—which I do not for one moment believe—there is fortunately independent evidence to show that Druitt was in London for one of these murders, at least.

According to an article by Irving Rosenwater in *The Cricketer* in January 1973, he was playing cricket at Blackheath at 11.30 a.m. on the very morning that Annie Chapman was murdered at 5.30 a.m. only half a dozen miles away. This fact alone is enough to destroy the uncorroborated gossip of McCormick's witness that he could not have killed Annie Chapman because he was living in Bourne-mouth when the first two murders were committed. Even if we concede to McCormick's theory that Chapman was the third victim and not the second (he makes Martha Tabram the first) there is again the confirmatory evidence from the cricketing records that he is play-ing in a match at Canford on the same day that Nichols' body was found. Either fact is reasonable justification for dismissing the claim that Druitt could not have committed the murder because he was living in Bournemouth.

More difficult to explain away is Macnaghten's assertion that Druitt was probably a doctor. This is one of the most puzzling state-ments in the whole case and since much the same thing has been said not just once but many times, it is tempting to ask if there might be some truth in the story. Did he begin to study medicine after the ap-parent collapse of his career as a barrister? He was only a young man, not yet thirty-two, and with a degree behind him could certainly have qualified in medicine by the time that he was thirty-six years old. After all, the 'cramming' job at Blackheath could never have been more than a temporary stop-gap for a man of his education and background.

If so, if Druitt was a medical student and one of the two that were questioned by the police, this might explain one of the most puzzling factors about the whole case.

Nichols, it will be recalled, was murdered on 31 August; Chapman on 8 September; Stride and Eddowes on 30 September. Logically, if this pattern of dates had continued the next murders should have been on 8/9 October, 30/31 October and 8/9 November (which was the date that Mary Kelly was murdered). Instead, there were none at all in October. This immediately prompts the question 'Why not?'

Assuming still that Druitt was one of the medical students that had been traced, this would fit in with the dates in so far as we know them from Abberline's report, which is dated 1 November. As he is only answering the Home Secretary's queries about the *third* medical student it is a reasonable assumption that the reports about the two who had been traced must have been forwarded at least two weeks before that and consequently the enquiries must have been made in the first half of the month. If Druitt was questioned by the police at the beginning of October it would explain why there were no killings that month and why he waited until he could be sure that he was no longer under suspicion.

Would this pent-up frenzy explain the shambles of Miller's Court?

Tempting though this theory is, there are no hard facts to support it. As Donald McCormick rightly says, 'What other evidence is there to support Sir Melville's claim to name him as chief suspect? He was never seen in the vicinity of the crimes.'

This point was challenged by Dan Farson who says in his book *Jack the Ripper* that Montague's cousin, Dr Lionel Druitt, had a surgery at 140 Minories, on the City's eastern boundary. It was an important discovery, as the Minories is only a few minutes' walk away from Mitre Square, where Eddowes was murdered, and might have been Druitt's hide-out. Farson also quotes two 'Ripper' letters to support his theory. The first was sent from Liverpool on 29th September. It warned:

Beware, I shall be at work on the 1st and 2nd Inst. in Minories at twelve midnight, and I give the authorities a good chance, but there is never a policeman near when I am at work.

Yours,

JACK THE RIPPER

By a chance in a million, *while it was still in the post* Eddowes was murdered at about 1.30 a.m. on 30 September. As there were literally dozens of letters making similar threats it is unfair to pick this one out of the bag when there is no evidence whatever to suggest that the writer was in fact Jack the Ripper. Are we to assume that he posted the letter in Liverpool, told the police that he would commit a murder within twenty-four to forty-eight hours' time, but changed his mind on the train back to London and committed two murders instead that night?

Even less reliance can be put on the other letter Farson quotes. A few days later a second letter was sent from Liverpool:

> What fools the police are. I even give them the name of the street where I am living.
>
> Yours,
>
> JACK THE RIPPER

Following on from the first letter, the immediate conclusion is that the Minories is the address that the writer is referring to. Unfortunately, the address referred to is 'Prince William Street, Liverpool', which is written on the card, and does not leave room for any ambiguity.

Nor does Farson's main theory stand up any better. His new evidence is that Lionel Druitt was assisting Dr Thomas Thyne at his surgery in the Minories in 1879. Farson believes that Montague Druitt visited his cousin there and that later, when Lionel became a junior partner in Dr Gillard's practice at 122 Clapham Road, he stayed on and may even have rented a room there. This, if true, would explain the ease and speed of the Ripper's disappearance as he would be living on the City/East End boundary.

There are several factors which throw doubts on these conclusions. Only the Medical Register (1879) lists Lionel Druitt as being at 140 Minories. The Medical Directory, for the same year, does not mention him at all, although he is listed in the 1878 and 1880 editions; according to the 1879 edition the practitioners at the Minories address are Dr J. O. Taylor and Dr Thyne. In fairness to Farson, however, it would be reasonable to assume that the information in the Medical Register is correct as medical practitioners paid to have this information inserted whereas in the Medical Directory they apparently did not. Nonetheless, the discrepancy between the two volumes is something that ought to be explained.

Druitt's stay must have been a brief one as the following year

(1880) only Dr Thyne is listed at the Minories address. The Medical Register and the Medical Directory for 1880 give Lionel's address as 8 Strathmore Gardens, the same as in the 1878 editions.

A cursory stay then, if it took place at all, would explain his omission from the Register of Voters for the City of London, which includes the names of lodgers as well as of tenants and owners. I have searched these registers from 1878 to 1889 and have not found the name of Druitt mentioned anywhere. Clearly then neither Lionel and certainly not Montague were ever lodgers for any length of time— although there is always the possibility that they might have stayed there occasionally, as infrequent guests. Had Montague's stay, however, coincided with each of the murders then surely he would have come under suspicion. Unfortunately, without more facts this line of speculation is useless. The only conclusion that can be reached with any certainty is that Lionel Druitt was probably Dr Taylor's locum tenens when he resigned in 1879 (he is not mentioned in the obituaries) and that when he left after a brief stay the only practitioner in residence at 140 Minories was Dr Thyne, who is the only doctor registered at that address in 1880.

This still leaves us with Cullen's other alternative that he might have changed his bloodstained clothes in his chambers in King's Bench Walk. Yet this does not explain why, if he was going to the Temple, or even to the Minories, after leaving Mitre Square he should have walked in completely the opposite direction to both! The one fact which both men ignore is that he dropped part of Eddowes' apron in Goulston Street. This means that the Ripper, like a fox, was doubling back towards the police who were running in his direction. At some point, with so many police in the area, they must have met.

How, then, did he get away?

The only way he could have done so was by bolting into one of the hundreds of lodging houses in the area. There has been a general refusal to accept that this was possible because they were so public and he would have been too bloodstained to have escaped notice. But would he? On 11 September *The Times* published the following piece in a long article about Annie Chapman's murder and the enquiries that were then being made:

> The woman Chapman was known in appearance to the policemen on the night beats in the neighbourhood, but none of those who were on duty between 12 and 6 on Saturday morning recollect having seen her. It is ascertained that several men left their lodg-

ings after midnight with the expressed intention of returning who have not returned. Some men went to their lodgings after 3 o'clock, and left again before 6 in the morning, which is not an unfrequent occurrence in those houses. None of the deputies or watchmen at the houses have any memory of any person stained with blood entering their premises but at that hour of the morning little or no notice is taken of persons inquiring for beds. They are simply asked for the money, and shown up dark stairways with a bad light to their rooms. When they leave early, they are seldom noticed in their egress. It is then considered quite probable that the murderer may have found a refuge for a few hours in one of those places, and even washed away the signs of his guilt. The men in these houses use a common washing place, and water once used is thrown down the sink by the lodger using it. All this might happen in a common lodging house in the early morning without the blood-stained murderer being noticed particularly. The conviction is growing even, that taking for granted that one man committed all the recent murders of women in the Whitechapel district, he might in this fashion, by changing his common lodging house, evade detection for a considerable time.

It is also worth remembering that after the double event he washed some of the blood away in a street, as Henry Smith relates. Just how many other times did he do this? And depending on just how these murders were committed hangs the whole question of how blood-stained he would have been.

Trying to work out the practicalities that he must have faced when he killed these women gives some of the answers. Assuming that these women went with him expecting to have normal sexual intercourse, it is hardly likely that they—and certainly not their clients—would have been lying down on one of those filthy courts or alleys in autumn/early winter weather. The alternative is that it would have been performed standing up against some fence or wall. If so, the woman would have stood with her back to the wall and lifted up her skirts. Now, remembering that these were ankle-length skirts and that most of these women were wearing three or four garments of similar length (Catherine Eddowes, for instance, was wearing a skirt and three petticoats), they would have stood with these garments bunched up clumsily in front of them. The man would then stand close. Penetration would not be necessary as most prostitutes are experienced enough to grip the penis between their legs and cause him to ejaculate without penetration ever taking place. One prostitute is on record as saying that in several years of street work she was never penetrated more than three times! Alternatively he might be in such a state of excitement that sperm would not form; this condition is known as aspermia.

In this position she would have been completely vulnerable to any attack.

For a long time I assumed that she must have been standing so because of the bruising on nearly all the victims' faces and to explain away the absence of any stab wounds in the chest or throat. The bruising is generally one of the things which is ignored, although a contemporary newspaper said at the time of Eddowes' murder that one eye had been knocked out; this was wrong but certainly it was very badly bruised and swollen, as the mortuary photographs show. Polly Nichols and Annie Chapman were similarly badly bruised about the face. From this, I thought that probably the Ripper had punched them several times in the face, which would have stunned them and given him enough time to get his hands round their throats to strangle them. This would explain why Annie Chapman was able to call out, which she could not have done if she had been seized from behind and her throat cut. Once they had been strangled, into unconsciousness at least, it would have been a simple matter for the Ripper to have knelt by their head and swiftly cut their throats. This would explain why in the case of the four women he murdered in the street there was no bloodstaining except under the bodies. If they had been alive when their throats were cut the blood would have spurted out in about a three-foot jet.

On this evidence the indications are that the women were strangled first, with the probable exception of Mary Kelly.

There would be very little bloodstaining on the killer. Blood would have seeped on to the ground and been soaked up by the clothing, as did happen, and after the mutilation the Ripper would have had bloodstains on his hands, cuffs, the bottoms of his trousers and his boots. Much has been made of the question of whether he was ambidextrous or left-handed, but this is hard to judge, particularly if he was kneeling by their heads when he cut their throats, as I believe he was. According to Sir Melville Macnaghten, 'The theory that the Whitechapel murderer was left-handed, or, at any rate, "ambidexter", had its origin in the remark made by a doctor who examined the corpse of one of the earliest victims; *other doctors did not agree with him.*' According to the Westminster notes, the throats in the first four murders were cut from left to right, which makes the Ripper right-handed, and the women were lying down when murdered. Professor Cameron of the Department of Forensic Medicine at the London Hospital thinks, from the Mitre Square drawings and photographs, that he was right-handed as the incision drags to the right, as would happen, and is deeper as more viscera is exposed.

Both Professor Cameron and the late Professor Camps thought that the Ripper had probably always strangled his victims first. Professor Camps, however, pointed out a difficulty in *The Investigation of Murder:*

> The approach of the doctors in all the Ripper cases appears to have been on the basis of accepting the obvious. Viewed in the light of other sadistic sexual murders, strangulation would usually be a very significant feature. It seems very possible that the Ripper silenced all his victims by strangling them for, in at least two cases, obstruction to the mouth is mentioned and the absence of bleeding is also a matter for comment. In all cases there was no sign or sound of a struggle, which tends to confirm this. Yet no effort was made to trace the typical injuries associated with this, with the result that the knife became at once the murder weapon and the means of mutilation. If this hypothesis were correct and had been realised, it is possible that the later victims might have escaped their fate, for throat-cutting is neither silent nor neat, whilst all prostitutes fear strangulation. To look for such marks is not a matter of inspired guesswork but a simple extension of the maxim that it is safer to proceed by excluding all possibilities than by taking the short cut of accepting what is obvious. It is a major and very dangerous temptation to find what is expected and look no further.

The kind of injuries that Professor Camps was referring to are the showers of pin-prick haemorrhages (petechiae) which in cases of strangulation occur in the face and in and around the eyes, and the damage to the laryngeal structures, particularly the hyoid bone which is usually fractured. In fairness, however, to doctors such as Dr Phillips, the conditions they worked in were impossible. Most of their work had to be carried out in badly equipped workhouse mortuaries or in sheds like those which Dr Phillips and the coroner had protested about quite strongly at the early inquests, and which helps make the doctors' acceptance of the obvious at least understandable.

In discussing these points, Professor Cameron offered me an alternative theory of his own. It was based on a case that he had investigated in 1968. The insight that it gives into this particular killer's mind also suggests a motive for the Ripper killings that is at least as satisfactory as any other so far presented.

Briefly the facts of the case are:

On 7 February 1968 a young bride was found brutally murdered in the bedroom by her husband when he returned home to their flat in Bromley, Kent. It was a seemingly 'motiveless' murder. She had fourteen incised wounds in the throat and four stab wounds to the neck, one of which had penetrated through to the front of the spine on the right side. There was bruising round the neck which indicated that there might have been partial asphyxiation at or shortly before death. There were marks on the right side of her mouth which might have been done by the left hand, if she was gripped from behind, leaving the right hand free. A knife with a serrated edge was the probable weapon but this was never found. Nor was there any evidence of sexual assault.

A 26-year-old bank clerk was later convicted of the murder and sentenced to life imprisonment.

The case was discussed at a meeting of the Medico-Legal Society on 10 June 1971. During it, the following exchange took place, the relevance of which is immediately apparent:

Mr Taylor asked whether Dr Cameron was satisfied that the actual blows and wounds could have been inflicted in the way suggested. It seemed a rather peculiar attack from behind, with one hand over the mouth of a girl who obviously struggled, to use a long knife, which had to be low down quite far in front and pushed in, causing four wounds which were so very close together through the neck and all accurately placed. This was done to a girl who was, no doubt, screaming and struggling. There was also a slit across, which apparently would have been taken with a knife held in probably a different manner. It all seemed to be 'a bit too good to be true'.

   Dr Cameron recalled his remarks that the deceased had exhibited evidence of asphyxia in the form of petechiae (pin-point haemorrhages) and that there was bruising around the voicebox. On examination he assumed that she could well have been partially asphyxiated and rendered unconscious before the actual knife assault occurred.

He was under the impression that, if the knife assault was from in front, it would have to be from the left hand in view of the distribution of the fourteen undercut-from-below-up wounds that were partly superficial and partly deep across the neck. His opinion was that it was more likely to have been inflicted from behind or certainly, if the body was on the floor, from the head end, with the hand gripping the face to give the abrasions to the right side of the mouth. In that position, to cause the fourteen wounds in the neck would be a sort of violin-playing effect with the serrated edge of a knife and undercut from below up. It would not then require much force to bring an eight-inch blade into contact four times through the already gaping hole.

Professor Simpson said that he could support those views from a similar kind of case which occurred on a railway train from Basingstoke. He thought that Dr Cameron had given a soundly-based reconstruction of the infliction of the wounds.

The president asked whether there was a great deal of bloodstaining. The photographs did not appear to show very much bloodstaining in the room.

Dr Cameron replied that there was quite extensive bloodstaining, but it was only beneath the body. His impression was that the body had been assaulted actually in the bedroom, where it was found.

The president remarked that that suggested that 'the deceased was possibly at least semi-conscious before the knife attack took place'.

Dr Cameron said he would have thought that she was probably partially assaulted near the kitchen and ran, losing her slipper outside the door, towards the bedroom to get away. The bedroom was the furthest part of the flat, and probably that was where she was actually attacked.

The president asked whether the strangling component might have occurred first.

Dr Cameron replied that in his opinion, it did occur first.

The main points which have to be borne in mind are that there was a partial strangulation of the victim, bruising on the face and very little blood in the flat, most of it being under the body and soaked up by the victim's clothes, as happened with the Ripper's victims.

Now with this case in mind, Professor Cameron thought that the most likely position that the Ripper and his victim would have taken

up would have been with her bending forward and the Ripper standing behind her; again, remembering the heavy garments that she was
wearing—five in all—she would have found it easier in this position to
have flicked them forward over her back. Possibly, she might have
had anal intercourse—which used to be a common way of birth control with these women—rather than normal vaginal penetration. In
this position, anyway, it would have been a very simple matter for
the Ripper to have strangled her. As he was doing so, he could have
even battered their faces against the wall, which could explain the
facial bruising on three of them. It might even explain why Stride
was still gripping the bag of cachous, which in this position, she may
have gripped even tighter in her final spasms until she lost consciousness. If the Ripper had then cut their throats while still holding them
from behind, the risk of staining his clothes with blood would have
been minimal.

Such an explanation also gives us a possible motive for the murders
other than the normal one of sadistic cruelty. The murderer, in the
case referred to by Professor Cameron, had assaulted two previous
victims in precisely the same manner from behind and each time with
a knife. When he was seventeen he had been put on probation for
three years for breaking into a girl's house armed with a knife and
attempting to have sexual intercourse with her. Six years later he was
sentenced to three months' imprisonment for assault occasioning
actual bodily harm against a middle-aged woman whose bedroom he
had broken into. Apparently he was impotent but he could overcome
this by a sudden attack on a woman.

According to the Canadian graphologist's analysis of the 'From
Hell' letter that was sent to Mr Lusk, the writer was probably a latent
homosexual. Might this suppressed homosexuality have created a
similar impotency in Jack the Ripper and caused him to act in identical manner to the murderer just mentioned? Such a possibility makes
a much more acceptable theory than one which sees him as a social
reformer dedicated to the cause of slum clearance in Whitechapel
and the erection of model dwellings. Tom Cullen puts forward this
latter, very persuasive theory; but it ignores the reforms which had
been going steadily forward for more than a decade and wrongly
credits the Whitechapel murderer with reforms which rightly belong
to the newly created London County Council.

This has taken us slightly away from Montague Druitt but it does
help us towards a more convincing picture of the Ripper.

The question has already been asked as to whether the Ripper was homosexual. Alternatively, was Montague Druitt homosexual, and was it perhaps homosexual activity that brought about his sudden dismissal from the Blackheath school? Whatever it was, it was this dismissal and his letter to the headmaster threatening suicide that probably brought him to the attention of the police. Attempted suicide was a criminal offence and was then punished with a gaol sentence, but this would have been preferable to the tragic and unnecessary waste of this young man's life. Probably the headmaster, when he received Druitt's letter, tried to trace him through his friends who probably went to the police to help them only as a last resort, before they contacted Druitt's brother one week later. Naturally the police would have gone to the Temple and searched his rooms and it is there that they might have found either Druitt's bloodstained clothing or some other evidence which suggested that they had found the Whitechapel murderer.

And this is where my contribution to the Ripper story comes in.

When I was researching my first book I shared the Guildhall Records Office every Monday afternoon with the Inspectress of the Sir John Soane Museum, Miss Dorothy Stroud. At the time she was researching her book on George Dance. Gradually she discovered my interest in crime and one day she gave me Jack the Ripper's knife. I must admit that I groaned inwardly, as I thought it most unlikely that it was the actual weapon until she told me the following story. In 1937 she was an assistant editor on *Sporting Life*. The editor was Hugh Pollard, whose pro-Fascist sympathies had led him to fly Franco into Spain for the civil war. One day he was getting rid of many of his personal things. He came into the office and plumped on the desk in front of her a box which he said contained Jack the Ripper's knives. The box had two knives, of which I have one, and was lined with blue silk, heavily bloodstained. Miss Stroud took one knife and her friend took the other. They then burned the box because of the bloodstains! During the war Miss Stroud used the knife as a carving knife and later as a gardening knife. The blade became very nicked and eventually she broke it when cutting a privet bush. Fortunately she kept the pieces, which she gave to me. The Guildhall Museum, without knowing what it was, told me that it had been made in the last quarter of the nineteenth century. But it wasn't until I showed it to Professor Camps that I learned precisely what I had been given. The knife was a post-mortem knife with a thumb grip on the blade which is specifically designed for 'ripping' upwards.

Pollard was a partner of Robert Churchill the gunsmith, who was closely involved with Scotland Yard for many years as their 'gun expert'. I believe that Pollard, who played a similar role, was given the knives, possibly to destroy, but kept them because of what he had been told. His career would overlap with Macnaghten's. Although this is very circumstantial it is the sort of evidence which, if found in Druitt's room, might have turned a hunt for a potential suicide into a search for Jack the Ripper.

Unfortunately, as in so many other instances, there's no proof.

But if the police were already in possession of some such facts as these then it would explain why, when Montague's brother, William Druitt, gave evidence at the coroner's inquest, that he said that he was the only living relative. If he had been apprised by the police of the ghastly scandal that was waiting to be uncovered, it is not surprising that he should be doing his best to cover up the scandal and to protect the family's good name.

All this is very circumstantial. But then so are most theories. Yet strangely enough precisely the same pattern of evidence, even down to the suicide, appears with the main suspect in London's twentieth-century 'Jack the Stripper' murders.

But nobody has ever suggested that Jack the Stripper was heir to the throne of England!

Druitt is currently the firm favourite with most Ripperologists as the man most likely to have been Jack the Ripper. By chance, I happened to be looking through some old cuttings that were pasted in a battered three-volume edition of Griffiths' *Mysteries of Police and Crime*. Among them was one from the *People's Journal* issue of 26 September 1919, on the retirement of a detective named 'Steve' White who had spent many nights as a young policeman loitering about the evil-smelling alleys of Whitechapel in search of Jack the Ripper. His story is quoted below in full. Clearly it refers to the Mitre Square murder, as it is the only murder which fits the facts; it also confirms a long-held suspicion of mine that Constable Watkins was probably on the other side of Kearley & Tonge's warehouse door, either talking or drinking tea with the watchman who happened to be an ex-policeman.

Certainly White's description of the Ripper, when it is compared with the photograph of Druitt, is one of the most uncanny things about the whole story. One of his reports included the following passage:

For five nights we had been watching a certain alley just behind the Whitechapel Road. It could only be entered from where we had two men posted in hiding, and persons entering the alley were under observation by the two men. It was a bitter cold night when I arrived at the scene to take the report of the two men in hiding. I was turning away when I saw a man coming out of the alley. He was walking quickly but noiselessly, apparently wearing rubber shoes, which were rather rare in those days. I stood aside to let the man pass, and as he came under the wall lamp I got a good look at him.

He was about five feet ten inches in height, and was dressed rather shabbily, though it was obvious that the material of his clothes was good. Evidently a man who had seen better days, I thought, but men who have seen better days are common enough down East, and that of itself was not sufficient to justify me in stopping him. His face was long and thin, nostrils rather delicate, and his hair was jet black. His complexion was inclined to be sallow, and altogether the man was foreign in appearance. The most striking thing about him, however, was the extraordinary brilliance of his eyes. They looked like two very luminous glow worms coming through the darkness. The man was slightly bent at the shoulders, though he was obviously quite young—about 33, at the most— and gave one the idea of having been a student or professional man. His hands were snow white, and the fingers long and tapering.

As the man passed me at the lamp I had an uneasy feeling that there was something more than usually sinister about him, and I was strongly moved to find some pretext for detaining him; but the more I thought it over, the more was I forced to the conclusion that it was not in keeping with British police methods that I should do so. My only excuse for interfering with the passage of this man would have been his association with the man we were looking for, and I had no real grounds for connecting him with the murder. It is true I had a sort of intuition that the man was not quite right. Still, if one acted on intuition in the police force, there would be more frequent outcries about interference with the liberty of subjects, and at that time the police were criticized enough to make it undesirable to take risks.

The man stumbled a few feet away from me, and I made that an excuse for engaging him in conversation. He turned sharply at the sound of my voice, and scowled at me in surly fashion, but he said 'Good-night' and agreed with me that it was cold.

His voice was a surprise to me. It was soft and musical, with

just a tinge of melancholy in it, and it was the voice of a man
of culture—a voice altogether out of keeping with the squalid sur-
roundings of the East End.

As he turned away, one of the police officers came out of the
house he had been in, and walked a few paces into the darkness
of the alley. 'Hello! what is this?' he cried, and then he called in
startled tones to me to come along.

In the East End we are used to shocking sights, but the sight
I saw made the blood in my veins turn to ice. At the end of the
cul-de-sac, huddled against the wall, there was the body of a
woman, and a pool of blood was streaming along the gutter from
her body. It was clearly another of those terrible murders. I remembered the man I had seen, and I started after him as fast as
I could run, but he was lost to sight in the dark labyrinth of the
East End mean streets.

White's description of the suspected murderer, according to the newspaper, was widely circulated and used by the police at the time, but
the man was never seen. It alleged that it gave Sir Robert Anderson
his conviction that the murderer was a Jewish medical student, who
had taken this method of avenging himself on women of the class
to which his victims belonged.

The mystery, however, that baffled the police more than anything
was how the murderer and the victim managed to get into the alley
under the eyes of the watching police. It was clear that the couple
had not been in any of the houses, and they were not known to any
of the residents. Therefore they must have passed into the alley from
the Whitechapel Road, and the two police officers were positive that
in the four hours of their vigil not a soul had entered the alley. White
had his own suspicions regarding the truth of this declaration, and
his suspicions were shared by Sir Robert Anderson, who afterwards,
in comparing notes with White expressed the opinion that the murderer and his victim had entered the close during the temporary absence of the two watching policemen. The men afterwards admitted
that they had gone away for not more than a minute. It was a very
short absence undoubtedly, but it was long enough to give the murderer time to walk into the alley with his victim.

3. Dr Stanley

In 1929 Leonard Matters published *The Mystery of Jack the Ripper*. In it he claimed that his book was based on the death-bed con-

fession of an English doctor named Stanley that he was Jack the Ripper.

In his original introduction, Matters said that he had found the confession printed in Spanish in one of the journals in Buenos Aires where he had worked for some years on an English newspaper. In a revealing phrase Matters said that he had built up a story around that confession; and it is tempting to ask if his story did not come first and the facts, which were well researched and make up two-thirds of the book, come second. Certainly it is hard to escape from the conclusion that the Dr Stanley part of the book is fiction. Matters himself said that he could not vouch for the genuineness of the story but thought that it was entitled to some credence. He went on 'That such a man of such a character and such a life story did really exist in 1888 it is beyond my hope to prove'. He said that a search of the Medical Records of the General Medical Council of Great Britain had failed to find anyone who could be identified with this Dr Stanley but went on to argue that only by accepting the existence of this elusive personality was it possible to delineate the true character of the Ripper.

His story was allegedly based 'on the recital of an anonymous surgeon in Buenos Aires who claimed to have been a student in London under the doctor, and to have been present when he died in the Argentine capital some thirty years ago.'

Matters begins by asking three questions. Why were all the Ripper's victims prostitutes? Why did the Ripper kill only in the East End? Why did the murders stop after the murder of Mary Kelly?

His conclusions were: that it was only among prostitutes the Ripper could find the woman that he was looking for; that he knew that he would find her in the East End; and that the woman he was looking for was Mary Kelly.

Matters says that Dr Stanley's early career was an unbroken success. But his rapid fame as a brilliant young surgeon took a downward turn when his wife died when their son was only a few days old. This tragedy soured him and left him with a lasting contempt for his colleagues whose medical incompetence he blamed, to some extent, for her death. Gradually he withdrew into himself and lavished all his affection on his only son, Herbert.

Matters quotes an anonymous contemporary who knew him at this time. (As he could not prove that Dr Stanley ever existed this was certainly a wonderful achievement!) 'X' was taken to the doctor's house in Portman Square and shown his collection of pathological specimens in the doctor's private museum. One of Dr Stanley's self-appointed tasks was a compilation of the pathological history of cancer. His only regret was that life was too short to allow him to complete it but this would be done by his son who, as the doctor believed, would one day 'be hailed as a saviour of humanity!'

'X' was led to speculate: 'There was no doubt Dr Stanley had centred all his hopes on that boy, and, looking at his museum, he saw in it not only the proof that he was right in his theory and surgical methods but that his son's future was wrapped up in his own victory over those he imagined to be his enemies'. 'X' also wondered about the effect it would have on Stanley if anything happened to his son. Undoubtedly the consequences would be tragic. And this, Matters says, is precisely what happened.

Herbert Stanley met Mary Kelly on boat race night of 1886. He was then a brilliant medical student and only 21. They spent a week in Paris together before he discovered that she was diseased. This is the first big flaw in Matters' story. Kelly's post mortem showed no trace of any such disease. Matters continues that the disease had taken firm hold on the boy before his father found out a few weeks later what had happened to him. For nearly two years they fought the disease with different cures before young Stanley died of its effects. By then the father knew the details of the short-lived affair with Kelly.

From the dramatic way he talks about it, one would suppose that young Stanley was the only person ever to have been afflicted with this disease, the name of which Matters modestly withholds from his readers. The following facts should be borne in mind to put the story into some perspective. According to Dr Henriques, in *Prostitution and Society* Vol 3, about 50,000 people were treated anonymously for venereal diseases in the London Hospitals in the middle of the last century. In the same period, about 20 per cent of the army was infected with the disease, as compared with today's figure of about 4 per cent. Most men seem to have accepted the risk as a perfectly acceptable hazard.

Both Donald McCormick and Robin Odell make the point that venereal disease was a slow killer and that, if he had contracted the disease from Kelly, Herbert Stanley would not have died within so short a time as two years. But, as Odell points out, the main flaw in Matters' argument has always been that, according to the medical evidence, Kelly was not infected with venereal disease: the only disease that she was suffering from was alcoholism. But before jumping to the conclusion that she could not have passed on the disease to young Stanley, Odell cautioned: 'Too much faith should not, in all respect, be placed on Dr Phillips' remarks, for a woman can be a carrier of venereal disease without the disease itself being evident. Moreover, the causal organism of syphilis was not discovered until 1905, so that a doctor in 1888 could not have based his diagnosis only on clinical evidence, which is especially difficult to establish in a woman, not to mention a specific case where the woman had been cut to pieces. If modern pathological examinations and blood-tests could have been made, they might well have shown that Kelly was a syphilitic.'

The story goes on to describe Dr Stanley vowing to revenge himself on Kelly. This means scouring the East End for her. He spends a week or two to familiarise himself with the underworld and night life of London, creeping through alleys and back streets and learning how to dodge from one street to another without being seen. For his first encounter with a prostitute Stanley goes to Wardour Street where he knows that Kelly had once lived. To his dismay she is no longer there. He curses the woman now living in her old lodgings, and who, after she has listened to his tirade, slams her door and mutters, 'My God! I'm glad I'm not Marie. If I was that man would kill me. Somebody ought to tell Marie, but I don't know what's become of her.'

Clearly this is fiction.

In spite of his statement that he could not prove the existence of Dr Stanley, Matters neatly dovetails into his story the evidence of a Mrs North who describes her meeting with a man she thought was a doctor; he was a man of 45 to 47 years of age, sinewy and strong, of tremendous force and will. 'His eyes were dark and glowed with fire,' says Matters. Dr Stanley subsequently learns that Kelly is living in the East End, and disguises his appearance. 'A change of attire; a slouching gait; a garbled form of English . . . or an imitated foreign accent. . . .' At the same time he resolves to kill all the women whom he questions, it does not matter how many, so overwhelmingly strong is his desire for revenge. His first victim is Martha Tabram. Stanley panics and stabs her simultaneously with his surgical knife and triangular-shaped bayonet. Polly Nichols is his next victim and this time being calmer and more in control of himself he succumbs to another impulse and disembowels her for the specimen he wants for his surgical museum! He obtains further physiological specimens from Annie Chapman, Liz Stride and Catherine Eddowes who, before she is murdered, gives him the name and address of Kelly's lodgings. Here again there is a blending of fact and fiction, because the other name that Eddowes used was Kelly and it would have been easy for Stanley, if his story had been true, to have assumed that she was the woman that he was looking for. Eventually Stanley, after keeping observation on Mary Kelly, overhears her say that her man has left her and that she'll be out on the streets unless someone pays her rent.

He follows her to Miller's Court and, awaiting his chance, creeps into her unlocked room. Shaking her awake he reveals his identity and gives her a chance to speak before he kills her. She has only time to scream 'Murder' before he uses the knife.

His revenge is complete.

Afterwards Stanley wanders the world for ten years, apparently without his famous collection, and finally settles down in Buenos Aires. There he lives for some years and, recognising a former pupil of his, writes to him when he eventually succumbs to cancer, the disease for which he had striven to find a cure. When the pupil arrives to see him Stanley tells him that he has only an hour or two to live. He confesses that he is Jack the Ripper and gives the visitor a hundred pounds to pay for a modest funeral and the rest to do with as he likes. He wants his visitor to promise to do something for him, but he dies before he can tell him what it is.

As a postscript to this story it is worth including Leonard Gribble's theory, put forward in an issue of *True Detective* (January 1973), in an article which he called 'Was Jack the Ripper a Black Magician?'

Once again, the story is about a doctor avenging himself on the East End prostitutes who had given his son the disease from which he had died in an asylum for the insane. Each of his victims is a blood sacrifice; but, on top of this, the murders are committed in such a way as to coincide with certain phases of the moon since the doctor can build up an occult pentagram (this is the significance of the figure 5) to give himself immunity from discovery. In fact, there are six victims. Martha Tabram is the first. Her murder has an occult significance; apparently three times thirteen is an occult formula which is why she was stabbed 39 times. Stride, however, is not a victim proper. Because the Ripper didn't have time to complete his ritual slaying it was essential that he had to find a second victim quickly to make her death coincide with that particular phase of the moon. If he hadn't murdered Eddowes immediately afterwards the efficacy of the pentagram would have been broken.

Kelly's death and mutilation coincided with the final phase of the sacrificial period, which sealed the mystical pentagram and so brought the killings to an end.

4. George Chapman (Severin Antoniovich Klosowski)

George Chapman, whose real name was Severin Antoniovich Klosowski, was born on 14 December 1865 in the tiny Polish village of Nargornak. From December 1880 to October 1885 he was a surgical student in village practice. He completed his studies, which ended on 1 January 1886, with three months practical surgery at the hospital in Praga. He then applied for, but failed to get the degree of junior surgeon. At most he seems to have been a *feldscher*, a hospital attendant or 'barber surgeon'. (This was a relic from the days when the professions of hairdressing and medicine were intertwined.) After a brief spell of military service he emigrated to England, arriving in 1888. His first known job was as a hairdresser's assistant in a shop in the High Street, Whitechapel. For some reason he was known as 'Ludwig' Klosowski (or Zagowski), which the English pronounced 'Schloski'.

Nothing is known in detail about Chapman's career in Whitechapel at this time, except that it coincided with the Whitechapel murders. Ex-Detective Sergeant Leeson, in his autobiography, *Lost London,* conveys some information that is relevant. He says that 'Chapman lived in Whitechapel, where he carried on a hairdresser's business in a sort of "dive" under a public-house at the corner of George Yard. . . .' If true, then this has some significance as it was in George Yard buildings that Martha Tabram was stabbed to death. However, Leeson's statements must be treated with great caution, even when he is describing events with which he was intimately connected, such as the famous 'Siege of Sidney Street' some years later. (In my book about this episode, I was able to check contemporary police documents and statements against his later statements in these memoirs. I found such alarming discrepancies between them that I decided *Lost London* was almost entirely untrustworthy.) In connection with this statement about Chapman, it should be borne in mind that Leeson did not join the Metropolitan Police until October 1890 and was not posted to Whitechapel until February 1891, and his statement must therefore be treated as second-hand evidence.

It is known that Klosowski changed jobs and went to work for a barber in West Green Road, South Tottenham, and that he subsequently bought his own shop in the High Road, Tottenham. He was a poor business man and, the shop failing, he was reduced once more to the status of barber's assistant. He worked for a barber in Shoreditch and then moved on to another shop in Leytonstone.

In 1889 he was introduced to one Lucy Baderski at the Polish Club in St John's Square, Clerkenwell. After they had known each other for a very short time, less than four or five weeks, they were married on August Bank Holiday, 1889. Klosowski, however, already had a Polish wife whom he had left behind in Poland. She came to London and tried to oust her rival from his affections. For a short time both women shared the same house with him. Eventually, Klosowski's legal wife realised the hopelessness of her situation and left. Afterwards Klosowski and Lucy Baderski went to live in Cable Street, close to the docks, before emigrating to America in 1890. In February 1891 Lucy Baderski left her husband because of his infidelities and returned to England alone. According to Klosowski's story, he followed her in 1893 (though there is evidence to show that this happened a year earlier).

The couple were reconciled, but only temporarily. Klosowski did not try to get custody of the two children of the marriage, probably because this would not have fitted in too well with the image that he liked to project of himself as a widower or bachelor.

At the end of 1893 he met one Annie Chapman (not to be confused with the Ripper's victim) and they lived together for about a year. After they broke up in December 1894 she found out that she was pregnant. He refused to help her, even to the extent of denying her a reference so that she could support herself and the child. The only legacy of this affair was that Klosowski borrowed from his discarded mistress the name of Chapman. This was to shake himself free of his tangled affairs, which he did by suppressing totally the name Klosowski. Years later, when he was questioned by the police, and asked if he was Klosowski, he replied: 'I don't know anything about the fellow.' The change of name, says H. L. Adam, in his introduction to the *Trial of George Chapman,* may have been inspired by other more sinister ambitions having 'for their primary purpose and *idée fixe* the pursuit, capture, and the destruction of women.'

He met his first victim when he was lodging with the Renton family in Leytonstone in 1895. Mary Renton's married name was Spink. Her husband was a railway porter who left her, taking their son with him, because she was an alcoholic. Chapman had changed his lodgings, and soon after the breakup of this marriage he and Mary Spink were soon seen about a lot together. Eventually they announced that they were getting married. This was a polite fiction, since each was still legally married. After they had set up house together, Mary Spink had £250 advanced to her from a trust fund of about £600. A further £350 was advanced to her two years later, in 1897, only a short time before she died. Chapman and Mary leased a barber's shop in a poor part of Hastings but, because it was not very successful, they moved to a more affluent part of the town where the business prospered. Mrs Spink was a small blond woman with short cropped hair. She helped her husband by lathering and sometimes shaving the customers; she was popular with the customers and used to entertain them by playing the piano. These 'musical shaves' were very popular and the business prospered dramatically. In spite of this, Chapman gave it up within six months and returned to London as the landlord of the Prince of Wales tavern off the City Road.

While in Hastings Chapman had by no means neglected his casual love affairs. Shortly before moving to London, he purchased an ounce of tartar emetic from a local chemist. In London, Mrs Spink, who seldom suffered from anything but a hangover, began to experience severe vomiting and stomach pains. Gradually her health broke down under these attacks and she became very emaciated. Chapman was very solicitous for his wife's health and supervised the food and medicines that were given to her. She weakened steadily under these administrations and, on Christmas Day 1897, she died. The cause of death was given as phthisis due to her emaciated condition.

A few months later he hired a new barmaid named Bessie Taylor, who was soon installed as the new but unmarried Mrs Chapman. Like her predecessor, she soon acquired the same haggard condition. To avoid arousing suspicion among the customers who had known his first wife, Chapman gave up the Prince of Wales tavern and moved to Bishop's Stortford where he took over The Grapes. While they were there, Bessie Taylor went into hospital for an operation. Afterwards Chapman became even more brutal to her, to the extent of threatening her with a revolver. They moved back to London where Chapman leased the Monument Tavern in the Borough. He continued to ill-treat his wife. This aggravated her condition, and she became steadily thinner and more frail. None of the doctors who examined her realised that she was being slowly poisoned. On 14 February 1901 she died. Cause of death was given as 'exhaustion from vomiting and diarrhoea'.

Just a few months later Chapman met his final victim, a young woman named Maud Marsh, whom he hired as barmaid at the Monument Tavern. From a letter that was produced at his trial, it is clear that she held out against him for some time before moving in with him as Mrs Chapman No. 3. Her pathetic lie that they were husband and wife did not deceive her parents, who were suspicious of Chapman and never trusted him for one moment. Within a short time Maud began to suffer from the same pains and symptoms as had her predecessors. Solicitous as ever, Chapman insisted on preparing her food and medication himself. Mrs Marsh eventually suspected that her daughter was being poisoned and called in another doctor to examine her. His visit precipitated the final tragedy. Chapman gave his wife a final massive dose of poison and she died the next day. The local doctor, warned by telegram by Dr Grapel (who had examined her) that his patient was being poisoned, was too late to save her. He refused to issue a death certificate and Chapman's fate was sealed when the post mortem showed traces of arsenic. He was arrested on 25 October 1902, the day of Edward VII's Coronation procession through London. Only then was it discovered from his private papers that he was also Severin Klosowski. He was charged with the murder of Maud Marsh, and subsequently with the murders of Mary Spink and Bessie Taylor. Their bodies when exhumed were found to be in a remarkably good state of preservation, one of the surest indications of poisoning by arsenic.

Chapman's trial began on 16 March 1903 and lasted four days. His only friend, it seemed, was his Polish wife who begged to see him. This he refused to agree to. His defence counsel did not call for any new evidence or witnesses on his behalf. The only thing he could do was play for the jury's sympathy, by claiming that Chapman was a 'hated alien'. This line was unsuccessful, and the jury took only eleven minutes to bring in their verdict of guilty.

Chapman was hanged at Wandsworth prison on 7th April 1903.

Chapman has always been a leading Ripper suspect. This can be attributed to H. L. Adam who, when he edited the *Trial of George Chapman,* was able to draw upon the knowledge of ex-Chief Inspector Godley who had not only arrested Chapman but had worked with Inspector Abberline on the Ripper investigation. Godley is clearly the source for Adam's statement that Abberline thought that Chapman and the Ripper were one and the same person. When

Godley made his arrest Abberline told him 'You've got Jack the Ripper at last!'

The arguments in favour of Chapman being the Ripper can be briefly summarised as follows; that he was working in Whitechapel at the time and had the necessary surgical skill to have committed the killings and the mutilations both quickly and efficiently; that the description of the man who was seen with Kelly was—yet again!—an accurate description of Chapman himself; that the Americanisms in some of the correspondence such as 'boss' suggest an American background, which Chapman certainly had, although this carelessly overlooks the fact that he only acquired such a background two years after the murders; the callous joking of some of the Ripper correspondence, which was typical of his brutal humour; that the last murder was committed while Chapman was still in London (July 1889) and that similar murders were committed in the immediate area of Jersey City which was where Chapman opened his shop in America. This last point does not hold up, since a thorough search of contemporary records shows that the only murder which could be possibly referred to as such was that of 'Old Shakespeare' (see p. 182).

The case against Chapman's being the Ripper must necessarily hinge on the character of the Ripper himself, whoever he was. In an attempt to understand it, the following extract is taken from Krafft-Ebing's *Aberrations of Sexual Life,* edited by Dr Alexander Hartwich.

From the observations to be now recounted it emerges with utter clarity that the perverse urge in murders for pleasure does not solely aim at causing the victim pain and—most acute injury of all—death, but that the real meaning of the action consists in to a certain extent imitating, though perverted into a monstrous and ghastly form, the act of defloration. It is for this reason that an essential component of murders for pleasure is the employment of a sharp cutting weapon; the victim has to be pierced, slit, even chopped up. The correlation between pleasure-murder and defloration is further confirmed by the fact that the chief wounds are inflicted in the stomach region, and in many cases the fatal cuts run from the vagina into the abdomen. In boys an artificial vagina is even made in pleasure-murders.

Comparatively often the killing of the victim results from strangulation, that is to say, in the simplest manner, without any weapon being used, and certainly in some way linked with coitus, as before or after it, seldomer as a substitute. But it would seem as if the said act usually failed to satisfy the murderer, so that afterwards the corpse is hacked to bits, in which connection it is especially the genitalia, and in the case of women also the internal genital organs, which are concerned. In an extremely grisly manner one can connect a fetishistic element too with this process of hacking up the victim, inasmuch as parts of the body—and here again it is particularly the genitals which are concerned—are removed, and in a certain degree made into a collection. [My italics.]

It is obvious that individuals as seriously psychopathic as the perverts in this group may also display the most diverse other sex-deviations, such as e.g. homosexuality, paedophily and fetishism. At the same time there is a high degree of hypersexuality and especially before and during the act.

The point that I am making here is that this is an instantly recognisable portrait of the kind of man we know that Jack the Ripper must have been.

But can we also say that is a portrait of George Chapman?

Clearly it is not. Coincidences such as Chapman living in Whitechapel at the time of the murders seem meaningless once the portrait of the sadistic murderer has emerged. Jack the Ripper could never have made the change from a murderer of this type to the coldly calculating wife-poisoner of Chapman's ilk. It is impossible to fit the two characters into the same frame, and on this ground alone Chapman should not be considered a candidate for the Ripper.

5. Dr Pedachenko

To understand Donald McCormick's *The Identity of Jack the Ripper* it is essential to know something of the Klosowski/Chapman theory, since the author uses the latter as a springboard for his own theory. His primary source material was the (unpublished) three-volume *Chronicles of Crime* by the graphologist Dr Dutton, already referred to in connection with the handwriting analyses of the Ripper correspondence (p. 91). Unfortunately these 'chronicles' were either lost or destroyed after Dr Dutton's death in 1935, and when McCormick came to write his book, nearly twenty-seven years later, he was obliged to fall back on the notes which he had taken in 1932 and then forgotten about (but which had fortunately survived the war). McCormick described Dutton's *Chronicles of Crime* as being 'not a single narrative, but rather a collection of impressions and theories which he noted at various periods.' Apart from the Ripper case, 'they covered a number of other interesting cases.' So it is fair to assume that McCormick has built his theory on the notes that he took of Dr Dutton's jottings. This is a weakness of the book. The reader, if he is to have any confidence in these findings, has a right to expect an accurate recounting of facts that he can check. Unfortunately, where this is possible, McCormick is apt to undermine the confidence of his readers. The most glaring example is in his retelling of the famous 'Siege of Sidney Street' case, where he takes two well-documented incidents—the murder of three London policemen and the Siege itself—and turns it into a single incident, although the events happened several miles apart and with a time lag of nearly three weeks between them. He made the same mistake again in *A History of the Russian Secret Service,* published in 1972, which he wrote under the pseudonym of Richard Deacon.

According to McCormick, Dr Dutton was friendly with Inspector Abberline who discussed this case with him on more than one occasion. From Inspector Godley's statement we know that Abberline congratulated him on having caught the Ripper when he arrested Chapman in 1902. But, according to Dutton, he changed his mind—more than fourteen years after his original investigation, if Dutton is correct. McCormick goes on: 'What finally convinced Abberline that he had made a mistake in thinking Klosowski was the Ripper was his discovery that the Polish barber-surgeon had a double in London and that this double, a Russian and also a barber-surgeon, sometimes posed as Klosowski for reasons which were not apparent.' McCormick then asks: 'Could this be the same Russian surgeon hinted at by Sir Basil Thomson and others, the character named as Ostrog by Sir Melville Macnaghten? Or could it be the Russian named by William Le Queux as Dr Alexander Pedachenko?'

As the story is rather a complicated one I shall break it down, as McCormick did, into the Russian and English sources.

Russian source. In 1923 the journalist and amateur spy, William Le Queux, published his autobiography, *Things I Know About Kings, Celebrities, and Crooks.* He was a name-dropper on a grand scale as can be readily judged from some of his chapter headings—'What I Know about Kings'; 'Evenings with "Carmen Sylva", Queen of Roumania'; 'What the Sultan of Turkey told me'. In fact, he was a good high-society gossip columnist with a lot of readers, and there is probably truth in his claim that, after the murder of Rasputin, 'the

Kerensky government handed to me, in confidence, a great quantity of documents which had been found in the safe in the cellar of his house, in order that I might write an account of the scoundrel's amazing career.' Among the papers was an incomplete manuscript called 'Great Russian Criminals' which, to his amazement contained the truth about the Jack the Ripper murders. Here is part of the extract that he copied before he returned the manuscript.

The true author of these atrocities was disclosed by a Russian well-known in London, named Nideroest, a spy of our Secret Police, who was a member of the Jubilee Street Club, the Anarchist Centre in the East of London. One night in the club the identity of 'Jack the Ripper' was revealed to him by an old Russian Anarchist, Nicholas Zverieff. The mysterious assassin was Doctor Alexander Pedachenko, who had been on the staff of the Maternity Hospital at Tver, and lived on the second floor in the Millionnaya, but had gone to London, where he lived with his sister in Westmoreland Road, Walworth. From there he sallied forth at night, took an omnibus across London Bridge and walked to Whitechapel, where he committed his secret crimes.

Alexander Pedachenko, according to Zverieff—whose record appears in the reports of the Secret Police—was aided by a friend of his named Levitski, and a young tailoress, called Winberg. The latter would approach the victim and hold her in conversation and Levitski kept watch for the police patrols, while the crimes and mutilations took place. Levitski, who had been born in London, wrote the warning post-cards signed 'Jack the Ripper' to the Police and Press. It was through Levitski that Zverieff knew the truth.

Before giving the rest of the quotation, which is an explanation of the above, it is worth examining this statement in a little more detail, for every one of these facts comes from the man called Nideroest —even though he claims to be passing on the information that he has been given by 'the old Russian Anarchist Zverieff'.

The only information that Le Queux gave about Nideroest's background was a single sentence that he had 'found out that a man named Nideroest was a member of the Jubilee Street Club and was known in connection with the Anarchist affray at Tottenham, and also with the Sidney Street affair.' When his book was published, *The Star* was quick to comment that he 'lets a large cat out of the bag when he reveals that the disclosure of the author of these atrocities originates with a Russian well known in London, named Nideroest, a spy in the Russian police. . . .'

Nideroest first hit the national headlines in January 1909 when he used a false name to get into the hospital where one of the gunmen, who had shot two persons and wounded numerous others, was lying wounded. Nideroest did this by pretending to be his brother. He was arrested before he could get to the wounded man and there is a photograph of him in the *Daily Mirror* of 27 January 1909 being led away. In court next day Detective Inspector McCarthy said that he had known him for some years and that four years earlier he had concocted a bogus story about bombs being made in Whitechapel. He was not an anarchist but a casual journalist. Nideroest's only explanation for his behaviour was that he had gone to the hospital to work up a sensational interview and that it was only by pretending to be a relative that he could get in. The Bench discharged him with a reprimand. It was this and the Sidney Street incident, after which Nideroest claimed to have helped the famous Peter the Painter escape from the house, that led Le Queux's reviewers—who were clearly well aware of the facts—to denounce Nideroest as an 'unscrupulous liar'.

The other and more important point, which McCormick omits to mention, is that in 1909 Nideroest was only 24 years old, as his photograph confirms. This means that he was three years old in 1888! So, whenever that interview with Zverieff took place, it must have been at least fifteen years after the murders. Indeed, one can pin it down even more accurately. According to Nideroest, the facts were given to him in the Anarchist Club in Jubilee Street. This club was not opened until 1906, and so it must have been after that date. McCormick, later on, offers further proof of Pedachenko's existence by quoting an extract from an *Ochrana Gazette* which he had been shown by a Russian exile, Prince Belloselski (who had been given this lithograph copy by Myednikov, former head of the Moscow Ochrana). This gazette was a confidential Secret Police bulletin, issued twice a month to the heads of sections to keep them up to date on what was happening in revolutionary circles. McCormick quotes one of the items contained therein.

KONOVALOV, Vasilly, alias PEDACHENKO, Alexey, alias LUISKOVO, Andrey, formerly of Tver, is now officially declared to be dead. Any files or information concerning him from district sections should be sent to the Moscow Central District of Ochrana.

Such information, photographs, or identification details as may still exist might refer to KONOVALOV, PEDACHENKO or LUISKOVO either individually or collectively. If documents held by you do not contain these names, they should also be examined for any information concerning a man, answering to the description of the above, who was wanted for the murder of a woman in Paris in 1886, of the murder of five women in the East Quarter of London in 1888 and again of the murder of a woman in Petrograd in 1891.

KONOVALOV's description is as follows: Born 1857 at Torshok, Tver. Height medium. Eyes, dark blue. Profession, junior surgeon. General description: usually wore black moustache, curled and waxed at ends. Heavy, black eyebrows. Broadshouldered, but slight build. Known to disguise himself as woman on occasions and was arrested when in woman's clothes in Petrograd before his detention in the asylum where he died.

This document was dated January 1909, but the actual date of receipt most probably was in the latter half of the previous year. What makes a close examination of it so fascinating is that it is asking for —not giving—information about the wanted man! The authors are not even sure that any 'information, photographs, or identification details' exist. The names are the permutations under which they might find him; but if these failed to throw up any information then their files were to be searched for 'a man' answering the description and wanted for various murders. Even more astonishingly, they knew that he was arrested in Petrograd and that he died in an asylum. With this information available to them, why then had not they been able to trace him? Why did they have to put out a general appeal for any existing photographs, information or identification details? Clearly the answer is that they had not been able to trace him, which in turn strongly suggests that, between the two control dates of 1906 and 1908, Nideroest had fed back the story which he claimed had been told to him by Zverieff, and the Ochrana had published it in turn in the hope of finding some confirmatory evidence.

But if the records did not exist, then what is the explanation for the second half of Le Queux's statement:

The report of Nideroest's discovery amused our Secret Police greatly, for, as a matter of fact, they knew the whole details at the time, and had themselves actively aided and encouraged the crimes, in order to exhibit to the world certain defects of the English police

system, there having been some misunderstanding and rivalry between our own police and the British. It was, indeed, for that
reason that Pedachenko, the greatest and boldest of all Russian
criminal lunatics, was encouraged to go to London and commit
that series of atrocious crimes, in which agents of our police aided
him.

Eventually at the orders of the Ministry of the Interior the Secret
Police smuggled the assassin out of London, and as Count
Luiskovo he landed at Ostend, and was conducted by a secret
service agent to Moscow. While there he was, a few months later,
caught red-handed attempting to murder and mutilate a woman
named Vogak and was eventually sent to an asylum, where he
died in 1908.

After the return to Russia of Levitski and the woman Winberg the Secret Police deemed it wise to suppress them, and they
were therefore exiled to Yakutsk. Such are the actual facts of the
'Jack the Ripper Mystery' which still puzzles the whole world.

The opening sentence—that the police were greatly amused as they
knew the details of Nideroest's discovery—is clearly not true. If they
had known them, why should the Moscow Ochrana have appealed
for information about a man who had been brought to Moscow by a
secret service agent and had there been caught attempting to murder and mutilate a woman some months later? The question can be
put even more simply. Why should the Tsarist Secret Police not only
not find, but even doubt the existence of, one of their own men
when the secret police of the Revolutionary Government that over-
threw them were able to do so and to say just how 'amused' their
predecessors had been by the incident? The answer that immediately
springs to mind is that the Revolutionary police were discrediting
their predecessors as much as possible and that they were faking
extra evidence. In fact, Le Queux was the perfect 'fall-guy as well
as propagandist for the new régime'.

The genuineness of the Rasputin papers is open to doubt on several counts. They were written in French which Rasputin, according
to Prince Belloselski, 'was certainly not fluent enough in . . . to dic-
tate a narrative in that tongue. If he dictated this at all it must have
been in Russian.' Once the doubts have been raised then they harden
into near certainty that the papers were faked particularly when A. T.
Vassilyev, who was the Tsarist police chief, states in his book *The
Ochrana* that Rasputin's apartments were immediately searched after

his death for compromising documents and that none were found. This is not to say that Le Queux did not receive any papers from the Kerensky government. Indeed, that he might have done is confirmed by an independent source, C. W. Shepherd, whom Le Queux in his memoirs describes as editor of the Northern Newspaper Syndicate. ('Shep' ghosted three books for Le Queux and was highly amused when the publisher wrote to Le Queux, after the receipt of one of these manuscripts, 'I see the old hand has not lost its cunning'.) When I asked him if he had ever seen the Rasputin papers he told me that he had once had to make a flying visit to St Leonards or Hastings where Le Queux was then living (he could not recall the date) and while he was there Le Queux had pointed out the Rasputin documents to him. He said: 'I saw them in a terrific-sized envelope, sealed and plastered with signs and codes and all sorts of things.' Unfortunately Le Queux never opened it in his presence.

The only reason for Le Queux to have been sent these papers was, as Prince Belloselski says, to help 'show up the Tsarist Government in the worst light. Indeed, the only object for Kerensky to pass these documents on to Le Queux would have been for propaganda purposes.'

Le Queux must have realised that he was being used in this way. Although he was a money-spinner he was also a lavish spender and had to spend much of his time abroad to avoid his creditors. He was constantly hard up and yet, with this new evidence in front of him, he nowhere refers to it in his biography of Rasputin but chooses to wait five years before appending it as a sort of footnote in his autobiography. His only explanation for his startling decision is the rather lame excuse that he had only recently discovered that a doctor called Pedachenko actually did live in Tver.

One doubts him, just as one doubts the genuineness of the Rasputin papers. So what the Russian sources eventually boil down to is a collection of papers that only came into existence after 1906—eighteen years at least after the murders, and that the source for them was a well-known liar: Nideroest had been publicly proved as one on more than one occasion.

They have to be dismissed from the case.

The only point not so far discussed with respect to these sources, is what possible reason the Russian Secret Police had for sending Pedachenko to England to commit these murders. This was allegedly done to show up the defects in the English police system. This is such a preposterous argument, however, that it cannot be taken seriously.

McCormick suggests, slightly more plausibly, that Pedachenko was being used as an *agent provocateur* to discredit the anarchists who were using England as a base for their attacks on the Tsarist régime. He claims that Nideroest was a counter-espionage agent and that this was his role when he helped his colleague, the famous Peter the Painter, to escape from the house in Sidney Street which was done with the help and connivance of the English police. This is to suggest that the English police condoned the instigation of the original jewel robbery that led to the murder of three of their colleagues, among the worst crimes in English police history, and then let the real architect of it escape and two men die in the 'Siege' itself. The chief argument against this theory is that the anarchists and other aliens were not expelled to their own country, even when they were implicated in such plots. Of the Sidney Street gang, eight were tried for murder and, with one exception—and her sentence was quashed on appeal—all were acquitted. None of them was expelled and, in the case of the woman who was found guilty, the jury made a specific request to the judge that she should not be deported. To underline this point, one of those involved, the only one who was not an anarchist, was sent back to Russia in 1917 as the Bolshevik delegate from London; after the October revolution he became deputy head of the Cheka! It was British policy to tolerate these political refugees who included such names as Lenin, Litvinoff and, for a very short time, Stalin.

None of them was expelled as an undesirable and yet Nideroest was. This fact stands squarely in the way of McCormick's theorising. Nideroest was arrested in 1909 and expelled from the country in 1915.

British source. McCormick quotes an entry from Dr Dutton's diary of 1924. 'Another theory on the Ripper. This time by William Le Queux in *Things I Know*. It is a great pity that he did not follow up what is a useful clue. By failing to do so, and by taking the Rasputin MS at its face value, he has only made a fool of himself. Further examination might have shown that Pedachenko was Klosowski's double. The fact that Pedachenko was a doctor at a Russian hospital is neither here nor there. What Le Queux should have found out was that Pedachenko worked as a barber-surgeon for a hairdresser named Delhaye in the Westmoreland Road, Walworth, in 1888.'

McCormick found out that there was such a hairdresser as Dutton had described, but by itself this means little. He does not produce any evidence for Pedachenko's existence. Dr Dutton's source for his story was a Dr J. F. Williams, who told him that a Russian barber-surgeon named Pedachenko assisted him occasionally at St Saviour's Infirmary on an unpaid basis. Dr Williams believed that Pedachenko worked as a barber-surgeon in various establishments in South London and that he 'removed warts, treated skin diseases'—which is exactly what a *feldscher* might be expected to do.

Dutton also quotes the private evidence, again uncorroborated, of Wolff Levisohn who was one of the prosecution witnesses at Chapman's trial. He had first met Chapman when he was working in High Street, Whitechapel, in 1888. At the time Levisohn knew Chapman as 'Ludwig Zagowski'. They met from time to time up until 1890. At Chapman's trial Levisohn made one of the most damaging, and so far unquoted, statements against the whole Chapman/Ripper theory. He said: 'I talked to the accused about medicines, and he asked me if I could get him a certain medicine, but I said no, I did not want to get twelve years.' What did he mean? From such a remark the only inference that can be drawn is that Chapman was asking him to get a poison of some sort. It could not have been drugs, as it was not then a criminal offence to use them. As this request was made before 1890 it is a strong argument in favour of Chapman's having consistently stuck to the same method throughout his murderous career. It also makes one wonder whether he managed to get this substance from somewhere else and, if he did, who was his victim? Was there a murder of which we know nothing? Certainly such consistency of method is far more likely than the theory that he changed his nature from frenzied sadist with a knife to cold, calculating prisoner.

Levisohn saw Chapman once again in 1894 or 1895 when the latter was working in Tottenham and then lost sight of him from 1895 to 1903, when he was tried. According to Dutton, however, Levisohn told Abberline at the time of the Whitechapel murders that 'he should look for a Russian who lived somewhere in Walworth, did a certain amount of illicit doctoring and attended barbers' shops to cut out warts and moles.' This tallies with Dr Williams' story. There was apparently some resemblance between Pedachenko and Chapman, so much so that, according to Dutton, 'Abberline for a long time thought that Pedachenko and Klosowski were one and the same person.' And this is surely what they were. We do not know when Chapman asked Levisohn to get him some poison, but if it was early on in their relationship, and if Chapman was confident as well as careless enough (as the evidence throughout his trial showed that he was) to have done so, then this would have been sufficient for Levisohn to give his tip to Abberline. True, the name he gave Abberline was 'Ludwig Zagowski', but it is just possible that —Levisohn being a traveller in hairdressers' appliances—he had discovered that Chapman was working under an alias in the Walworth Road.

To sum up, the evidence from the British sources suggests that Pedachenko/Chapman was a single person and not two individuals as Dr Dutton maintains. Indeed the only person who tries to separate them is Dr Dutton. As McCormick says, 'Dutton's suggestion that "Klosowski" posed as his double, with the implication that the latter was Pedachenko, is not followed up by any explanation.' What Dutton has done is to blur some of the Chapman evidence and relate it to the Nideroest story and two documents that did not come into existence until nearly twenty years after the murder and possibly even later. It is significant, surely, that the reference to Pedachenko was not entered in his diary until 1923, which was the year following Le Queux's publication of *Things I Know*.

Unless Dr Dutton's *Chronicles of Crime* turns up there is no way of corroborating his statements, and until it does these have to be taken on trust.

6. Neill Cream

Dr Neill Cream is another famous murderer who has been suggested as Jack the Ripper. His chequered career of arson, blackmail, abortion and murder was finally brought to an end in 1892 when he was found guilty of the murder of four London prostitutes, whom he had picked up in the boroughs of Walworth and Lambeth (which led to his being called the Lambeth Poisoner) and poisoned with strychnine. On the scaffold he is said to have exclaimed 'I am Jack the—' just as the bolt was drawn. The hangman is said to have sworn that this was so. What makes the incident open to doubt is that among those who were present in their official capacity was the new Commissioner of the City of London Police, Sir Henry Smith, who boasted many years afterwards in his autobiography that nobody knew more about the Ripper case than he did. Smith, it will be remembered, had several times clashed with Warren on the latter's handling of the case. The fact that Smith does not mention this incident is surely significant.

Far more damaging to Cream's claims, however, is that from November 1881 to July 1891 he was serving a life sentence for murder in the Illinois State Penitentiary at Joliet in America.*

However, there is a further theory that he had a double, and that they provided alibis for each other. Early in Cream's career he was defended on a charge of bigamy by Sir Edward Marshall Hall who advised him to plead guilty. Cream refused to do so and protested that he had been in prison in Australia at the time of the offences. His description was sent to the prison in Sydney, where he claimed to have been, and the prison confirmed that a man of that description had been in prison at the times in question. Cream was released but was recognised again by Marshall Hall when he was tried on the charges of murder many years later. Marshall Hall's theory, according to his biographer Edward Marjoribanks in *The Life of Sir Edward Marshall Hall,* was that 'Neill Cream had a double in the underworld and they went by the same name and used each other's terms of imprisonment as alibis for each other.'

This has led to the suggestion that while Cream was serving his life sentence in America, his double was committing the Whitechapel murders. As the double had given Cream an alibi for the bigamy charge, Cream subsequently tried to repay the debt by shouting those last words from the scaffold.

7. Clarence, Stephen and Gull

In 1970 Dr Thomas Stowell caused something of a public sensation when he published, in *The Criminologist,* his 'A Solution' to the Jack the Ripper mystery. His source material was apparently the private papers of Sir William Gull who had been Physician Extraordinary to Queen Victoria. Throughout his article Stowell referred to the suspect only as 'S'. However, he dropped enough clues to show that he was pointing a finger at H.R.H. Prince Albert Victor ('Eddy'), Duke of Clarence, the eldest son of the future King Edward VII. When asked to confirm or deny this interpretation, Stowell would do neither, apparently on the grounds that he did not want to embarrass the present Royal Family. Moreover, Stowell died within a few days of publishing his theory, and his notes were burned, unread by his distressed and mourning family.

Fortunately it was possible to verify from other sources that Stowell had indeed been referring to Clarence, as was generally supposed. He had discussed his theory at various times with other people, among them Colin Wilson who had met him in 1960 when he

* For a new theory about Dr Neill Cream, see p. 229.

was writing a series of articles for the London *Evening Standard* called 'My Search for Jack the Ripper'. This research was to be the raw material for his masterly novel, *Ritual in the Dark*. Stowell invited Wilson to lunch and in the course of their conversation it became clear that he thought Wilson had reached the same conclusions as himself about the Ripper's identity. In fact, the 'clues' in Wilson's articles to which he attached so much significance were quotes from the newspapers of the time, which Stowell might easily have found out for himself. This illustration of the casualness of Stowell's research goes some way to explaining the not infrequent errors which he makes—a casualness that might be attributed to his age, however, for Stowell was already in his seventies. Wilson found him a friendly and likeable man and for a long time was under the impression that Stowell was a surgeon, which is how he had introduced himself, although Wilson wondered from the way that his hands were shaking as he cut his steak just how much longer he would be able to continue operating.

Stowell's greatest discovery, or so he claimed, was that Clarence had not died in the great 'flu epidemic of 1892, as the history books stated, but in a private mental home near Sandringham, from 'softening of the brain' due to syphilis. If true, this information could not have come from the private papers of Sir William Gull, who died in 1890 at the age of 73, two years *before* Clarence. Presumably then it came from some other source. It is lamentable, in view of the claim's startling nature, that this source was not identified.

Stowell is often wrong on small but important points of detail. For instance, he says that 'S' was forced to resign his commission when he was 24—which Clarence never did—shortly after the raiding of a male brothel in Cleveland Street catering to aristocratic and wealthy homosexuals. Clarence is generally considered to have been one of its patrons because one of those involved was his personal equerry, who was forced to flee the country to avoid prosecution. In the publicity that inevitably followed these revelations, there was a newspaper smear which alleged that among those involved but not named was 'the highest in the land', which has always been taken as a direct reference to Clarence, but again without proof.

Whether Clarence was homosexual or not is open to doubt. As Michael Harrison says in his biography, *Clarence,* 'the destruction of Eddy's [Clarence's] correspondence, and the discreet silence maintained about his private activities, have made the task of assessing his character no easy one . . .' His homosexuality must remain 'not proven' and so too, without the benefit of Sir William Gull's papers, must Stowell's most damaging allegation that Clarence became infected with syphilis at one of the shore parties that he attended while on a visit to the West Indies. In time, this alleged syphilitic infection, so Stowell believed, sent him insane and led him to commit the Whitechapel murders.

Stowell alleged that the Royal Family definitely knew after the second murder, and possibly even after the first, that Clarence was the murderer. Within a few hours of the 'double event' on 30 September, Stowell goes on, Clarence was placed under restraint and shut away in a private mental home. Stowell's critics were quick to point out that Clarence was shooting game in Scotland on those dates, and also that from 3 to 12 November, during which period Stowell would have him escaping from the asylum and committing the Miller's Court murder, he was at Sandringham taking part in his father's birthday celebrations. Clearly if he was the madman that Stowell says he was, and that if he was locked up once more after Miller's Court, it becomes impossible to explain why or how, immediately after these celebrations, Clarence should have been sent abroad as his father's personal representative to Denmark.

Stowell stressed the similarity in appearance between 'Collar and Cuffs', as Clarence was called, and some of the eyewitness descriptions of possible suspects, particularly of those wearing deerstalker hats, which he suggests that Clarence may have worn as a kind of ritual vestment. (Should he, one wonders, have been called Jack the Hat!) Certainly there is a startling similarity in appearance between Druitt and Clarence. Indeed, the resemblance between them is so overwhelming that the argument can go both ways, and is just as favourable to the Druitt theory as to Clarence. Clarence's skill in disembowelling prostitutes, Stowell continues, might have been acquired by his observing and learning the art of dressing deer (another reason for wearing a deerstalker) when he had been out hunting, which might in turn have stimulated his psychopathic rages as well as given him the necessary dexterity to perform the mutilations.

Throughout Stowell's article the characters of 'S' and Clarence wheel about, like two moons through the heaven, occasionally overlapping sufficiently at the edges to show that there might be some common linkage but breaking away almost at once to reveal the internal contradictions of much of the evidence. Stowell says, for instance, that 'S' recovered sufficiently to go on a five-month cruise on which he was accompanied for part of the time by his parents. Clarence did, in fact, go as far as Port Said with the Prince and Princess of Wales when he made a journey to India in 1889. In the following year he was formally installed as the Duke of Clarence and Avondale, yet, according to Stowell, Sir William Gull, who was treating him, told his father while he was away that his son was dying of syphilis of the brain. Now paresis (softening of the brain) is usually reckoned to appear fifteen to twenty years from the time of infection, symptoms being manifest for two to three years before death. Obviously there can be no absolute time scale for such a disease; some venereologists put the earliest time for the onset of paresis at ten years after infection but the general rule is fifteen. Clarence was a victim of the great 'flu epidemic that swept through Europe in 1892 and he died of pneumonia on 14 January 1892, aged 28. If he had caught the pox, in the West Indies in 1879, and died as a result of it in 1892—and there is no evidence to show that he did—then Stowell's theory is possible—just!

Clearly the evidence is thin indeed for supposing that Clarence was Jack the Ripper, and yet he plays an equally prominent role in at least two other theories. Of these the more important was that aired in Michael Harrison's biography of Clarence, which examined the question of whether or not he was Jack the Ripper. Harrison concluded that he was not, but was convinced that the Ripper was somebody close enough to Clarence to have been confused with him. Harrison's researches convinced him that Stowell's 'S' was Clarence's tutor at Cambridge, James Kenneth Stephen, with whom he believes Clarence had a homosexual relationship, not necessarily a physical one, and that the murders were committed by Stephen out of a twisted desire for revenge because of the gradual cessation of this relationship.

Stephen's father was Sir James Fitzjames Stephen, the judge who is remembered nowadays for his mishandling of the Maybrick trial in 1889. It was so gross that he had to be given police protection from an outraged public. He was forced to retire from the Bench in 1891 because of the brain disease which had been gradually creeping up on him. Within a year of his retirement his son died in an asylum for the insane. Cause of death, so the medical certificate stated, was a mania lasting two and a half months, the persistent refusal of food for twenty days and exhaustion.

According to one of his contemporaries Stephen had 'added to his father's powers and force of intellect a cultivated taste in the delicacies of scholarship. He was no mere bookworm, but a man with a natural bent towards dainty and exquisite language in prose and verse'. (After which it comes as no surprise to learn that his cousins were Vanessa Bell and Virginia Woolf.) In 1883 he was chosen to be Clarence's tutor at Cambridge, where the Duke was sent for two years. University was regarded more as some kind of finishing school than as a place to improve his mind, which a former tutor had once described as 'abnormally dormant'. According to Harrison there was a sexual scandal of some kind between tutor and pupil, but there seems to be little evidence of such a scandal. The accusation seems chiefly to be based on Harrison's interpretation of the old rugby song 'They Called the Bastard Stephen' which he thinks refers to Stephen and Clarence!

At the end of his two years at Cambridge, on 17 June 1885, Clarence was gazetted to the 10th Hussars, and the relationship with Stephen, whatever it was, gradually petered out.

Two years later Stephen had a serious accident that caused serious brain damage. According to Quentin Bell, the nature of the accident was not definitely known. Family tradition has it 'that he was struck by some projection from a moving train.' Harrison, however, claims that while Stephen was out riding near Felixstowe his horse shied and backed him into the moving vane of a windmill. After treatment he made what seemed to be a perfect recovery. Only much later was it realised that the brain had been permanently damaged and that Stephen was slowly going mad.

Quentin Bell says in his biography of Virginia Woolf: 'One day he rushed upstairs to the nursery at 22 Hyde Park Gate, drew the blade from a sword stick and plunged it into the bread. On another occasion he carried Virginia [Woolf] and her mother off to his room in De Vere Gardens; Virginia was to pose for him. He had decided that he was a painter—a painter of genius. He was in a state of high euphoria and painted away like a man possessed, as indeed he was. He would drive up in a hansom cab to Hyde Park Gate—a hansom in which he had been driving about all day in a state of insane excitement. On another occasion he appeared at breakfast and announced, as though it were an amusing incident, that the doctors had told him that he would either die or go completely mad.'

Harrison says that it was after this tragic accident that Stephen became Sir William Gull's patient. This was apparently after Gull had suffered his first stroke in 1887. At the time of his accident,

Stephen had been a fellow of his college and a barrister, looking ahead to an excellent career. Now, like Clarence, he lacked concentration, vacillating between one interest and another, but with bouts of lucidity in between. He told his father that he intended to be a professional man of letters, and published a weekly journal called *The Reflector* which only ran for a matter of weeks before folding for lack of support. His father had to settle its debts. Possibly with a view to curbing some of his son's excesses, his father appointed him to a Clerkship of Assizes on the South Wales circuit, one of his reasons being that this would give him some practical experience of life at the bar. In fact, Stephen's illness and other absences effectively prevented his taking up his duties and in 1890 he resigned. In 1891, still under treatment, he published a pamphlet defending the compulsory study of Greek at the universities, and brought out two slim volumes of poetry, *Lapsus Calami* and *Quo Musa Tendis*. As Harrison points out in his analysis of these poems, Stephen shows both his parvenu snobbery as well as his pathological hatred of women, one of whom he suggests in a poem should be 'done away with, killed, or ploughed'.

Later the same year he was committed to a mental asylum where he stayed until the following year, 1892, when he died on 3 February.

What evidence then is there for Harrison's theory that Stephen was the Ripper? His explanations are elaborate, ingenious and often amusing; but they cannot be taken too seriously. Harrison argues that the inevitable termination of the homosexual relationship which might have existed between the two men aggravated Stephen's jealousy and made him look for ways of revenging himself on Clarence. But why, one asks, should the brutal murder of five unknown East End prostitutes upset the heir to the throne? Harrison argues that Clarence may have been pressured by the Royal Family to curtail his friendship with Stephen. If so, then Stephen may have been offering up some kind of blood sacrifice. 'There is the fact that the first (Smith) was "offered up" on the Feast of the Great Mother, a savage deity whose temples were served by castrated priests who, after their ritual castration, dressed as women. There is also the fact that the tenth and last "offering" (Coles) was made on the 13 February, the Ides of February, the Roman Feast of Terminalia in honour of Terminus, patron of limits, boundaries, treaties, and *endings*. It was customary, though forbidden by King Numa Pompilius, who had established the feast, to *offer blood sacrifices*—usually a young lamb or pig. Unless it is the wildest coincidence, the "sacrifice" that the classical scholar, Stephen, offered to Terminus on the morning of the Ides of February, 1891, bore a name which made her markedly suitable as a victim—Coles: Latin *coleus,* from Greek κολεός, "a sheath", which in latin is "vagina". It was in this same year that J. K. Stephen published his very able pamphlet, *Living Languages,* in defence of the compulsory study of Greek at the universities.'

Another of Harrison's arguments is that one of Stephen's poems, called 'Air; Kaphoozelum', suggests that when Stephen wrote it he was thinking of the ribald old verses which were as familiar then as they are today to anyone who takes part in a pub crawl or plays any sport, and whose chorus runs:

> Hi ho, Kaphoozelum,
> Kaphoozelum, Kaphoozelum,
> Hi ho, Kaphoozelum,
> The Harlot of Jerusalem.

The villain of this song killed ten harlots, and Harrison suggests that Stephen did the same, his other five victims being Emma Smith (who said that she was stabbed by five men!), Alice Mackenzie, Frances Coles, Mellett or Davis (murdered 28/29 December 1888) and Farmer. In order to get the arithmetic right, Stride and Eddowes are perversely counted as one victim! Amelia Farmer is also counted as one when, in fact, she was not murdered at all! According to *The Times* report of 22 November:

> Considerable excitement was caused throughout the East End yesterday morning by a report that another woman had been brutally murdered and mutilated in a common lodging-house in George Street, Spitalfields, and in consequence of the reticence of the police authorities all sorts of rumours prevailed. Although it was soon ascertained that there had been no murder, it was said that an attempt had been made to murder a woman of the class to which the other unfortunate creatures belonged by cutting her throat, and the excitement in the neighbourhood for some time was intense.
>
> The victim of this last occurrence fortunately is but slightly injured and was at once able to furnish the detectives with a full description of her assailant. Her name is Annie Farmer and she is a woman of about forty years of age who lately resided with her husband but on account of her dissolute habits was separated from him. On Monday night the woman had no money and, being un-

able to obtain any, walked the streets until about half-past seven yesterday morning. At that time she got into conversation in Commercial Street with a man whom she describes as about thirty-six years old, about five feet six inches in height, with a dark moustache, and wearing a shabby black diagonal suit and hard felt hat. He treated her to several drinks until she became partially intoxicated. At his suggestion they went to the common lodging-house, 19 George Street, and paid the deputy eight pence for a bed. That was about eight o'clock and nothing was heard to cause alarm or suspicion until half-past nine, when screams were heard proceeding from the room occupied by the man and Farmer. Some men who were in the kitchen of the house at the time rushed upstairs and met the woman coming down. She was partially undressed and was bleeding from a wound in the throat. She was asked what the matter was and simply said, 'He's done it,' at the same time pointing to the door leading into the street. The men rushed outside but saw no one except a man in charge of a horse and cart.

The sequel was reported next day.

The man who committed the assault on Annie Farmer on Wednesday morning has not yet been captured. It is now believed that the wound to Farmer's throat was not made with a sharp instrument; also that the quarrel arose between the pair respecting money, as when the woman was at the police station some coins were found concealed in her mouth. The authorities appear to be satisfied that the man has no connection with the recent murders.

Clearly the woman had faked the attack to divert attention from the robbery. And if—as I suspect—this woman was the same Amelia Farmer who had been Annie Chapman's friend and was one of the last people to see her alive (see p. 30), an explanation is soon forthcoming. As she had been accepted as a police witness at the coroner's inquest, she probably thought she stood a better chance of getting away with this piece of petty thievery than she otherwise would have done. When she was caught she tried to bluff it out and pretend that she had been attacked. The fact that the police took her to the station and not to hospital suggests that they knew quite clearly what she was up to. They must have done, to have caught her with the coins in her mouth!

But the weightiest argument against such elaborate conjecturing is that nowhere does Harrison make a point-by-point comparison of

Stephen and Stowell's 'S' to see if they were the same person. He had done this with Clarence. Had he done it in Stephen's case he would have seen at once that they could not be one and the same man. Stephen never went on a world cruise, was never commissioned in the army, for example.

Yet Harrison insists that there is a scarcity of factual evidence, and that the case against Stephen must therefore be argued from internal evidence.

He makes two final points. First, that there is some similarity between Stephen's handwriting and that in the two Ripper letters beginning 'From Hell' and 'Old Boss', which he reproduces. He finds a striking similarity, indeed, between the forming of the letter 'K' in the letters and the initial 'K' of Stephen's christian name in signature. The other point he makes is that there is stylistic similarity between Stephen's poetry and the verse of some of the anonymous Ripper letters. The main objection to these points is that very little reliance can be placed on a handwriting comparison. The handwriting of the German murderer Peter Kürten, who was known as the Düsseldorf Ripper because of the way that he imitated his notorious predecessor, changed completely after each murder, so much so, indeed, that he used to point out to his wife the anonymous letters that he wrote to the police, and which were reproduced in the newspapers, so confident was he that she would never recognise them—nor did she, which would seem to deny Harrison's theory the support of even this flimsy strut.

The other name which frequently crops up in these theories is that of Sir William Gull, who first came to public notice in 1871 when he successfully treated the Prince of Wales for typhoid fever. Queen Victoria was so grateful for his 'great services' to the Crown that she rewarded him the following year by creating him Baronet and Physician Extraordinary to the Queen, in addition to his existing title of Physician in Ordinary to the Prince of Wales and to the Royal Family generally.

Stowell says that Gull was seen more than once in Whitechapel on the night of a murder and suggests that he may have been there for the express purpose of certifying the murderer insane. Who saw him there, one asks? Stowell was quoting from Gull's own papers, so are we to assume that the doctor was watching himself? And if 'S' was insane and Gull was treating him, why should the latter wait in Whitechapel to catch him when he could have done so much more easily and with far less fuss in his own consulting rooms? One can hardly believe that it was necessary to catch 'S' in the act of murder to prove his insanity.

Stowell quotes a story about the medium R. J. Lees, a spiritualist who, according to Fred Archer in his book *Ghost Detectives,* used to hold seances for Queen Victoria. Apparently Lees had three visions of the coming murders. On the first occasion he claimed to have seen the murder committed. He described the murderer as wearing a dark tweed suit and a light coloured overcoat, which he used to cover up his bloodstained shirt. Lees was apparently so shaken by this experience that he went abroad, only to bump into the murderer on his return while boarding a London omnibus at Shepherd's Bush! His wife who was with him and who seems to have had a refreshing degree of scepticism only laughed at him when he pointed out the man as Jack the Ripper, as did also a policeman whom Lees tried to persuade to arrest the man. While they were arguing the man jumped into a cab and drove away.

The police apparently took Lees' story a little more seriously when he told them—without knowing that they had received a letter threatening to clip the next victim's ears off—he had seen in another vision that the ears were mutilated. This apparently convinced them that his powers were genuine, and they took him seriously when he told them of a third vision, this time of Kelly's death. They allegedly used him as a human bloodhound after the body had been found, in an attempt to trace the murderer's flight from Miller's Court. He took them to a fashionable house in the West End belonging to a highly reputable physician. Under questioning, the doctor's wife told them that her husband had 'sudden manias for inflicting pain'. On one occasion she had caught him torturing a cat, and on another brutally beating their son. She had noticed that her husband's absences from home coincided with the murders.

The doctor, when he was questioned, admitted to sudden losses of memory. He had found bloodstains on his shirt and on another occasion scratches on his face which he could not account for. When his wardrobe was searched the tweed suit and light overcoat which Lees had seen in his first vision were found among his clothes. The doctor wanted to kill himself when he realised what he had done. Instead, a specially formed commission on lunacy found him to be insane and he was committed to an asylum where he died many years later.

There are several variants of this story but the general outline is the same in each. Stowell went on to speculate as to whether the house that Lees had gone to was Gull's house at 74 Brook Street. His own variant of this story had been told to him by Gull's daughter who said that her mother had been subjected at the time of the murders to a cross-examination by a medium and asked a lot of impertinent questions. Sir William Gull who came downstairs while she was being questioned admitted that he had had losses of memory since a slight stroke in 1887 and on one occasion had discovered blood on his shirt. Stowell speculated that this might have all have been a deliberate attempt on Gull's part to divert suspicion from Clarence, although one would have thought that this was carrying self-sacrifice a little too far, especially when there was every chance of the murders continuing.

Medically the slight stroke that Gull had in 1887 was the first attack of severe paralysis. Although he recovered from it, its effects were serious enough to prohibit him from further medical practice. Taken with the fact that he was seventy years old at this time, this is surely enough to cast doubts on the story of his roaming about Whitechapel trying to catch his patient. There is enough internal evidence in the story to show that the doctor referred to could not possibly have been Gull. According to Lees, the wife complained that she had caught her husband brutally beating their small son; Gull's son was by this time a barrister, and so could hardly have been the child referred to. Finally, Gull did not die in a lunatic asylum. He died at home on 29 January 1890, after a third stroke which left him speechless.

However, in spite of these doubts, Gull played an even more sinister role in a story told by Joseph Sickert, son of the painter Walter Sickert, in a BBC television series, *Jack the Ripper,* that was investigated by television's fictional detectives Charlie Barlow and John Watt. Sickert told viewers that the murders had been committed by Gull with the help of a coachman named John Netley. The programme's researchers discovered that Netley did exist and was twenty-eight years old at the time of the murders in 1888; he was accidentally kicked to death by a horse when he fell from a van that he was driving in 1903. Sickert claimed that the Duke of Clarence had been a regular visitor to the artist's colony in the Cleveland Street area, where his grandfather had lived, and had fallen in love with a girl named Ann Elizabeth Crook who worked in a tobacconist's shop nearby. She became first his mistress and then his wife, in 1888. Their affair had to be kept secret, since the girl was a Catholic—public knowledge of such a marriage might have endangered the throne.

This marriage broke up, apparently after the Cleveland Street raid, and Ann Elizabeth was committed to Guy's Hospital for four months and subsequently to Fulham Hospital, where she died in 1921.

There is just a chance that, at this point, Gull might have been involved in such a scheme. In the early part of his career at Guy's Hospital, with which he retained close links until his death, he had been the superintendent of a small lunatic asylum for twenty women. If he did have a hand in the forcible detention of Ann Elizabeth then this would explain why she was committed for those first four months to that particular hospital. But how, one asks, does this explain the murders? Sickert said that one of the witnesses to the marriage was a servant girl, Mary Kelly, and that she was killed as part of a cover-up plan by high-ranking government officials. Frankly, this is hard to swallow. Surely if officialdom could commit Clarence's wife to an asylum for thirty-three years then it could have avoided murder by doing the same with a servant girl.

Sickert went on to say that his mother was Ann Margaret, the daughter of this secret marriage. She was born in 1885 and so must have been conceived in 1884 when Clarence was at Cambridge—just about the time that Harrison says Clarence was having a homosexual relation of sorts with Stephen. In 1892 Ann Margaret is alleged to have been run down by the coachman John Netley. But for whom is he then supposed to have been working? Gull had been dead for two years. At any rate, she survived this murderous attack and was brought up by Walter Sickert, who later married her.

What value can then be placed on Sickert's claim that he once lived in the same lodgings as Jack the Ripper (see p. 122)? If he knew the truth about Clarence's marriage and his affair with Ann Elizabeth—which must have lasted from 1884, when Ann Margaret was conceived, to 1889, the time of the Cleveland Street scandal—why did he draw this red herring over the trail and why, if he knew the truth, was he himself never silenced?

But there is an even greater flaw in this theory. Why should any agent of the Crown or State have resorted to murder to remove this 'threat' to the throne when the Royal Marriages Act was still on the statute book? Under this Act, any such marriage as that between Clarence and Ann Elizabeth could have been set aside as illegal, since (1) Clarence was under 25 years old at the time of the marriage; and (2) he had married without the Queen's consent. The Act had, in fact, been specifically designed by George III to prevent his sons from entering into marriages of which he disapproved; and it had also been used to nullify the marriage of Augustus, Duke of Sussex, even though a second child had been born to the marriage in lawful wedlock! In addition, the Act of Settlement of 1700, still in force, expressly excludes any person who shall marry a Roman Catholic from 'inheriting the Crown.'

Clearly this story is going to win acceptance only if the marriage certificate, with Kelly's name as witness, can be produced. Until it is, it must remain, like the other theories, just an interesting story.

8. Deeming

Frederick Bailey Deeming killed his first wife and four children in 1891. Before emigrating to Australia with wife number two he had disposed of their bodies by burying them under the kitchen floor of their home at Dinham Villa, Rainhill, near Liverpool. His second wife was murdered within a month of their landing in Australia. She was buried under the bedroom floor of a house near Melbourne. Deeming's prospective third wife was already on her way to meet him when the body of wife number two was discovered. Deeming was arrested, tried, and executed on 23 May 1892. In prison he claimed to be Jack the Ripper but this was just boasting, since he had been in prison at the time of the Whitechapel murders. After his execution a plaster death mask was forwarded to New Scotland Yard, apparently because of the persistence of these rumours, and for many years it was pointed out to visitors as the death mask of Jack the Ripper; it is now in the famous Black Museum. This has helped to perpetuate the myth, which was also reinforced by the following piece of doggerel verse:

> On the twenty-first of May,
> Frederick Deeming passed away;
> On the scaffold he did say—
> 'Ta-ra-da-boom-di-ay!'
> 'Ta-ra-da-boom-di-ay!'
> This is a happy day,
> An East End holiday,
> The Ripper's gone away.

9. The Slaughterman

In *Jack the Ripper in Fact and Fiction*, Robin Odell suggests that the killer was a Jewish shochet, or ritual slaughterman, who was never caught or identified. In doing so, he makes the perfectly valid point

that a current preoccupation with identifying Jack the Ripper has
sometimes led to exaggerated accounts of the murders and to a lack
of interest in the murderer's probable motives and character.

In Whitechapel in 1888 there was a Jewish abattoir in Aldgate
High Street where the slaughtering of animals regularly took place
and where there must have been many shochets to cope with the demands of the expanding immigrant population. Possibly the shochet
in question may have been a refugee from Eastern Europe who fled
to America in the great wave of persecutions following the anti-
Jewish decrees of the early 1880s. He may have stayed there for just
one or two years before moving on to Britain and finally settling in
London. This temporary residence in America might help to explain
some of the obvious Americanisms in some of the Ripper letters,
such as 'Boss'. Such expertise in slaughtering would explain why the
police, in at least two of the murders, were baffled by the lack of
blood. Odell attributes this to the manner in which the victims were
handled—he compares it to the way in which the Japanese kicked
away the trunks of the people they had just beheaded—in such a way
as to prevent the murderer's clothes from becoming bloodstained.
Unfortunately he completely omits to suggest that the victims might
first have been strangled. Any blood would then seep onto the
ground and be soaked up by the victim's clothes, which, the police
reports confirm, is actually what happened.

In explaining his theory, Odell begins by quoting Dr G. Sequiera,
the police surgeon who examined Eddowes, that the killer was no
stranger to the knife. Shochets, in fact, had considerable expertise
with the knife—as they showed when performing the shechita, or
ritual slaughtering, which was 'designed to drain the meat of blood
which was sacred to God.' In the abattoir the animal was prepared
for slaughter by hobbling its legs with ropes and 'casting' its throat
for the knife, which was long-bladed and carefully honed to give a
razor-sharp edge. To comply with Talmudic law it had to be free of
any nicks or blemishes, since to kill with an imperfect weapon would
invalidate the slaughtering and the meat would be forbidden to Jews.
The blade was tested by being drawn backwards and forwards across
the index finger of the other hand and when the shochet was satisfied
that the blade complied with the religious law he would give the Ben-
ediction and draw 'the razor-sharp knife across the prescribed area
of the animal's throat. A quick forward and backward stroke, and
the work was done: the throat was cut through to the bone. Death
was immediate, and as the shochet stepped back the animal's life-

blood gushed to the ground from the severed arteries and veins.'

Having done this the shochet had to make a post-mortem examination, or bedikah, of the animal. First he had to make sure that the throat had been cut correctly and that the windpipe and gullet had both been severed. Next, he had to make an incision in the chest and examine the heart and lungs for injury or disease. A third incision was then made in the abdomen so that the stomach, intestines, kidneys and internal organs could be similarly examined. If there was any sign of disease or injury the meat was trefah, or forbidden; if not, the meat was marked kosher, or 'fit'.

Some anatomical knowledge and a degree of skill were clearly necessary to remove these and other parts of the body, as prescribed by Jewish law, and, as Odell remarks, 'if there were any doubts about equating the elementary anatomical knowledge displayed by Jack the Ripper with the skill of a slaughterman, surely these must now be dispelled.' Clearly, the shochet's expertise would account for the skilful butchering of his victims.

This may be so, but such expertise was not confined to a shochet. Judging by the following letter, written by a contemporary of the Ripper's to the harassed police, it would have been possessed by any good professional butcher. The letter is interesting and worth quoting at length. Although it shows how a shochet may have worked —assuming for the moment that Odell's theory is correct—at the same time it disposes of Odell's argument that an ordinary butcher or slaughterman would not have had the literacy to write the one or two genuine Ripper letters.

The writer was R. Hull, of 4 Bloomfield Road, Bow. The letter is dated 8 October, 1888:

From the age of 14 years till past 30, I was a butcher so that I can speak with some authority. Doctors, I think, but little know how terribly dextrous a good slaughterman is with his knife. There has been nothing done yet to any of these poor women that an expert butcher could not do almost in the dark. It is not known perhaps to the medical fraternity that a slaughterman is a dexter handed man. Consequently Doctors are misled. And as to the time taken by the murderer to do the most difficult deed done as yet, I think it would be reduced to about one third of the time stated by them if done by a practical man, which according to their own evidence it must be or some one connected with their own craft. I cannot think that inexperienced men could do it. I have never seen the inside of a human being, but, I presume there is little difference between such and a sheep or pig. I could when in the trade, kill and dress 4 or 5 sheep in one hour. Then as to the blood, do not be misled, if done by a butcher he will not have any or very little upon his person. I have many a time gone into the slaughterhouse and killed several sheep or lambs and scarcely soiled my clothes, that is when the weather has been fine and the skins have been dry. It likewise occurs to me, that if done by a butcher he would know his work too well to attempt to cut the throat of his victim whilst standing up, but when they have laid down for an immoral purpose, then with one hand over the mouth and the thumb under the chin, then with, what is known in the trade as a shaking (striking) knife, which is a terrible weapon in the hands of a strong butcher, in the twinkling of an eye he has cut the throat, then turning the head on one side, like he would a sheep, the body would bleed out whilst he did the rest of his work, from which the blood would flow. The only fear of making a mess would be the breaking [of] a gut or intestine and that would not be done by one knowing his business. The slaughterman's knives consist of a set of three; the Sticking knife which is about 6 or 8 inches long in the blade, with a thick back to keep it from bending whilst severing the Pith or Spinal cord. The next is a Dressing knife, a little shorter and wider than the Siding knife, which is longer one than either of the others, curved at the end so that it shall not go through the hides. This knife is only used just for one particular work in dressing breasts. They all have wooden handles rivetted through the tang of the blade.

A shochet was a minor cleric, a person of high respectability and some education, and possessing a deep religious faith. Although he would be of some standing in the community it is unlikely that his income would have been much greater than that of the lower-class elements among whom he lived and worked. In appearance, his dark clothes and black frock coat would have given him the slightly shabby and faded respectability that matches some of the descriptions of Ripper suspects. Because he was such a familiar figure, and a person to be trusted, this might explain why the victims were willing to trust themselves to go with him and were temporarily lulled into a sense of false security. Odell points out that a well-dressed stranger might have worked his charm on one or two occasions; but that he should continue to do so goes against all common sense. Yet this is precisely what did happen, in fact, many years later when the Boston Strangler was terrorising that city. It went against all the rules that he should have been able to persuade these women to open their doors to him, a perfect stranger, especially when their doors had been reinforced with locks and chains for the very purpose of keeping him out! How much easier it must have been in London's East End for the Ripper to have persuaded women to go with him when they were starving, cold and ill, desperately in need of the few pence that he would give them for some food and perhaps even shelter.

Odell's theory is that the Ripper was possibly a psychopath suffering from some sort of religious mania: 'A ritual slaughterman steeped in Old Testament law might have felt some religious justification for killing prostitutes.' He draws a colourful picture of this man's background and mental state:

> Lurking behind the respected character of the ritual slaughterman was the mind of a sexual sadist tormented with hideous desires. The tiger's heart was filled with cunning, premeditation, and fiendish delight in the perverted, and these were the tools of his ambition. His distorted mind drove him to seek gratification for blood-lust in a manner that mirrored his professional ability. Jack the Ripper did not commit those terrible crimes because he was a slaughterman. He killed because he was a psychopath, but inevitably his perversions drew strength from his training and skill as a slaughterman.
>
> Remorse was an alien feeling to the Ripper, for his mind was filled with an overpowering appetite that only death could end. In his twisted way he could claim, too, a sense of religious justification in clearing the East End streets of harlots. In such ways do wretched prostitutes become the butt of the sexual psychopath's inadequacy. Incapable of normal sexual relations, and inferior to the task of seduction, these perverts often seek the easy acceptance of prostitutes, and then in a cruel travesty of morals claim justification for killing them.

Unfortunately it is impossible to agree with his final assertion that of all the potential murderers in London in 1888 the hypothetical shochet alone possessed all the requirements of motive, method, and opportunity to murder prostitutes in the East End. The methods have already been discussed, and as we have seen, an ordinary butcher had precisely the same expertise as the shochet and could wield a knife with equal dexterity. Motive and opportunity are even more

easily disposed of: a similar case could equally easily be made against
any unknown living in the East End at that time, and would be just
as difficult to disprove. If the Ripper did strangle his victims—and
the evidence suggests that he did—then Odell's theory falls to the
ground completely. It is only by agreeing with Odell's argument totally and uncritically that we can accept it. Unfortunately the facts
are too few to do this.

In explanation of the Ripper's ceasing his activity, after Miller's
Court, Odell suggests that he was discovered by his own people who
may have dealt with him according to their own brand of justice in
preference to having him before the English courts. This would have
effectively countered any of the outbreaks of anti-Semitism that Sir
Charles Warren had feared might lead to rioting in the East End
and which had prompted him to rub out the message on the wall.
According to Sir Robert Anderson in his memoirs, *The Lighter Side
of My Official Life,* the Ripper was a Polish Jew and it was also
'. . . a remarkable fact that people of that class in the East End
will not give up one of their number to Gentile Justice.'

Even more tantalisingly, he goes on to say that he is 'almost
tempted to disclose the identity of the murderer. . . . But no public
benefit would result from such a course, and the traditions of my
old department would suffer. I will merely add that the one person
who ever had a good view of the murderer unhesitatingly identified
the suspect the instant he was confronted with him; but he refused
to give evidence against him. In saying that he was a Polish Jew I
am merely stating a definitely ascertained fact.'

From this, one would assume that the killer's identity had been
discovered after the carnage in Miller's Court. Fortunately Sir Robert
has prefaced his remarks in such a way that it is clear that he is
saying that the killer's identity had been unmasked after the *second*
killing, the victim of which was Annie Chapman. He says, 'During
my absence abroad the Police had made a house-to-house search for
him, investigating the case of every man in the district whose circumstances were such that he could go and come and get rid of his bloodstains in secret. And the conclusion we came to was that he and his
people were certain low-class Polish Jews. . . .' As Anderson returned immediately from Paris when the Home Secretary telegraphed
him to come home, the morning after the double event, it is clear
that these searches were carried out during the investigations into the
first two murders.

From these facts, it seems abundantly clear that Anderson was accusing John Pizer (Leather Apron) of being the Ripper. As he had already been accused and acquitted at the time, this seems a remarkable assertion to make and one which Anderson, probably through ignorance or fear of libel, preferred to cloak under the guise of official secrecy and claim that 'no public benefit would result from such a course, and the traditions of my old department would suffer'.

Is he really saying that the police knew the identity of the murderer and let him commit three more murders without bringing him to justice?

In case there are any doubts as to who Anderson was referring to, let the reader check back over the period of the first four murders and see who else it could be but Leather Apron. Crowds were waiting outside the police stations for the latest news of the Ripper; they were flocking to the scenes, they were greeting trains bringing back suspects from other parts of the country, and the newspapers were publishing every piece of gossip as fact. The only Polish Jew to be arrested, and to fit the facts, was John Pizer. More important still, and this identifies him absolutely as Anderson's 'Polish Jew', *The Times* on 12 September gave details of the identity parade and the confrontation of the 'murderer' with this witness who positively identified him and who, according to Anderson, subsequently refused to give evidence against him.

According to this report, this witness was half-Spanish, half-Bulgarian, giving the name of Emanuel Delbast Violenia. He told the police that he, his wife and two children had tramped to London from Manchester and found lodgings in Hanbury Street preparatory to emigrating to Australia. Early on Saturday morning he was walking along Hanbury Street when he heard a man and a woman quarrelling and the man distinctly threaten to kill her by sticking her with a knife. The woman he was referring to was evidently Annie Chapman. After her body had been discovered later that same day he had communicated these facts to the police.

At 1 p.m. on 11 September he was taken to Leman Street Police Station to try to identify the man she had been quarrelling with. Pizer was brought up from the cells—he is described as a short man with black whiskers and a clean shaven chin—and took his place in a line up of half a dozen men, who were predominantly Jews. Violenia unhesitatingly identified him as the man that he had heard threatening the woman with murder. After Pizer had been taken back to the cells, Violenia was taken to the mortuary to see if he could identify the woman he had seen as Annie Chapman. Apparently he could not.

So far the facts agree with Anderson's story. He then alleges that this witness refused to give evidence against Pizer. So he did, but not for the reasons that Anderson is suggesting. According to *The Times*, 'Subsequently [in fact the same afternoon], cross-examination so discredited Violenia's evidence that it was wholly distrusted by the police, and Pizer was set at liberty.'

In effect, all the facts suggest that Anderson was relating a story got at third hand. As such, it can be ignored.

Perhaps the last word on this particular theory should be left to the anonymous scribbler who wrote the following verse:

> I'm not a butcher,
> I'm not a Yid,
> Nor yet a foreign skipper,
> But I'm your own light-hearted friend,
> Yours truly Jack the Ripper.

10. Jill the Ripper

William Stewart set himself a more modest objective. He didn't try to prove the Ripper's identity but only the *class* of person that he might have been. He began by asking four questions. (1) What sort of person was it that could move about at night without arousing the suspicions of his own household or of other people that he might have met; (2) who could walk through the streets in blood stained clothing without arousing too much comment; (3) who would have had the elementary knowledge and skill to have committed the mutilations; and (4) who could have been found by the body and yet given a satisfactory alibi for being there.

At first glance, the solution would seem to be a policeman. The only objection to this might be a low score under (3) but even this could be overcome if it is remembered that most policemen were ex-army men with enough overseas experience of war to have given them a working knowledge of slaughtering, both of animals and men, and the treating of wounds. However, Stewart's choice was for a woman who was or had been a midwife. Such a woman might also have been an abortionist. Stewart postulates that she might have been betrayed by a married woman whom she had tried to help, and sent to prison; as a result, this was her way of revenging herself on her own sex.

Stewart argued that such a woman would have had the theoretical knowledge for committing the mutilations. She could have moved about the streets at night without arousing suspicion, and she would have had the confidence of her victims. Her bloodstained clothing could have been explained away by a difficult birth or from her examination of one of the victims to see if she was alive. Alternatively, the clothes of the period would have enabled her to turn her skirts and cloak inside out to conceal the bloodstains.

Stewart makes a great deal of the point about bloodstained clothing, but he never seems to have considered the possibility of strangulation. He always assumes that the murderer must have walked away bespattered with blood. The nearest he comes to recognising that something such as this could have happened is when he says that the murderer 'would have been easily able to almost instantly produce unconsciousness, particularly in persons given to drink, by a method frequently used on patients in those days by midwives who practised among the extremely poor.' This remark is never explained, but presumably he is suggesting that midwives partly throttled their patients by exerting half-pressure on the pressure points.

Stewart's main premise that the Ripper was a woman stems from the fact that Kelly was three months pregnant and that, being a young woman in danger of being evicted, she wanted to terminate her pregnancy. He suggests that the midwife/abortionist was called in to abort the foetus and once inside Miller's Court seized her opportunity and killed Kelly as she was lying helplessly on the bed. Afterwards she burned her bloodsoaked clothing in the grate and escaped wearing Kelly's clothing. The chief objections to this line of argument are that Kelly's clothes were left behind and that the only clothing destroyed, judging from the ashes in the grate, were the shirts, petticoat and bonnet belonging to Mrs Harvey (whom Stewart does not mention). Certainly if bloodstained clothing had been burned in the grate it would not have given off enough heat to melt the spout of the kettle, as actually happened. Stewart's theory is an attractive one if only because it would explain the sighting of Kelly—in fact, the midwife in disguise—at 8 a.m. the next morning, a few hours after Kelly's death.

Stewart's secondary points are to underline his main contention that the murderer was a woman. He says that Nichols' bonnet must have been given to her as she would not buy a hat and leave herself without the money for the bed. He ignores the fact that nowhere is there any evidence to suggest that Nichols bought the hat herself. Her exact words were, 'I'll soon get my doss money, see what a jolly bonnet I've got now.' From this Stewart deduces that the donor was not a man, since if it had been she would have boasted of the fact, but a woman. The other point that he makes is even weaker. Chapman's pockets, he says, were turned out because there was something inside them, such as a name, which could have identified the murderer. Seeing the contents scattered on the ground gave the murderess the idea of arranging them at her victim's feet and adding the rings to the neatly laid-out pile, just to create another mystery.

The chief flaw in the whole theory is that once again, with the exception of Kelly, none of the women is known to have been pregnant. In fact, in view of their age (most of them were in their forties), living hard and drinking equally hard, it would have been surprising if they were. Stride certainly was not, and it is equally doubtful that Chapman could have been, particularly after the beating, including a kick in the stomach, which had put her in the Infirmary for several days.

Stewart's theory was up-dated in a series of articles written for *The Sun* newspaper in 1972 by ex-Detective Chief Superintendent Arthur Butler of New Scotland Yard. He claimed that the murders were committed by an abortionist who had been living somewhere in the Brick Lane area and that four out of the seven victims (he includes Emma Smith and Martha Tabram) died because of bungled abortions and had not been murdered at all! In fact, the mutilations were an attempt to conceal her mistakes! Two of the other three victims were murdered because they knew too much, he claimed, and the third, Long Liz Stride, was not a Ripper victim at all.

Butler's source for this theory is unconfirmed gossip. None of his sources is given, except for a reference to nephews of people who were living in the area at the time, and it is difficult to judge, without knowing more of the facts, what sort of value judgement to put on his statements. However, he begins by saying that Emma Smith was murdered by the abortionist and her accomplice because she tried to blackmail them for more cash, as apparently she had done in the past. He complicates the story slightly by giving Emma a partner with the unlikely name of 'Fingers Freddy' who, among other things, was a street conjuror. Freddy disappears, possibly into the Thames says Butler, soon after Emma is murdered by the abortionist's accomplice. Butler has ignored Smith's own evidence that she had been attacked by four men, as well as the testimony of the witnesses who took her to hospital. Instead he paints a harrowing death-bed scene with a constable sitting by her bedside waiting for any other clues that she might give him as to the identity of her murderers. Apparently Butler was unaware of the fact that Smith was dead and in her coffin and that three days had passed before the police were told about the original assault, and then only because the inquest was to take place.

Martha Tabram was similarly murdered, according to Butler, because she knew too much about the abortionist's activities. Allegedly a friend of hers named 'Rosie Lee' went to the abortionist on the Bank Holiday Monday for her pregnancy to be terminated. Later, when Tabram called back for her, she was told that Rosie had been treated and had left. When Martha still could not find her friend after several hours of searching she went back to the abortionist and had a flaming row with the woman, the inference once again being that the abortionist had bungled her work. (Since Rosie had apparently disappeared without trace, it is surprising that the abortionist, having once found a foolproof method of disposing of unwanted bodies, did not use the same disposal method for her other 'failures'.) Martha is killed the same night to stop her from talking.

Butler goes on to say that although he has no evidence that Polly Nichols was ever pregnant he knows (but does not give his source) that she had visited an abortionist twice in the previous two years.

Apart from murdering Smith and Tabram and possibly 'Fingers Freddy', the abortionist's accomplice comes in useful for removing the bodies in a pram and dumping them in the street. Annie Chapman was apparently trundled through the streets like this, and, says Butler, this accounts for a handkerchief being tied around her neck, as a measure to stop her almost severed head from dropping off completely.

Butler objected to Stride's being included as a Ripper victim on two grounds: first, that the throat was cut from left to right, which is in the opposite manner to the other victims (though without knowing the respective positions of murderer and victim this is hardly a valid point); and second, that he would not have killed Eddowes if he had murdered Stride, because of the hue and cry that was going on in Berner Street. This assertion seems to display a complete lack of understanding of the nature of the sadistic murderer.

His final points about Kelly's death are much the same as those that were made by Stewart.

To sum up, without knowing the precise nature of Butler's sources it is impossible to know just how much weight can be given his theory. Certainly Mr Butler would put everyone in his debt if he committed his sources to paper and so ensured that his theory be not dismissed as just another story.

GASLIGHT GHOULS

One of the most original stage productions in recent years was offered by the Bubble Theatre Company when it toured the London boroughs in 1973. It was called *The Jack the Ripper Show* and was one of several plays that the actors scripted themselves and performed in two molecular-shaped tents which they pitched in the local park, or on any open space, as they moved from borough to borough.

To get the full flavour you had to go on a wet and windy night, as I did. Wooden folding chairs stood in rows around the stage, which was in the middle of the tent. The stage itself was a simple platform about two feet high. There was no scenery. As the audience came into the tent they were met by the cast who were in period costume and full make-up and singing music hall songs to the accompaniment of a jangling piano. Everyone was given a cup of wine upon entering. As I knew some of the cast I was given two (which lulled a sneaking suspicion that all was not well when they isolated me in a gangway seat on the front row).

The play is about the Sharp family of Victorian strolling players. Since there are only four of them they have obvious difficulties when playing Shakespeare: their bowdlerised productions are known as 'Sharp's Short Shakespeare Shows'. The son suggests that instead of Shakespeare they perform a 'Jack the Ripper' show. A stranger whom they spot lurking outside the tent is hired to play the Ripper. (While he was waiting for his cue, this actor was kept busy chasing off the local kids who kept peering through the canvas and racing round the tent, shrieking and whooping, like Indians round a wagon train).

The stranger is—naturally—Jack the Ripper!

For the new 'production', the play within the play, the title of the show is changed to the much more dramatic 'Sharp's Short Shocker'.

An equally dramatic change comes over the cast. The son, in particular, wears make-up, pouts, leers and grimaces with as much verve as the master of ceremonies in 'Cabaret'.

Highlight of the second half is a parade of Ripper suspects. First is the mad Russian with a waist length ginger beard concealing the Hammer and Sickle tattooed on his chest. Second is Montague Druitt who changes his identity as frequently as he changes his hat, from a deerstalker to a bowler and back again. Third is the Duke of Clarence—one of the girls in pink tights, top hat, black underwear and a cardboard moustache. Fourth—but there was no fourth.

At this point I knew why I had been put in the front row.

Before I could move, a large No. 4 was dropped on to my shoulders and I was yanked on to the stage. There were cheers and shouts as the audience was asked to show by their applause if they thought that I was Jack the Ripper. Naturally they did. All I could do was bow and accept the prize which was presented to me on a covered tray—a glass of tomato juice.

Mistakenly, I thought they had finished with me. They had not.

Just before the end of the show, Jack the Ripper ran away! As the show could not end without him, and the audience had already indicated that they thought that I was the Ripper, I was forced back on to the stage again to take his place on the gallows. After I had been 'tried' and protested my innocence—which nobody believed!—I was 'hanged'. (Not at all painful and worth being revived by the bird in black tights.)

From which you may gather that any resemblance between this and the real-life murders was purely coincidental.

The best known of all Ripper-orientated books, plays and films is Mrs Belloc Lowndes' story 'The Lodger', which originated at a dinner party when she overheard one of the guests telling another that his mother's butler and cook, who were husband and wife and took in lodgers, believed that they had let one of their rooms to Jack the Ripper! This snatch of conversation inspired her tale, which was published in *McClure's Magazine* in January 1911. She did not get one favourable review. She mournfully complained that for the American edition she hadn't been able to find 'even one sentence of tepid approval'. Gradually public opinion swung in her favour, so much so that two or three years later the reviewers were perversely complaining that each of her new books was a disappointment, and why didn't she write a new 'Lodger'!

By 1923 the sixpenny edition alone had sold more than half a million copies. It was turned into a stage play called 'Who is He?' and

then into a silent movie. The director was 26-year-old Alfred Hitchcock who helped to adapt the story. Today it is hailed as the first
true Hitchcock-style movie. The star was England's leading matinee
idol, Ivor Novello, and because of his following the storyline had to
be changed to show that he was not the murderer. Throughout the
film, commercial interests dictated that his innocence be spelled out
in big letters. (The same problem cropped up sixteen years later when
Hitchcock made 'Suspicion' with Cary Grant.) Hitchcock would have
liked Novello to have been the murderer, as in the book, but dramatically this change was probably a better arrangement as, Hitchcock
says, a cinema audience finds it easier to identify with an innocent
man who is wrongly accused than with a guilty man on the run. There
is a greater sense of danger.

When it was first shown to the distributors they hated it. They
thought it too heavy and Germanic. Bookings that had been made
on the strength of Novello's reputation were cancelled and the film
was put back on the shelves. Several weeks later they had second
thoughts about it and showed it to the trade who went into ecstasies
over it and hailed it as the most important British film to date. It
was a smash hit with critics and public alike.

Its most famous effect, and for which it is chiefly remembered, is
a shot 'through' the ceiling of the lodger pacing backwards and forwards in his room and making the chandelier in the room below move
with him. Hitchcock achieved this by shooting from below through
a 'ceiling' of inch thick plate glass. He had to do it this way because
the film was silent, whereas if he had been doing it with sound he
would have shot just the swaying chandelier.

The biggest problem which all writers and directors have had to
face is just how to portray the Ripper. Most have opted for the detective story ploy of using a character, sometimes as narrator, who is
'below suspicion'. (A good example occurs in Edgar Wallace's *The
Ringer,* in which the Scots doctor who is 'helping' the police is in
fact himself the Ringer.) In Robert Bloch's short story 'Yours Truly,
Jack the Ripper', the Walrus and the Carpenter of the tale (which
is how they are described) are Sir Guy Hollis and John Carmody,
a Chicago psychiatrist. Hollis has followed the Ripper to Chicago.
Carmody, who is the narrator, finds this incredible as the murders took
place *fifty-seven years* earlier! Hollis' incredible theory is that Jack
the Ripper is a practitioner of Black Magic and has been given eternal
youth provided he makes blood offerings at the right times. His
murders to date total eighty-seven! 'The trail is there, the pattern. Un-

solved crimes. Slashed throats of women. With the peculiar disfigura-
tions and removals. Yes, I've followed a trail of blood. From New
York westward across the continent. Then to the Pacific. From there
to Africa. During the World War of 1914–18 it was Europe. After
that, South America. And since 1930, the United States again.' His
motive for hunting him down is obscure until the last page when he
reveals that his mother was one of the 'nameless drabs' that the Ripper slew in 1888. He and his father had hunted for this pathological
monster to revenge her. His father had been stabbed to death in a
brawl but Hollis knew whose hand had struck the blow. In fact, his
dogged determination to hunt the Ripper down is such that Carmody,
in a fog-ridden alley in Chicago, pulls out a knife and bears down
on him swiftly.

'John,' Hollis screams. 'Never mind the "John",' Carmody whis-
pers, raising the knife. 'Just call me—Jack.'

Some of the American stories originated with the murder of a
prostitute in New York in 1891. She was known as 'Old Shakespeare',
so called from her habit of quoting the Bard when she was drunk.
Her mutilated body was found in a Manhattan hotel on 24 April
1891. Next day the newspapers were proclaiming in screaming headlines that Jack the Ripper had arrived in America. This, if true, was
seen as a challenge to Police Chief Inspector Byrnes who, at the time
of the Whitechapel killings, had boasted that if the Ripper came to
New York he would be arrested and in prison within thirty-six hours.
He had an Algerian Frenchman named Ameer Ben Ali arrested on
suspicion of murder. At his trial evidence was given that he had
known 'Old Shakespeare' and that he might have committed the murder by lodging opposite her room, creeping across the corridor after
her client had gone, killing her, and after robbing her, going back
the way he had come. Ali complicated matters by pretending that
he didn't speak English, although during his trial there were times
when it was obvious he did. Eventually the jury brought in a verdict
of second degree murder. On 10 July 1891 he was sentenced to life
imprisonment. Soon afterwards he was transferred to a prison for the
criminally insane. However, ten years later, new evidence came to
light which threw doubts on the prosecution's case. In the circumstances, Ali was pardoned and shipped back to his Algerian home.

His capture in the first place undoubtedly owed something to the
Americans' somewhat arrogant boast that in the same situation they
would do better than Scotland Yard. Theodore Benson capitalised
on these facts in his short story 'In the Fourth Ward'. His narrator

is Benn Higgs, an old sailor who is telling what happened when he first went to sea as a young boy. In New York he went ashore with an older seaman called Thomas Goolden, who had been a butcher's assistant until his mother died, but had then gone to sea. In his sea-chest Goolden kept pictures of his brother and a girl—the latter defaced with red chalk to look like gashes. In a tumbledown bar they meet a prostitute known as 'Old Shakespeare'. Ben Higgs gets drunk. His drink has been doctored and, when he wakes up, head splitting, he finds himself tied up in a cellar of the Fourth Ward Hotel. Creeping towards him is a man with a knife. Close to, he sees that it is his old seafaring mate, Thomas Goolden, who cuts him free. As they stumble into the street he hears Goolden say, 'Here's to you, Mr Byrnes', after which he slips away, never to be seen again. All that Higgs knows is that when Goolden cut him free he left fresh blood on his hands and wrists from the knife that he was carrying. Later he hears that 'Old Shakespeare' was murdered in room 31 above him.

This type of story, however well told, is of very limited appeal because the ending is too obvious and the suspense cannot successfully be maintained. A subtler approach was chosen by Kay Rogers in 'Love Story', where the storyteller is the real-life victim Long Liz Stride. She is ghost-ridden by the girl Elizabeth that she once was, clean, virginal and loving, with bright dreams for the future. Now she is just a gin-sodden old harridan. But however much she soaks up the gin she cannot stop this other self from haunting her. Liz will only be free if she can find for Elizabeth the pure love that she once dreamed of and still craves. Eventually she does so, in a Whitechapel courtyard. In the eyes of Jack the Ripper she sees pure *scarlet* love. In that instant, Elizabeth flees her forever, laughing in triumph and revenge, and leaves Liz with the man who is about to kill her.

In Alban Berg's opera *Lulu,* the heroine is an amoral creature who has a disastrous effect on all men. Her first husband dies of a heart attack after seeing her in the arms of another man. Her second husband commits suicide. She shoots her lover and, on her release from prison, becomes a street-walker, only to meet her death at the hands of Jack the Ripper. In describing his opera, which was inspired by two plays by the German dramatist Frank Wedekind, Berg said of Lulu that she is 'a glowing fireball, singeing everything that comes into contact with her.' She is a destructive agent who has to be destroyed, even as she has herself destroyed others. In fact Berg, to emphasise this point, wanted four victims from the earlier part of the opera to be shown as clients later when she has sunk to the depths and become a street-walker. According to one critic, however, 'The trouble is that if such a monster [Lulu] is not to horrify, our sensibilities are apt to jump the tracks, so that she becomes less an object of odium than a figure of fun. If one is not to be appalled when Lulu absent-mindedly inquires, as the son of the lover she has killed buries his head in her breasts, "Isn't this the sofa your father bled to death on?" it is hard to restrain a giggle.'

Intentionally or not, this is the way a number of the stories end up. One of the most hilarious is 'Jack El Destripador', which is of German-Spanish origin. The story opens with Mr Warren bringing Sherlock Holmes up to date on the thirty-eighth Ripper murder. Holmes's police rival is Detective Murphy. They wager £1000 as to who will catch the Ripper, and Warren throws in twenty-five bottles of champagne as a bonus.

In the bedroom of the victim (singer Lilian Bell) Josias Wakefield, the funeral director, is measuring the body. He finds the singer's false tooth and deduces from it that she smoked opium. Under the bed he discovers, too, the disguised Murphy who rages at the funeral director—none other than Sherlock Holmes!

Holmes then goes to an opium den, where he blackmails the half-caste woman who supplies him with the drug into telling him that the singer was getting her drugs from a mysterious person known as 'The Indian Doctor'. Suddenly there is a scream, and in the next room another Ripper victim is lying. The Ripper himself has escaped by jumping onto a moving train.

This thirty-ninth victim is Comtesse de Malmaison, who is identified by her shoes. She has been having an affair with her American riding instructor, and the only other person who knew of her assignations with him was a West End doctor with an Indian background called Dr Fitzgerald who was to examine her for a contemplated abortion. Holmes follows this doctor's wife, and discovers that she is having an affair with an army captain. He disguises himself as a soap manufacturer and warns the doctor of his wife's pending elopement. The doctor falls into a rage, denouncing all women as serpents of Eve, and has to be quieted with morphine. Holmes successfully manoeuvres the doctor's wife away from her next rendezvous with her lover, and takes her place disguised as a woman. When Dr Fitzgerald sees him with a street-walker's strolling gait, he screams 'My wife—on the streets!' The Ripper side of his personality takes over and he attacks Holmes, who fortunately is wearing a steel cuirasse under his female attire. Still in this garb, he drags the doctor back to

Warren's office where Detective Murphy suddenly acknowledges that Holmes has won the bet.

In spite of this nonsense, the idea struck a sympathetic cord with Ellery Queen, whose *A Study in Terror* (published in Britain in 1966 under the drab title of *Sherlock Holmes versus Jack the Ripper*) pits Holmes' ingenuity against the Ripper's fiendish cunning. It is an interlocking story of past and present events. The main narrative is formed by Dr Watson's unpublished account of the case; the sub-plot concerns the giving of the manuscript to Ellery Queen so that he can make investigations to clear the name of the man whom Watson has wrongly identified as the Ripper. The sub-plot was discarded, as was Ellery Queen's solution, when a film version was made in 1965: Dr Watson's 'false' ending made for a simpler and better story. The book ending is unsatisfactory, however, for at the final dénouement six of the principal characters are tidily disposed of in less than four pages. One impales himself on his sword stick, four more are burned to death and the sixth is stabbed by somebody pretending to be Jack the Ripper!

Naturally enough the story begins in 1888, when Holmes is sent a surgeon's instrument case from which the post-mortem knife is missing. Stamped into the lid is the coat of arms of the Osbournes, one of England's oldest and noblest families. When Holmes tries to return the instrument case to the head of the family, Kenneth Osbourne, the Duke of Shires, he is told that it probably belonged to the black sheep of the family, the Duke's youngest son, Michael Osbourne. From the Duke's eldest son, Lord Carfax, Holmes learns that Michael disgraced the family name by marrying a prostitute and that, as far as their father is concerned, he is 'dead'.

Holmes' investigations take him to Whitechapel. In a soup kitchen, financed by Lord Carfax, he finds the shambling idiot 'Pierre', a derelict who is none other than the missing Michael Osbourne.

Gradually he pieces together the following story.

The surgeon's instrument case had been sent to Holmes by Michael Osbourne's prostitute wife, Angela, in the hope that he would follow the trail to the man whom she suspects of being the Ripper, a Whitechapel thug named Max Klein. Klein is also her protector and, some months previously, had taken her to Paris where she had met and fallen in love with Michael Osbourne, who was then a medical student. Klein had seen in their romance the perfect opportunity for blackmail. He had forced Angela to marry Michael. After they were married he revealed the details of her sordid past to Michael and had threatened to reveal it also to Michael's father, the Duke of Shires, unless he gave in to his blackmail demands. Michael, however, had more backbone than Klein had anticipated and attempted to murder him. He failed in his attempt and was given a brutal beating which resulted in his permanent loss of memory. He would have been killed if Angela had not intervened. Klein punished her by mutilating her face with a knife. Subsequently he took Angela and Michael back to Whitechapel, as he had further plans for them. But instead of using Michael in his other schemes as he had planned, Klein abandoned Michael, who drifted unrecognised about the streets until he found refuge in the hostel.

Klein had found a more lucrative source of income—he had discovered the identity of Jack the Ripper, and was blackmailing him instead!

The grand dénouement sees Holmes and Watson in the evil Klein's clutches. Holmes and Michael Osbourne, who is with them, are taken away to be slaughtered, and poor Watson is tied to a chair in the same room as Angela Osbourne (who is too scared of Klein to set him free). Through the door bursts Lord Carfax with a knife in his hand.

'The Ripper! Oh, God in Heaven! It is Jack the Ripper!' screams Angela Osbourne.

Watson confesses with shame that his first reaction was one of relief. Then the ghastly truth dawns on him as Lord Carfax tears away Angela's clothing and plunges his knife into her bare breast. Watson notices that his clumsy efforts at dissection lack the skill of his previously performed mutilations and were best not described. Lord Carfax then sets fire to the room. As the flames rise about him Watson consigns his soul to his Maker. Instead he is cut loose and thrown through the window!

'Tell them that Lord Carfax is Jack the Ripper,' is the last cry that he hears before he hits the ground and is knocked unconscious.

When he recovers consciousness, it is to find that Holmes has escaped (how is never satisfactorily explained), that Michael Osbourne, Max Klein and one of his henchmen have also died in the flames, and that Lord Carfax has stabbed himself to death with his swordstick.

Watson is most annoyed when Holmes refuses to let him publish the story, but is partially mollified by a new Holmes story, *The Case of the Peruvian Sinbad*. His unpublished manuscript becomes part of the Osbourne papers, and it is Lord Carfax's spritely 80-year-old daughter who, believing in her father's innocence, eventually gives them to Ellery Queen to investigate.

Queen's final solution is that Jack the Ripper was none other than the Duke of Shires, who stabbed himself when Lord Carfax found out the truth about his father. Lord Carfax had certainly killed Angela Osbourne, whom he had been hunting, believing her to be the family's evil genius; by telling Watson that he was Jack the Ripper, and consigning himself to death in the flames, he had tried to protect his father's name and reputation.

Frankly, it made a much better film.

This was made in 1965 and released under its American title *A Study in Terror*. The Ellery Queen part of the story was discarded completely and the story-line faithfully followed Watson's narrative.

Another period reconstruction, *Dr Jekyll and Sister Hyde,* by Hammer Films, scrambled Stephenson's story of Jekyll and Hyde with that of Burke and Hare and Jack the Ripper. Plus sex.

Dr Jekyll, in seeking for the elixir of life needs female hormones for his experiment. At first he manages to obtain these from the local morgue. To his horror he discovers that his 'elixir' turns him into a woman, beautiful Sister Hyde. He continues his experiments and to get more hormones, uses the services of body snatchers Burke and Hare until the one is lynched and the other blinded by an angry mob. Only then does Jekyll become the Whitechapel murderer, stalking the streets in search of victims and disguised as Sister Hyde. But gradually Jekyll finds that she is taking him over. An already bizarre situation is further complicated when Dr Jekyll and Sister Hyde each falls in love with the brother and sister living in the apartment above Jekyll! Finally Jekyll tries to get rid of Sister Hyde. To do so, however, he must kill again and in a rooftop chase he falls to his death. When the police examine the body they find that it is a hideous mutation, neither man nor woman.

Just how the story can be developed for the future is very hard to see. In 1973 the Half Moon theatre, appropriately located in Whitechapel, staged a play called *Ripper*. The emphasis throughout was on the squalor, the doss houses, the overcrowding and the black, grinding poverty of the East End. Characters included crude stereotypes—the stupid policeman, the anarchist—and there were many hilarious exchanges of dialogue, such as the following one between Queen Victoria and the Duke of Clarence.

VICTORIA: Why did you resign your army commission?

CLARENCE: I was found in that beastly men's club in the Tottenham Court Road.

VICTORIA: Oh yes, a strange reason.

CLARENCE: A strange club, Mummy dear.

VICTORIA: We hear you have unacceptable women.

CLARENCE: Friendly, Mummy.

EQUERRY: Sir William Gull, your physician, Ma'am.

VICTORIA: Ah, Gull.

GULL: (nervously) I've had a narrow squeak, Ma'am. Some quack medium led the police to my house!

VICTORIA: Tsk, tsk, ridiculous.

GULL: I had your son's blood on my hands at the time, Ma'am.

VICTORIA: Edward—I thought we had sent you on another world tour?

CLARENCE: (petulantly) I'm sick of touring, Mummy.

VICTORIA: (to Gull) You have examined the Duke of Clarence?

GULL: He has an infection, Ma'am.

VICTORIA: What, Gull?

GULL: Syphilis, Ma'am.

VICTORIA: We think that is on the organs of generation?

GULL: Not in his case, Ma'am.

VICTORIA: Where, Gull?

GULL: In his brain, Ma'am.

After this it seems that the Ripper story can only be developed through the medium of science fiction by taking on sci-fi elements.

A good example of this kind of juggling with time is found in Donald Henderson's short story 'The Alarm Bell'. An alarm bell is the heaven and hell of his mysterious strangler in a mackintosh. He is a man who dislikes the tedium of his life—the routine drudgery of his job and the dreary little streets of houses which he has to pass through on his way to work. One morning he makes a detour through wartime Shepherd's Bush and, as he passes a small house with dirty green blinds, he hears an alarm bell. The ringing triggers off his killer instinct, which he is unaware of, and his last point of contact with reality is the knowledge that his hands are sliding their way up the unlatched window.

Inside the dingily lit ground floor room he hears breathing. His large muscular hands, which normally look incongruous when they're thrust into his excessively small mackintosh pockets, grope for the long thin mound of the man's throat. He is disappointed at how tamely the man dies, but his pleasure reawakens when he realises that there is someone else in the bed—and the woman sits up in bed and begins to scream.

Upstairs Mr Randall thinks that the newlyweds, Bob and Vera, are having 'marriage larks' or else that Vera is yelling at her husband, which she frequently does. He lies in bed smoking listening for Uncle George's footsteps on the stairs, hoping that the latter will bring him a cup of tea.

Uncle George has slept badly. He blames it on his drinking too much the previous night. He has a premonition that the alarm bell ringing by his head means an awful sort of danger. First of all he thinks it means a fire, and next approaching murder. He starts thinking about how tragedies happen for no apparent reason, and opens his bedroom door. He freezes with horror when he sees on the landing the staring eyes of a man in a mackintosh. The strangler is holding the limp figure of Sid, the lodger in the basement, by the throat. The strangler drops him as a cat drops a little mouse because he has seen a nice, long, trembling thin one that has lost even the power to squeak. Uncle George's last thought as his head almost bursts with the pressure on his throat is that as the strangler's victim his story will be in the *News of the World* on Sunday.

Imagine missing it!

Old Mr Randall puts up more of a fight when the strangler grips him from behind. He heaves and plunges about his bedroom with the strangler gripping him by the throat. The two men tumble downstairs, by which time Mr Randall is turning green. His body is dumped by the kitchen door and the strangler lets himself out through the front door just as the milkman enters by the back, taking in the morning's milk as the Randall family have always asked him to.

When he finds the bodies he hurries into the street. There he sees a man in a mackintosh leaning by the fence, taking in great gulps of air, tells him what has happened and asks him to fetch a policeman.

The strangler does so. But he is returning to normality and is deeply distressed by what has happened. As if the day was not sordid enough without starting it with several murders! As he mingles with a crowd he thinks about a police theory that it's possible for a man to commit murder without knowing it—but surely that is going a bit too far?

What was he thinking about?

He remembers. Bells.

Why bells?

Heavens, he'll be late for work!

Finally, perhaps the best of the Ripper short stories, and one that certainly grows on the reader. This is Harlan Ellison's 'The Prowler in the City at the Edge of the World'. Jack is transported forward in time to the last city in the world, a place of antiseptic aluminium cubes from which the Whitechapel slums have disappeared and where there are only metallic buildings and a metallic sky. He is glad because (here the story is following Cullen's theory) he was motivated to commit the murders to bring about social reforms. But something is wrong. Suddenly there is a time transference and he is back in Whitechapel again, committing murder once more. As he does so he understands what has happened. He has been brought forward in time by a group of hedonists so that they can batten and feed on his unspoken thoughts and sensations. This leads up to the most sensational motivation ever attributed to the Ripper, and one worth ending on.

'He hates them all, every one of them, something about a girl, a venereal disease, fear of his God, Christ, the Reverend Barnett, he . . . he wants to fuck the Reverend's wife!'

9

BEYOND THE GRAVE

In November 1972 a detective went into a Maida Vale flat in London and discovered the body of a young girl, well known for her casual sexual relationships. She was lying on the floor, her head covered with a towel, her skirt rumpled up about her waist, her brassiere undone and her underclothing pulled down. There was a torn stocking around her neck. Her body glistened from a quantity of yellow, lemon-smelling, domestic fluid that had been sprayed over her and was running down her legs. The room had not been greatly disturbed, but on the wall was a message, done in the same yellow liquid that was on the body. There was only one word: 'Ripper'.

The sinister undertones of the Whitechapel murders are increasing rather than diminishing. For example, some years ago a man left a message with my colleagues asking if I would go to see him as he had a 'Ripper' collection. Naturally enough I was sufficiently intrigued to go to his house. It was on a bright Saturday morning in early summer. My host, a short, dark haired man with a heavy jaw, was waiting outside his house to greet me. We went upstairs to his first floor flat and he shut the door. Although it was only 11 a.m. there were heavy blankets, doubling as curtains, pulled across the window to keep out the light. There was very little room to manoeuvre. Behind the door was a double bed and at the bottom, wedged in between the wall and the bed, there was a table of which only one side could be used. I sat at this table while my host pottered about, making coffee; sensing my unease, he eventually pulled out his 'collection'. It could be broken down into three categories. The first consisted chiefly of a series of photographs of himself at the various murder scenes, pointing out dramatically the 'spot' on the twentieth-century pavements.

The second category consisted of tracings of the *Illustrated Police News* drawings of the Ripper's victims. Each of the bodies had been slashed with red ink to simulate the mutilations and was lying in a large pool of red ink; at some point he had run out of the red ink and had changed over to green. He told me that he was hoping to make models of these, beginning with Mary Kelly.

The final category was probably the most frightening of all. He knew that I was interested in the affair known as 'the siege of Sidney Street', and so he had made a similar tracing of the shooting of the three policemen. Underneath it were other tracings of victims of the Nazis and Japanese war crimes. Most of these had been copied from Lord Russell of Liverpool's books *Knights of the Bushido* and *Scourge of the Swastika*. I particularly remember one of a Chinese man who had been bound against a tree, his eyes gouged out. As was the case with all these tracings, the only colouring in them was to indicate the mutilations.

By the time I had leafed through them all—I just did not grasp at first what I was looking at—I was feeling decidedly uncomfortable and a little bit scared. Suddenly I realised that neither of us was talking any longer, and that my host was staring at the tracings in my hand. His eyes glazed and he pushed his heavy jaw forward.

'I've always wanted to see a dead body,' he said.

Without once turning my back on him I rose to my feet (happily I was bigger than he was), made some polite excuses and left. I have not seen him since. Some years afterwards I was told that he was working in a hospital as a mortuary attendant.

Clearly, interest in the Ripper can be unhealthy. This is a fact often overlooked by those, such as myself, who enjoy playing 'Hunt the Ripper'. On 12 March 1974, Terence Collins, aged 21, was found guilty of battering a 79-year-old woman to death with a tombstone as she knelt by a grave in a Surrey churchyard. After killing her he ran into the street and screamed at a schoolteacher into whom he bumped: 'Don't look at me. I will cut your face. I have got the devil in me today.' He then went into an antique shop and said that he wanted a swordstick, sharpened to a fine point, and a black cloak with a red silk lining, 'Like the one that Jack the Ripper wore.' When he was arrested and questioned the next day he told the police: 'Sometimes I think I am the devil; sometimes Jack the Ripper or a vampire or something like that.' The court was told that he had been in a mental hospital three times and was suffering from a psychopathic disorder. Collins pleaded guilty to manslaughter, with diminished responsibility, and was sent to Broadmoor indefinitely.

Three months later, on 4 June, 18-year-old Thomas Hopkins was jailed at Manchester Crown Court for life after pleading guilty to wounding with intent a 67-year-old woman. The judge told him that there was some dispute among the doctors about just how mentally ill he was, but all of them agreed that he needed treatment of some kind in prison. The prosecution said that when detectives searched his home they found documents relating to Jack the Ripper and a tea caddy containing photographs of Hitler. One of the documents read: 'Jack the Ripper. I have returned from the dead. I will kill again—I hate women (bitches).'

Echoes of the Whitechapel murders can be found in these and many other cases. Yet only two can be considered as genuinely Ripper-style murders. These can perhaps be defined as (1) those where all the victims are prostitutes; and (2) where the murderer had consciously imitated his famous predecessor and has said that he has done so. Even so this definition has its drawbacks, as there have been many prostitute killers especially in continental Europe, where the Ripper has become something of a cult figure.

One of the earliest was in the France of the Second Empire, when Louis Napoleon was Emperor. The first three murders were spread over the period 1861–64, but it was not until much later that they were connected. All three victims were mutilated. In the case of Jeanne Heris (a prostitute, and the first victim), there was some medical evidence that she had been strangled before her throat was cut. The police confessed themselves baffled. 'If,' said the investigator, 'we had the most minute description of the murderer, and if that description pointed to the most phenomenal cast of countenance and the most misshapen body, we should not be able to pick him out from among a million and a half people unless he belonged to the habitual criminal classes; and I am personally convinced that he does not belong to these. He is a monomaniac, but at ordinary times as sane as other people. Accident, and accident alone, will bring him into our hands.' In spite of this pessimism, several lives might have been saved had not a number of warnings gone unheeded.

The murderer was, in fact, Joseph Philippe, a servant, a man of soldierly bearing, not more than 35 years old. His motive was robbery. After the initial murders he tried to strangle at least three other prostitutes, all of whom suspected that he was the man wanted by the police, but none of whom was prepared to inform on him nor willing to go with him, not even when he liberally backed his advances with offers of money.

All of Philippe's victims were murdered indoors. After murdering another two women, he shifted his activities to another part of the

Paris suburbs. On 6 November 1864, between 6 and 7 a.m., terrible shrieks and screams were heard coming from one of the tenements in the Faubourg St Antoine. This was such a commonplace occurrence that no attention was paid. Even some workmen who were passing by ignored the woman who was shrieking and screaming out of the window above them, and whose cries for help were mingled with the tearful howling of a child in the same room. She was holding on to the window-sill, and as they walked below some drops fell on their upturned faces. Wiping them away they saw that they were red. They thought she had been drinking wine! Some little time later, she and the child were found hacked to death.

Only a few hours earlier, Philippe had aroused the suspicions of another prostitute in the same quarter. She thought that he was an ex-convict and told the police. For the first time they had a description of the murderer, although it was described as being no more than a 'rush-light in a cathedral'. His face was slightly pockmarked, with a scar across it; he had frizzy hair, a moustache and goatee beard; and there was a tattoo on his left arm, of a flower with the words 'Born under an unlucky' and then a star to finish the sentence.

Doubtless because of the publicity given to this description, Philippe committed no more murders for the next eighteen months. When he resumed it was in another part of the city.

On 8 January 1865 he murdered his eighth victim in a house in the fashionable Faubourg St Honoré. The body was still warm when it was found; the victim had evidently been strangled, for her face had turned black before her throat was cut from ear to ear. Before rifling the room her murderer had carefully washed his hands in a bowl of water, which he left unemptied. He had also left behind his razor.

Three days later Philippe got into an artist's studio on the Rue d'Erfurt, using some pretext, and when the woman there had turned her back on him he had dropped a small bolster case over her head and tried to strangle her with his hands. With some difficulty she had managed to fight him off and raise the alarm. Some people who had heard the woman's cries gave chase to him in the street, and he was caught. In his pocket was a long sharp table knife.

For some hours the police did not realise that they had their hands on the man who had terrorised Paris for the past four years. It was only when his apartment was searched that the evidence was found that sent him to the guillotine in July 1866.

According to the medical men who examined him, 'he was glad to die: . . . life, shorn of its usual debauches, would be irksome to him.'

Few cases can compare with the next two. Both have enough fascination to stand by themselves and yet in the context of this story they gain by being bracketed with it. Both men committed more murders than the Ripper and yet the more revolting criminal of the two, Peter Kürten is probably the one least well known to the general public.

Jack the Stripper

There are obvious similarities between the London 'Nude' murders of 1964–65 and the Whitechapel killings of 1888. Neither murderer was caught and, in both cases, the police investigation was abruptly terminated for apparently the same reason—that the murderer was thought to be dead. The victims of both men were prostitutes. Jack the Stripper's had an extra peculiarity: they were all between 5 ft and 5 ft 3 in tall. In both cases there was the same intensive man-hunt. Eight senior detectives, ranging in rank from Commander to Superintendent, led the Nudes inquiry investigation; between them they had solved between seventy and a hundred murder cases.

The six Nudes murders occurred in inner London between February 1964 and February 1965, when they ended abruptly. All the women were from the Bayswater and Notting Hill area. Initially it was thought that there might have been eight victims, murdered over a much longer period. The two victims that were discounted were Elizabeth Figg, who was murdered in June 1959, and Gwynneth Rees, who was murdered in November 1963. Figg's partially clothed body was found on a river walk between Chiswick Bridge and Duke's Meadow. She solicited in the Notting Hill area, as did Rees. There were many similarities between their murders and the other six, but there were also enough inconsistencies in the murderer's modus operandi (such as leaving the bodies partly clothed) to make it advisable for the police to exclude them altogether from the Nudes investigation and to concentrate on those with a defined and well established pattern.

The first Nudes murder was that of Hannah Tailford who was last seen alive when she left her home at Thrulby Road, West Norwood on 24 January 1964. She was a former part-time waitress from Northumberland who had drifted into prostitution. For a time she had lived with a man named Walter Lynch and they had a three-year-old daughter. She used various pseudonyms, including Teresa Bell and Anne Taylor, and generally solicited in the Bayswater Road. Her body was found on 2 February 1964 in the Thames near Hammersmith Bridge. The flame-coloured blouse, dark skirt, dark blue coat and hat which she had last been seen wearing were missing. She was still wearing stockings, which were around her ankles, and her briefs had been stuffed into her mouth to stop her from crying out. From the injuries to her head it was thought that she might have been knocked unconscious and thrown into the river somewhere along the riverbank of Duke's Meadow, which was about half a mile away, and which was a local spot for prostitutes and their West End clientele as well as for courting couples.

At first there was a strong suspicion that she might have been killed because she was blackmailing a client. She had a reputation for attending 'kinky' parties and in a flat she rented in Victoria for purposes of prostitution the police found cameras and studio lighting equipment. Strong though these suspicions were, the coroner's inquest jury was impelled to return an open verdict. The bruising on her face was not conclusive evidence that she had been attacked. It might just as easily have been the result of a fall. It was equally possible—though there were strong reasons for doubting it—that she had committed suicide by undressing and stuffing her briefs in her mouth to stop herself from screaming in case she lost her nerve, which frequently happens with a certain type of suicide.

About seven hundred people were questioned in this initial investigation.

The post mortem showed that she was pregnant. So was Irene Lockwood, whose naked body was found on the Thames foreshore ten weeks later on 8 April at Duke's Meadow, about three hundred yards from where the first body had been found. She had been in the water for about twenty-four hours. She was identified by her fingerprints and the tattoo on her right arm, reading 'John in Memory'. She had been strangled.

She was found to have been friendly with a girl who had been murdered a year before named Vicki Pender. They had both been car prostitutes and taken part in the 'blue films' racket. At first it was thought that, like Hannah Tailford, she might have been killed because she had tried to blackmail a client with photographs. Vicki Pender had been beaten up a number of times for precisely this reason.

While this investigation was under way a man confessed to the first murder. At his trial, this 54-year-old bachelor said that he had only confessed because he was 'fed up', but the more likely explanation was that he had done it out of loneliness and for the need of some attention. The police took his confession more seriously than they do the usual imitative confession, which are common enough during a murder investigation, because some of his descriptions of the girl, including details of her accent and clothing, were uncannily accurate. After a six-day trial he was found not guilty and acquitted. He told reporters as he left the court: 'I was confused and depressed although I shall never really know why I said I did it.'

The main proof of his innocence was that, while he was in custody, the Stripper struck again. This time his victim was a convent-educated girl named Helen Barthelemy, who had run away from home to Blackpool and had worked there on the Golden Mile as a strip-tease artiste. She had moved to London about a year before she died. Shortly before doing so she had been sentenced to four years' imprisonment for her part in a robbery, but the sentence had been quashed on appeal. She was a prostitute in the Shepherd's Bush and Notting Hill area. Her body was found in an alley in Brentford—sixteen days after Lockwood's body had been dragged from the river. She had been asphyxiated and, from discolouration marks on her body which had been left by her underclothes, it was certain that her clothes had been removed after death.

Another factor, which was to be found in the later murders, was that four of her teeth were missing—and one, broken off, was lodged in her throat—although there was no evidence to suggest that this was the result of a blow. Apart from its being the first of the bodies to be found away from the river, she also gave the police their first and apparently their only clue. On her naked body were flakes of paint. From the analyst's reports, it emerged that the body had been kept in or near a paint spray shop, perhaps a motor repair works.

Until now, the public and press had not realised that this killer was on the prowl. New Scotland Yard, however, took the unusual step of calling a press conference and giving the widest publicity to the three previous murders. In particular, the police emphasised their fear that if they did not get the information they wanted then another woman might soon be murdered. They stressed: 'This is urgently directed to all women whose means of livelihood places them in danger of meeting the same fate.'

As a result of this appeal, quite a lot of information was given to the police, particularly by prostitutes, about known deviants. For three months there was an uneasy lull, thanks to this publicity and to the increased police patrols in North London. Then on 14 July the Stripper struck again.

His fourth victim was Mary Fleming. She was last seen alive in the early hours of Saturday, 11 July. Her body was found—in a half-squatting-half-sitting position—outside a garage in a cul-de-sac in Chiswick. When she was first spotted at 5.30 a.m. from a bedroom window opposite, the man thought that she was a discarded tailor's dummy. Moments later, a motorist had to brake sharply as a small, dark-coloured van drove out of the cul-de-sac, narrowly missing him. He was so incensed by what had happened that he called the police. Minutes later they were dealing not with a dangerous driving charge but with a murder case.

Again there were some teeth missing from the victim, although this time they were from her dentures.

This case was still being investigated when the body of the fifth victim, Margaret McGowan, was found under some debris in a car park in Kensington on 25 November 1964. The body was badly de-composed—she had been missing since 23 October—and her hands had to be severed and taken away in plastic bags to be finger printed. There were tattoo marks on her arms, and the words 'Helen, Mum and Dad'.

McGowan was a Glasgow girl who had come to London and lived in Shepherd's Bush. She had three illegitimate children and several aliases, including that of Frances Brown, which had been the name she used when she gave evidence at the Stephen Ward trial, which saw the culmination of the notorious Profumo scandal two years be-fore. (I can remember her pacing up and down outside the Old Bailey, on the pavement opposite the main entrance of the Central Criminal Court, puffing away on a cigarette. She was a tough, hard-faced little Scot, wobbling precariously on her high stiletto heels, with those incongruous looking tattoos on her bare arms which were poking out of tiny puff sleeves.)

The closest the police came to a lead was through a girl she had been with twenty-four hours before she disappeared. They were picked up in the Portobello Road by two men who, so the police later thought, might have been businessmen connected with the Earl's Court Motor Show. Certainly the two men seemed to know each other. They drove off together with one girl in each car. McGowan's car was lost in the traffic. Probably the driver was inhibited by his social standing from coming forward later; it is highly unlikely that he was the killer, but certainly the police would have liked to eliminate him from the inquiry.

The sixth and last victim was Bridie O'Hara, last seen alive outside the Shepherd's Bush Hotel after the public house closed at 11 p.m. on 11 January 1965. Yet her body was not found until 16 February behind a workshop on the Heron Trading Estate only a short distance away. The man who found her saw both feet sticking out from under a bush and he too thought they belonged to a tailor's dummy. The post mortem showed that she had been asphyxiated and strangled. Some of her teeth were missing.

The same day Detective Chief Superintendent John Du Rose, known to his subordinates as 'Four-Day Johnny' because of the speed with which he normally solved his murders, was brought back from vacation to lead the investigation.

The most remarkable thing about this last murder was that the body had been partly mummified because of the conditions in which it had been kept. Rose's problem was to find out where. Similar paint traces and dust particles to those found on Barthelemy's body were present. There were also traces of oil. The bodies must have been kept in a factory or small shop where car repairs were carried out. From the spray pattern the police knew that the bodies had been kept in a small room next to the paint shop. Every garage, factory and repair shop which used a paint-spraying process was searched. Thirty-six detectives swept through the twenty-four square miles of London west of Paddington to find it. Hundreds of samples of paints were sent away for laboratory analysis but, with one exception, there was always some slight difference. Meanwhile extra reinforcements were drafted to the area.

A system of 'flagging' was introduced as a check on cars. Any that turned up more than once in the same area during the night became suspect vehicles; three times or more and they were 'red flagged' and the drivers put down for questioning. If this system had been introduced earlier the killer might perhaps have been caught.

Eventually the spot where O'Hara's body had been kept was found. The place was in a transformer building at the rear of a factory on the Heron Trading Estate and opposite a paint spray shop. Analysis showed that the paint used here was the same as that found on the body. However, it seemed that this major clue was only incidental to the killings. The body had certainly been stored in the transformer, but this did not lead to the identification of the killer—although he clearly had a specialised knowledge of this private estate of about seven thousand people. Policemen carried out checks on cars that passed through the estate and concentrated their efforts more and more on this small area. Du Rose waged a war of nerves on the Stripper. He didn't know his identity but, in a steady stream of press releases, he let it be known that the number of suspects had dropped from twenty down to three, of which the Stripper was one.

Du Rose guessed that the man he wanted was about forty years old and of strong sexual urges. Each of his victims had died at the moment of his frenzied orgasm. One theory which has been postulated is that some of the teeth had been taken out after death in order to permit further oral sexual release. Possibly if just one of his victims had died through this particular perversion he might have been acquitted of any charges that might have been brought against him. Another theory was that he might have been revenging himself on these women who had all at some time had venereal disease, and that he had become infected. A third possibility was that he was challenging the police to catch him by flaunting his killings, which he might have committed for a grudge motive. Nothing was too bizarre to be considered.

Yet instead of the murders continuing it became clear just a week later that they had stopped altogether. Gradually the number of police patrols in the area were reduced, and a degree of normality began to return to north-west London.

The Stripper had been stopped—but how? Was he dead, in prison, ill or had he fled the country? 'Four-Day Johnny' ordered an investigation to be made of all men who had been jailed since February 1965, and asked for details of London inquests for the same period on young and middle-aged men. It was while they were checking the background of a South London suicide that certain facts suggesting that he might have been the Stripper began to emerge.

This man had had the ideal cover. He was a security man. On the nights when the women had been murdered, he had always been on duty between 10 p.m. and 6 a.m. His motives for suicide were obscure. He left a suicide note saying that he was 'unable to stand the strain any longer'. However, there was no obvious reason for his death. Why should he take his life? And why, if he wasn't the Stripper, had the murders stopped since his death?

In spite of intensive searches of this man's home and garage nothing turned up, such as clothing or jewellery, which might have linked him firmly with the murdered women. His bewildered family could not explain the reasons for his sudden death and there was as much of a mystery about him as before.

The remarkable similarities of this case with the Ripper case are obvious and show just how the Victorian police, working on the same lines, could have back-tracked to Druitt. At least it shows that an apparently motiveless death, a note threatening suicide, and the perfect cover for murder are not such unusual phenomena.

The Düsseldorf Ripper

On Friday 23 May 1930, Frau Kürten met her husband, Peter, in the Hofgarten, in Düsseldorf. After a meal, which she didn't feel like eating, they went for a walk across the Rhine bridge. They were an oddly contrasting couple. She was a gaunt, raw-boned woman, prematurely wrinkled, and he was a short, well-dressed man, wearing a hat, as was the fashion, partly to cover his neatly pomaded hair which was parted in the middle and partly to protect the powder and rouge on his face which made him seem much younger than he was. For once in his life Kürten seemed unnaturally dejected. He was deep in the grip of an uncontrollable urge to share his terrible secrets with someone else. His wife was the only confidante he had. Until a day or two before not even she had had the slightest suspicion that he might be the Düsseldorf Ripper, the Vampire or the Werewolf, as the press called him. Even now, when he told her that he was the man who had committed the series of murders and attacks that had paralysed the city for the past fifteen months, she couldn't believe what he was saying. Finally, to convince her that he was indeed the man that the police were looking for, he took her step by step through the killings, giving her such a mass of detail that she was forced to believe him.

Kürten said later that his love for his wife wasn't based on sex but 'on respect for her noble character.' Probably his infidelities and his years of imprisonment and theft as a petty criminal had drained her of emotion. Her reaction now to his tale of horror was not one of fear for his safety, as one might have expected, but of fear for her own old age, unemployment and starving alone. Her grief was inconsolable. The only advice that she could give him was that he should kill himself and that she should do the same, too, as there was no hope left for her in this life. Eagerly, Kürten told her that there was, that he could help them both. He pointed out that there was a large reward being offered for his capture and that, if she told the police what she knew, then she would be entitled at the very least to a large part of it. He did not find it easy convincing her that this was not a betrayal in the true sense of the word. But after extracting from her a promise that she would not kill herself, he arranged to meet her outside St Rochus church the next afternoon.

Next morning he bathed, had his hair cut and dressed himself neatly for the meeting. He spent part of the morning walking up and down outside the house of a widow whom he had marked down for his next victim. He was arranging in his mind the grand finale to his terrible career, but had not yet decided whether to kill the widow only or her family as well. He was surprised at what he considered to be his premature arrest. He had not expected his wife to carry out his wishes quite so soon. The immediate area surrounding the church was filled with armed policemen and, as his wife arrived and they stood talking, four policemen with revolvers rushed forward and seized him.

His reign as the Düsseldorf monster was at an end. But the fame which he had sought, when, as a teenager he had stood in front of some wax models of murderers and had boasted that one day he would be famous like them, did not elude him.

In the past fifteen months he had carried out a series of sex murders and attacks which are almost without parallel in the annals of crime. He was a pyromaniac, a fetishist, a masochist, a sadist and a sex killer. The best brains in the Berlin Alexanderplatz had been engaged in running him to earth, as well as Düsseldorf's own efficient police. Nearly three thousand clues had had to be followed up, and over thirteen thousand letters of help had poured in from a terrified public. Nothing, not even spiritualists, mediums and amateur graphologists had been too bizarre to be used in tracking down this sadistic killer.

Peter Kürten was born in 1883 in Muhlheim on the Rhine. He was the third child in a family of thirteen. His mother's family were normal, hard-working people. But his background on his father's side was an abnormal one: the family was noted then for its arrogance, violence and megalomania, while criminal tendencies, feeble-mindedness, paralysis and delirium tremens characterised it. His grandfather had served several prison sentences for theft and his children, Kürten's uncles and aunts, were alcoholic psychopaths.

Kürten's father was by profession a moulder, and he forced Kürten, who wanted to be a draughtsman, to be apprenticed to the same trade, much against his wishes. He was also a brutal, over-sexed alcoholic. For long periods his large family of ten lived in one room.

Besides the constant brutality and the drunkenness, his long-suffering wife was often forced to have intercourse with him in front of the children when he came home drunk. Kürten said that if it had not been for the marriage bond, his father's aggressive brutality to his mother would have constituted rape. Eventually, when Kürten was in his teens, she divorced him.

Kürten's sisters were also heavily over-sexed. According to his own confession, one of them actually made sexual advances towards him. In 1897 his father was sentenced to fifteen months imprisonment for attempted incest with one of his daughters, who was then only thirteen and a half years old. (It was this incident which seems to have given his wife the grounds for divorce.) Kürten himself tried to commit incest with the same daughter, his sister.

When he was only eight years old Kürten ran away from home for several weeks, sleeping, for part of the time, in furniture vans. In the next six years, he frequently repeated this episode. Some of the time, before he reached his teens even, he lived as a street thief, snatching purses and handbags from his victims, mostly women and young girls.

After he came out of prison his father's drunken brutality towards him became even worse and on more than one occasion he was attacked by him with a knife. He began to threaten that he would cut off his head and once, Kürten said, he was only prevented from doing so by the screams of the other children. Kürten, by now fourteen years old and already apprenticed to a moulder, decided to escape yet again. He absconded with several hundred marks belonging to his employer but was caught and sent to prison. He was ashamed at first of the humiliation of being led through the streets in handcuffs. In prison, however, during the first of the seventeen sentences that were to take up twenty-seven of the forty-seven years of his life, he was so impressed by the hardened professionalism of the criminals he met there that he had himself tattooed like them.

In prison he began to think about how he could revenge himself on society. While he had been on the run he had lived with a prostitute who had submitted to his sadistic practices. Even as an adolescent, Kürten's sexuality was abnormal. As a boy his family had lived in the same house as a sadistic dog catcher. Dogs that were picked up on the streets and not claimed by their owners were killed for meat or for their fat, which was used as a special ointment by the superstitious. The dog catcher showed Kürten how to torture the animals, and the boy derived even greater pleasure from watching them killed. Gradually, through reading and talking about his feelings, he began to understand his own character. Instead of attempting to control his impulses he gave free rein to them. From the age of thirteen to sixteen he practised bestiality with sheep, goats and pigs. His greatest pleasure, he discovered, was having intercourse with a sheep and stabbing it simultaneously.

According to his own statement, Kürten had already committed his first murders when he was nine years old. He had gone swimming with two boys and had pushed one of them into the river. When the other one had tried to rescue him, he had managed to push both of them under the raft, and they had drowned.

Of his time in prison, he wrote: 'I did myself a great deal of damage through reading blood-and-thunder stories, for instance I read the tale of *Jack the Ripper* several times. When I came to think over what I had read, when I was in prison, I thought what pleasure it would give me to do things of that kind once I got out again. . . .'

(Consciously or not, he imitated the Ripper when he began his own reign of terror. A good omen was that the sky was blood red over Düsseldorf when he returned to the city in 1925, as it was over London in the autumn of 1888.)

When he was released from prison in August 1899 he resumed his career of petty thieving. He lived with a woman twice his age. Significantly for Kürten's development, she was a masochist, and whereas Kürten's other mistresses had unwillingly submitted to his perversions, this woman positively demanded them from him, which only served to increase his sadistic leanings.

In the November after his release he committed his first adult murder. He was then sixteen years old. He tried to strangle a girl while he was having intercourse with her in the Grafenberger Wald. He thought that he had left her for dead, but as no body was ever found and no case of murder ever reported for that month, it is probable that she regained consciousness and staggered home without ever revealing her terrible experience.

Kürten certainly thought that he had killed her. For the first time he had discovered that he could obtain maximum sexual release in this way, and from this point on he was prepared to go to these lengths to have such orgasms. It is significant that this first murder was committed within such a short time of his release from a long prison sentence. As a prisoner, Kürten had frequently committed minor breaches of prison discipline so that he could be further punished by spells of solitary confinement. In the darkness of his cell he could weave his fantasies and dreams of revenge. While indulging in these fantasies he would have seminal discharges. This, he confessed, would happen if he had imagined that he had cut somebody's stomach or injured him in some way. It gave him final and complete satisfaction. He also invented a number of schemes for smashing bridges, poisoning reservoirs and schools of children with poisoned chocolates, each of these mass killings involved hundreds and thousands of victims. He made no attempt to control these perverted imaginings and steadily got more pleasure out of them. Behind them, there was a completely illogical theory of revenge which he called 'compensatory justice'. For example, if he killed somebody, such as a child, who could in no way be blamed for his (Kürten's) imagined wrongs, then society, if there was such a thing as compensatory justice, must feel it in the same way even if they did not know who had committed the crime.

Soon after his release he was given two minor sentences for fraud and petty theft, and these were followed by a more severe two-year prison sentence for trying to intimidate a girl by firing shots at her and, through a window, at her family. After he was released in 1904 he was called up as a conscript, but soon managed to desert. He went to live with a woman who joined him in his thieving activities until he was caught and sentenced to a further seven years in prison.

In May 1912 he was released again, but a few months later was convicted of attempted bodily harm when he shot at a waiter who had tried to interrupt a conversation that Kürten was having with a woman he was trying to pick up.

So far, he had not been linked with any sexual offences.

He next began to specialise in robbing from certain kinds of buildings, preferably those with a public house on the ground floor and rooms or flats above them.

On 25 May 1913 he went to the Cologne suburb of Muhlheim, where he had been born. He found a suitable house to burgle in the Wolfstrasse and managed to get upstairs between ten and eleven o'clock. In one of the bedrooms he found 13-year-old Christine Klein asleep. He seized her by the throat and strangled her for about a minute and a half. She struggled and then lost consciousness. Kürten slashed her throat four times and penetrated her vagina with his fingers. The whole incident lasted about three minutes. One of the tragedies of this case was that her uncle was accused of the crime but acquitted for lack of evidence. He died with the stigma still attached to his name. On the evening of the murder he had quarrelled with his brother and, in a rage, had sworn to do something that his brother would remember all his life. The police found by the girl's body a handkerchief with the initials P.K. which they assumed to be the name of the girl's father—Peter Klein. As it was just conceivable that his brother might have borrowed the handkerchief, this was one of the points of evidence which led to Otto Klein's acquittal.

A few months later Kürten crept into a bedroom where there were several children and a young girl of seventeen asleep. In a rush of feelings which he was later unable to explain he fell upon the girl and tried to strangle her before escaping unobserved. The bruises on her throat testified to the seriousness of the attack. In the summer he broke into another house and was about to strangle another girl, but somebody heard him upstairs and forced him to flee. In the same period he attacked an unknown man and an unknown woman with an axe, in both cases reaching orgasm at the sight of their blood. He also tried to strangle two women.

In 1904 he had already committed his first cases of arson, setting fire to barns and hayricks. He found great delight in the sight of the flames, but more exciting still were the attempts to put out these fires and 'the agitation of those who saw their property being destroyed'. Soon after the axe attacks he burned another haywagon and hayrick.

The next eight years he spent in prison. He boasted subsequently that he poisoned some of the patients in the prison hospital where he went to work as a volunteer nurse. After his release he went to Altenberg, where his sister lived, and told her he had been a prisoner of war. She believed him and introduced him to the woman who became his wife. She was a hard-working woman, and she rejected his first advances because of his obvious success with other women. Apart from being a very frugal person, she was also a very jealous one. She had been engaged to a gardener for eight years and had been his mistress; when he had refused to marry her she had shot him and had served four years of a five-year prison sentence. When Kürten threatened to kill her if she didn't marry him, she gave in to him and stuck loyally by him to the end. She didn't know of his prison sentences when they were married in 1923 and later regarded this as some sort of penance in expiation of her own earlier sin. He struck her only once in their married life, but the incident made her realise that there was a violent side to his character. Philosophically, she shrugged off the gossip about her husband's conquests, knowing them to be true, and stubbornly justified her behaviour by arguing that without her he would go under completely.

For the first two years of their marriage Kürten was a steady and reliable worker. He stayed at home in the evenings and joined the trade union. The only discordant note was when he left the Catholic Church, which he decided to do because of a fund-raising church tax. He had no friends and was an extremely self-contained person. He was dismissed from his job because of general unemployment, and in 1925 he returned to Düsseldorf. He was delighted to see that the sky was blood red on the night of his return. It was a good omen for him and it marked the beginning of Düsseldorf's reign of terror. It started slowly. The first attacks were carefully spaced over the four years until 1929, when they accelerated into truly horrific proportions. Between 1925 and the end of 1928, Kürten later confessed, he had been responsible for three cases of attempted strangulation of women, and seventeen cases of arson involving barns, hayricks, haywagons and, on two occasions, houses.

At the beginning of 1929 he committed six more crimes of arson. Then on 3 February, a woman, Frau Kuhn, was walking home from a friend's house when she was caught by the sleeve and savagely attacked. She was stabbed twenty-four times and lay in hospital for some weeks, unable to give any information as to what had actually happened. Kürten remembered that he had been feeling particularly excited that evening. 'On that evening, if an animal had crossed my path I would have fallen upon it and killed it,' he said. He had leapt at Frau Kuhn with a pair of scissors, which he drove into her head several times. As he hurried away he had seen her pick herself up and stagger off. Kürten found afterwards that he had broken off the point of his scissors.

He had them ground down to a point again.

Ten days later, on the Tuesday of Carnival Week, he bumped into a forty-five-year-old mechanic, Rudolf Scheer, who was helplessly drunk. Kürten stabbed him twenty times with his scissors. On 8 March he had a different pair of scissors with him when he killed eight-year-old Rose Ohliger. He took her to a building plot and strangled her before he stabbed her thirteen times. Later the same evening he went back and tried to burn the body. This attempt was unsuccessful, and so was another when he went back to the spot for the third time early the next morning. Because of the damp the clothes would only char.

The local press, when they picked up these stories, also began to publish stories about Jack the Ripper with whose activities there were obvious parallels. In time they would refer to Kürten as the 'Düsseldorf Ripper'. Some newspapers, as the savagery of the attacks increased, also referred to him as the 'vampire' and 'werewolf'. The police were puzzled by the apparent inconsistencies of the attacks. It was clear that this was the work of no ordinary sex maniac. The victims, so far, had been a man, a woman and child. Yet the stabbings in the temples, and the similarity of the cuts, all pointed to the attacks being the work of one man. In spite of hundreds of interrogations and plain-clothes police observations, there were no real leads.

In July Kürten tried twice more in the space of twenty-four hours to strangle two more women. A sixteen-year-old girl was lassooed from behind and dragged backwards to a hedge where her attacker knelt by her head and tried to strangle her with his hands. She caught hold of him by his nose and fought him off until she could get to her feet. Twenty-four hours later Kürten attacked another woman in an identical manner. She remembered afterwards that he had knelt down by her head and listened to hear if she was still breathing. Because of the tightness of the rope she couldn't open her mouth or scream. As he dragged her over the ground by the rope which was still around her throat, a couple out walking saw him and, although they couldn't make out what he was dragging along, except that it was large and heavy, they went to investigate and Kürten was forced to flee.

From their description the police arrested a twenty-one-year-old epileptic named Hans Strausberg, who was living in a home on the outskirts of Düsseldorf. He couldn't read or write and had a cleft palate and a hare lip. When he was questioned he confessed not only to the attacks but to the killings as well. The discrepancies in his statements and vagueness of response to some of the questions that he was asked were put down to the loss of memory which is a frequent condition of epileptics, and he was committed to a lunatic asylum for life.

Only a few weeks later the reign of terror began again.

On 30 July a prostitute named Emma Gross was found lying naked in her room. She had been strangled. Kürten was not, as it happened, the murderer but the killing set off a new wave of panic. On 21 August three people were stabbed from behind, at different times during the day, by an unknown assailant. Two of the victims were women. One was only slightly wounded but the other was more seriously hurt by a thrust through her liver and stomach. A man, who was the third victim, was stabbed in the small of the back; but fortunately the injury was lessened to some extent by the heavy leather braces (which were cut through) which he was wearing.

There was an immediate outburst of press and public comment criticising the police. Some people were already saying that the police had got hold of the wrong man and there were demands for Strausberg's immediate release. Faced with such a barrage of hostile criticism, the police intensified their efforts to catch the Düsseldorf Ripper. A special watch was kept on the fairs where intended victims might be picked up.

On 24 August the bodies of two foster sisters, one aged fourteen and the other five, were found on an allotment not far from their home. The youngest one had been strangled and stabbed and the older had been stabbed. Kürten later described how he had persuaded the older girl to go and buy him some cigarettes from the fair. While she was away he had killed her five-year-old sister and, when the older girl had come back, he took her to the same spot and stabbed her. She had run away screaming but he had chased after her and killed her by stabbing her in the back four times. On the Sunday that the bodies were discovered, Kürten, who was still feeling sexually excited, picked up a servant girl named Schulte and introduced himself to her as Fritz Baugmart. In a wood he tried to have sexual intercourse with her but she told him that she would rather die first. 'Well die then,' he said, and stabbed her several times. The last savage thrust broke off the point of his knife which lodged in her back. Fortunately some young men nearby had heard her screams for help and came to her rescue. Kürten ran away. The woman could only give a confused description of her attacker. The only thing it seemed that she could remember about him was that he had a tooth missing from his upper jaw.

The police conviction that there was more than one maniac at work was now strengthened. It seemed inconceivable that the same man would kill two children on a Saturday and, just over twelve hours later, try to commit a third murder.

Nearly a month later Kürten struck again. A domestic servant named Ida Reuter went to Düsseldorf to spend the afternoon and evening there. When she was found on the Monday morning it was apparent that she had been dragged from a footpath into some nearby woods and battered to death with a hammer. Kürten's explanation for using the hammer was that he thought that he might get more enjoyment out of it. Her handbag and knickers were missing.

Ten days later Elisabeth Dorrier was killed in the same way. She was still breathing when she was found but she died before she regained consciousness. Her hat was missing, as were some fragments of her coat, which had been torn to ribbons.

On 25 October a thirty-four-year-old woman, Frau Meurer, was accosted by a man in a lonely street in Flingern. 'Aren't you frightened? So much has happened here!' he said. Before she could turn her head, Kürten battered her unconscious with his hammer. She knew nothing more for an hour or two until she woke up in hospital. The force of the blows had broken the skin and had exposed, but not broken, the bone. This attack had not given Kürten quite the satisfaction he wanted. Later the same evening, he attacked a woman in a park in the centre of town. He hit her four times, knocking her unconscious with the first blow, but when his hammer broke he left her alone.

On 7 November, five-year-old Gertrude Albermann was reported missing from her home. Her body was discovered, two days later, lying in some brick rubble and nettles, close to a factory wall. She had been strangled and stabbed thirty-six times with a pair of scissors.

Still more horrific was the news that the killer had sent a letter to a communist newspaper telling them exactly where they could find the body of a child *as well as the body of another victim*. There can be no doubt that at this point Kürten was imitating the Ripper's tactics. Kürten forwarded a sketch map showing where the body could be found; he drew it on some greyish-white wrapping paper and marked it: 'Murder at Pappendelle. In the place with a cross a corpse lies buried.' The police began to dig at once in the lonely meadows indicated on the map. A farmer handed in a bunch of keys and battered straw hat which he had found some weeks before and these were soon identified as belonging to a domestic housekeeper, Maria Hahn, who had been missing since 14 August. There was a further storm of criticism about police failure to catch the Düsseldorf murderer, and the story of Jack the Ripper (which had been a newspaper standby almost since the murders had begun) now took a new turn as stress was laid on the fact that the Düsseldorf Ripper had copied him to the extent of writing to the police in exactly the same way. Kürten said that writing the letter had given him a sadistic satisfaction. On 14 November the body of the missing woman was found in a shallow grave. She was naked and had been stabbed twenty times in the temples, throat and breast.

All the resources of the Alexanderplatz, Berlin's equivalent of Scotland Yard, were now thrown into the biggest manhunt that had ever been launched. Nine thousand people were questioned in Düsseldorf alone, and in the fifteen months covering these attacks more than nine hundred thousand people were denounced as possible suspects in different parts of the country. Only three out of these nine hundred thousand denunciations were made against Kürten. One was made by a fellow prisoner who had once heard Kürten talking about sadistic practices. The second was by a woman who had known Kürten when she was a girl. From the descriptions of the stranglings she thought she recognised his habit of playfully strangling his girlfriends as they used to go walking in the woods. At his trial quite a number of women gave evidence about this playful strangling. The woman was told, when she reported it, that nobody of Kürten's name existed at his address! The third informant was Christine Heerstrasse whom Kürten had half strangled and thrown into the river. When she reported this incident to the police she was laughed at and fined for her 'gross nonsense' and only escaped payment of this fine on appeal!

The police still thought that there were several maniacs at work—namely, the strangler, the killer with a knife, the hammer-wielding fanatic and a fourth who was using a weapon which they had not been able to identify but which with hindsight they knew to be the scissors. Kürten had gone out of his way to blur his tracks and to create this sort of confusion. He later admitted: 'I hoped by changing the method to bring about the theory that there were several murderers at work.' More importantly, he thought that these variations would give him still greater sexual satisfaction. The police carried out intensive raids on the underworld to find him. They even dressed a tailor's dummy in the clothes of one of his victims and took it around the dance halls, cinemas and theatres in the hope that somebody might be able to identify her mysterious escort.

Soon afterwards Kürten made the mistake that led to his capture. On 14 May 1929, twenty-year-old Maria Budlick travelled to Düsseldorf to look for a new job. A friend who had arranged to meet her did not turn up, but a man who spoke to her in the station told her that he would show her the way to a girls' hostel. He took her through the main streets of Düsseldorf but when he turned into the Volksgarten, a public park, she became alarmed. She hung back, and refused to go any further with him, remembering the stories of the Düsseldorf monster. Fortunately a second man came along at this point and offered his help. It was Peter Kürten. Gratefully the girl explained what had happened and, as the first man scuttled away, she thankfully accepted Kürten's offer of a temporary rest and some food at his flat in the Mettmannerstrasse. She was disappointed to see how poorly furnished his attic rooms were, but after some milk, bread and ham she insisted on leaving as it was now after eleven o'clock and she had to find lodgings. They went the last part of the journey by tram. But instead of going towards the centre of Düsseldorf they were going, in fact, towards the Grafenberg woods. Kürten was taking her to a dell which was known locally as the Wolf's Glen. After they got off the bus and had been walking for only a little way Kürten suddenly stopped and tried to kiss her. He told her that she could scream as nobody would hear her. She struggled violently and Kürten tried to have intercourse with her standing up. Suddenly he let go of her throat and asked her if she remembered where he lived. She said no.

The lie saved her life, and trapped Kürten.

He showed her the way out of the woods and let her go.

Instead of going to the police and telling them what had happened, the girl said nothing at all about this incident to anyone. It was only when she wrote about it in a letter to a friend that it came to light. Fate took a hand. The letter was wrongly addressed and the woman who opened it immediately realised the letter's probable significance and handed it to the police. The police just as quickly contacted the girl and asked her to identify the house. She remembered the name of the street, as she had seen it by the light of a lamp, but she hadn't seen the number of the house. She walked up and down the street several times before picking one house out. It wasn't until she was at the top of the four flights of stairs that she felt almost certain that she had picked the right house. When she was shown into Kürten's flat she immediately recognised it as the one that she had been brought to. As she came out onto the landing she saw, coming upstairs, the fair-haired man who had picked her up and attacked her. He started when he saw her and hurried downstairs again, walking briskly away. The landlady wrote his name down on a piece of paper.

Peter Kürten.

Seventy-two hours later he was arrested.

The same evening Kürten went to call for his wife, who normally worked until 4.30 a.m., and told her that he would have to leave the flat for a while because of this girl. It was only an assault case, he explained, but with his record it would mean a fifteen-year sentence. He walked about the streets all Wednesday night, and hid in a room which he rented close-by until the Friday morning when he met his wife as arranged. She told him that the police had searched their flat and that he wasn't to go back there as she didn't want him to be arrested at home. It was then that he told her that he was wanted for the other attacks and persuaded her to go to the police.

There had never been anything sexual in their own relationship. She could never understand what other girls saw in him. She never suspected his perversions and Kürten had been obliged to fantasise acts of sadistic violence in order to go through with their irregular bouts of marital intercourse. However, she was used to his infidelities. Soon after they were married she had had to persuade a girl to drop an assault charge. Less than a year before she had publicly slapped a girl's face when she saw her give her husband a rose in the street. (Kürten had playfully brushed it against her cheek as he had turned on his heel and walked away. At the time he had a pair of scissors in his pocket, with which he was planning to stab the young girl if the opportunity arose.) Later that same afternoon he half strangled a girl he picked up, and she later gave evidence that for days afterwards the marks of his fingernails were clearly visible on her neck.

The women witnesses who came forward and testified against him clearly enjoyed being treated brutally. Brutality, Kürten had told them, 'belongs to love'. His charm and fascination were undeniable. Sometimes to demonstrate that the blame wasn't always his, he would arrange a rendezvous with a girl and take his wife with him as his sister, so that she could see how the women ran after him. Occasionally these outings were likely to end in a scene as the love-making wasn't always one way. On one occasion she had come home unexpectedly and caught him in bed with a girl, but Kürten had as gracefully as ever extricated himself from this compromising situation with a facile explanation which she had docilely accepted.

He boasted once to a fellow workman 'Come with me to the Rhine meadows and I'll show you, on a Sunday afternoon, I can count them —ten to each hand'.

His trial opened on 13 April 1931.

In accordance with German custom, it was presided over by three judges. The courtroom itself was the drill hall of Düsseldorf police headquarters, specially converted for the occasion. The dock was a hastily improvised wooden compartment resembling a cage. In a room behind the court was the Kürten Museum. In *The Monster of Düsseldorf: the life and trial of Peter Kürten,* Margaret Seaton Wagner writes: 'Here were the prepared skulls of his victims showing the various injuries inflicted by scissors or hammer blows, the weapons themselves, articles of clothing belonging to the dead women and children, and the spade used to bury Maria Hahn.' After the jury had been sworn in, the charges were read to him. He was indicted for nine murders and seven attempted murders. Forty cases of arson were omitted from the indictment! There was some speculation that Kürten might retract his confession, as he had done once before while awaiting trial, but now that the spotlight was on him he didn't hesitate to play to the hilt the role of monster.

Among the women who testified against him was a woman referred to as Charlotte U. Unwittingly she testified to the ease with which Kürten could persuade women to go with him to a lonely spot, even at the height of the terror. Margaret Seaton Wagner quotes his statement in court: 'I met a girl, and we had a glass of beer together and then went to the Grafenberg woods. I was able to calm away her fears of the dark and the murderer; I said there were always couples about the woods. At the spot called "Beautiful View" I gave her a blow with my hammer on the right temple. She dropped with a scream; I left her lying there after hitting her several times. The hammer was as big as those I had been using before. I saw the blood flowing.'

She had seen him take something out of his pocket and when he hit her she felt the blood running down her face like water from a tap. She was able to save her life by protecting her head with her hands. Afterwards she bandaged it up with her underskirt and hid for a fortnight until the wounds healed. She didn't dare go to the police.

If she had done so, she might have brought about Kürten's arrest much sooner.

An interesting point that came out at the trial is that killing was not always necessary to Kürten's sexual relief. This explained why again and again his victims were allowed to recover consciousness, or even why, when they were battered and stabbed, were still allowed to get up and stagger away while Kürten still had them in view and could have quite safely killed them. The question that the court had to decide was whether Kürten acted with premeditation before or after these attacks. Professor Karl Berg, who examined Kürten, said that with the exception of the Klein case in 1913, these acts were not the acts of irresistible impulse. Kürten was always fully in command of the situation. Occasional lapses of memory in some of the details he recalled were attributable to sexual excitation. Neither insanity nor irresistible impulse could be put forward as a defence for these murders.

Some of the details he revealed were quite horrifying. Once, when he could not find a victim, he cut the head off a sleeping swan and drank the blood. In another dream he pictured himself as saving the city from the Düsseldorf murderer, and of a torchlight procession being given in his honour and himself nominated as a commissioner of police. Margaret Seaton Wagner says: 'He pictured himself being badly wounded in a fight with the vanquished mass-murderer, lying ill in a hospital with the populace storming the building to do honour to Kürten, whose recovery was hampered by their attentions. At the time of his arrest he had probably reached the climacteric of his sexual life.'

In the prosecution's address it was revealed that twelve thousand individual clues were followed up; that two hundred people gave themselves up for the murders and that about two hundred and fifty accusations were received by the police on average each day.

The case ended on 23 April. The jury deliberated for one and a half hours and when they returned Kürten was sentenced to death nine times for murder. The judge, giving detailed reasons for the verdict, underlined the point that Kürten had always acted with premeditation. He always armed himself with a weapon, he was always capable of leaving off an attack and there was always a carefully thought out plan of flight and concealment of evidence. Throughout the trial he had 'created the impression of cleverness, calmness, and considered deliberation. Kürten is normal,' he said.

For a time it seemed as if the death sentence would not be carried out. There was a storm of controversy about the execution, which would have been the first to be carried out since 1928. Kürten meanwhile was being bombarded with letters, most of them anonymous, including love letters, poems and requests for autographs; he also received in equal numbers letters elaborating on the most horrible ways that he could be made to die.

Kürten appealed against his sentence but on 30 June 1931 the Prussian Ministry of Justice, in secret session, turned it down. The information was leaked to the press that he was to be executed at 6 a.m. on 2 July.

Kürten was not told of the decision until twelve hours before his execution. He received the news quite calmly and spent the time he had left writing to the families of thirteen of his victims asking for their pardon. He claimed that since his arrest his sleep had not been disturbed by any more sado-erotic fantasies. His last meal, the Henkers-Mahlzeit, or Hangman's meal, consisted of Wienerschnitzel, fried potatoes and white wine. Kürten enjoyed it so much that he had a double helping.

At 6 a.m. as the 'poor sinners' bell' began to toll, Kürten was led into the inner courtyard of Klingelputz prison in Cologne where the Magdeburg executioner was waiting for him, and walked briskly to the guillotine. His hands were tied behind his back and he was asked if he had any last wish to make. He said 'No' in a quiet, firm voice.

He was strapped on to the bascule and tipped forward. A few seconds later his head tumbled into the canvas bag.

His last wish, he had told his psychiatrist, would be that he might have the pleasure of hearing his own blood running into the bag.

10
CONCLUSION

I have tried throughout this book to take a long, hard look at what is known about Jack the Ripper, and attempted to clear away some of the many obscurities that bedevil researchers. My modest objective has been to return to basics, and to encourage others to do the same, while we are still close enough to the Ripper's time to add—with luck —just a few more facts to the precious few that we do know about him. Nobody can stop the 'legend' of Jack the Ripper from finally triumphing over these facts. Indeed, it can be argued that it has already done so. Jack the Ripper, within a hundred years of his crime, is already part-folk hero, part-myth.

There is only one fact of which we can be sure. Children chant it every day in skipping games in the East End of London.

> Jack the Ripper's dead,
> And lying on his bed.
> He cut this throat
> With Sunlight soap.
> Jack the Ripper's dead.

BIBLIOGRAPHY

ADAM, H. L., Trial of George Chapman, London: William Hodge, 1930.

ANDERSON, SIR ROBERT, The Lighter Side of My Official Life, London: Hodder and Stoughton, 1910.

ARCHER, FRED, Ghost Detectives: crime and the psychic world, London: W. H. Allen, 1970.

BARNARD, ALLAN (Ed.), The Harlot Killer, New York: Dodd, Mead & Co, 1953.

BARNETT, HENRIETTA, Canon Barnett, his life, work and friends by his wife, London: Murray, 1921.

BARNETT, SAMUEL & HENRIETTA, Practicable Socialism: essays on social reform, London: Longmans, 1888.

BELL, QUENTIN, Virginia Woolf: A Biography, London: Hogarth Press, 1972.

BESANT, WALTER, East London, London: Chatto & Windus, 1903.

BOOTH, CHARLES, Life and Labour of the People in London: East, Central and South London, London: Macmillan & Co. Ltd, 1904.

BOOTH, CHARLES, Conditions and occupations of the people of the Tower Hamlets, 1886–7, London: Stanford, 1887.

COBB, BELTON, Critical Years at the Yard, London: Faber & Faber, 1956.

CROW, DUNCAN, The Victorian Woman, London: George Allen & Unwin Ltd, 1971.

CULLEN, TOM, Autumn of Terror, London: Bodley Head, 1965.

DEW, WALTER, I Caught Crippen, London: Blackie & Son Ltd, 1938.

DU ROSE, JOHN, Murder Was My Business, London: W. H. Allen, 1971.

FARSON, DAN, Jack the Ripper, London: Michael Joseph Ltd, 1972.

GODWIN, GEORGE, Peter Kürten: A Study in Sadism, London: Acorn Press, 1938.

GRIFFITHS, MAJOR ARTHUR, Mysteries of Police and Crime, London: Cassell, 1898.

HARRISON, MICHAEL, Clarence, London: W. H. Allen, 1972.

HENRIQUES, DR FERNANDO, Modern Sexuality: Prostitution and Society, Vol. 3, London: Macgibbon & Kee Ltd, 1968.

JONES, GARETH STEDMAN, Outcast London, Oxford: Clarendon Press, 1971.

KEATING, P. J., The Working Classes in Victorian Fiction, London: Routledge & Kegan Paul, 1971.

KEATING, P. J. (Ed.), Working-Class Stories of the 1890s, London: Routledge & Kegan Paul, 1971.

KELLY, ALEXANDER, Jack the Ripper: A Bibliography and Review of the Literature, London: Association of Assistant Librarians, S.E.D., 1973.

KRAFFT-EBING, Aberrations of Sexual Life (ed. Dr Alexander Hartwich), London: Staples Press, 1959.

LEESON, BENJAMIN, Lost London, London: Stanley Paul, 1934.

LE QUEUX, WILLIAM, Things I Know about Kings, Celebrities and Crooks, London: Eveleigh, Nash & Grayson Ltd, 1923.

LONDON, JACK, The People of the Abyss, London: Thomas Nelson & Sons Ltd, 1902.

MCCORMICK, DONALD, The Identity of Jack the Ripper, London: Arrow Books Ltd, 1970.

MACNAGHTEN, SIR MELVILLE, Days of My Years, London: Edward Arnold, 1915.

MAGNUS, PHILIP, King Edward the Seventh, London: John Murray, 1964.

MARCUS, STEVEN, The Other Victorians, London: Weidenfeld & Nicolson, 1966.

MATTERS, LEONARD, The Mystery of Jack the Ripper, London: W. H. Allen, 1948.

MEARNS, ANDREW, The Bitter Cry of Outcast London with leading articles from the Pall Mall Gazette of October 1883 and articles by Lord Salisbury, Joseph Chamberlain and Forster Crozier. Ed. by Anthony S. Wohl, Leicester University Press, 1970.

ODELL, ROBIN, Jack the Ripper In Fact and Fiction, London: Harrap & Co Ltd, 1965.

PEARSON, MICHAEL, Age of Consent, David & Charles, 1972.

SMITH, LIEUT. COL. SIR HENRY, From Constable to Commissioner, London: Chatto & Windus, 1910.

STEWART, WILLIAM, Jack the Ripper, Quality Press, 1939.

WAGNER, MARGARET SEATON, The Monster of Düsseldorf, London: Faber & Faber Ltd, 1932.

WHITTINGTON-EGAN, RICHARD, Contemporary Review (Nov, Dec 1973 and Jan 1974).

WILLIAMS, MONTAGUE, Leaves of a Life, London: Macmillan, 1890.

WILLIAMS, MONTAGUE, Later Leaves, London: Macmillan, 1891.

WILLIAMS, WATKIN W., The Life of General Sir Charles Warren, Oxford: Basil Blackwell, 1941.

WILSON, COLIN and PITMAN, PATRICIA, Encyclopedia of Murder, London: Arthur Barker Ltd, 1961.

WINSLOW, L. FORBES, Recollections of Forty Years, London: John Ouseley Ltd, 1910.

INDEX

AUTHOR'S NOTE

As this book went to press, Donald Bell proposed a new Cream/Ripper theory in his article entitled 'Jack the Ripper—The Final Solution?' which appeared in *The Criminologist* (Vol. 9, No. 33, 1974).'

Bell points out that racketeering and corruption flourished in the Chicago of the 1880s and argues that Cream might have bribed his way out of prison, or escaped. In corroboration, a major handwriting expert, Derek Davis, asserts that Cream's writing matches that in two of the Ripper letters.

Yet the evidence of the Governor of Illinois, the prosecuting attorney, contemporary newspapers, Cream's relatives, and Cream himself proves that he was not released until 1891.

There is further evidence of his continued imprisonment in a petition sent by Cream's solicitors to the Home Secretary while Cream was in Newgate Prison, shortly before his execution on 15 November, 1892. This petition included a sworn affidavit from Thomas Davidson, an accountant-bookkeeper with Messrs John Ross & Co., Quebec. He stated:

> That, as one of the executors under the will of the late William Cream, of Quebec, I found on the testator's death [1887] his eldest son, Dr. Thomas Neill Cream, a life prisoner in Iolat Prison, State of Illinois, U.S.A., for complicity in murder. That being desirous of assuring myself as to his guilt or innocence I applied to the authorities connected with his trial and conviction for the evidence upon which such conviction was based and received such documentary evidence as convinced me of his innocence. That I then exerted every legitimate influence I could command to secure his liberation, and succeeded eventually in getting him released in the early part of the summer of 1891. That he came immediately to me in Quebec on being liberated, and that at my first interview

230

with him I concluded he was unmistakably insane, and stated my conviction to his brother, Daniel Cream, in whose house he was stopping.

The other relevant affidavit was made by Jessie Cream, the sister-in-law in whose house Cream had stayed after his release. She said that Cream had been released from the Joliet Prison in Illinois on or about 29 July, 1891. He had stayed with her family until he sailed for England in September, 1891.

Besides these two affidavits, there are the facts that in December of 1890, Cream wrote from prison to Pinkerton's National Detective Agency, asking that someone be sent to see him. That on 12 June, 1891, his life sentence was commuted to one of seventeen years, which, with time off for good behaviour, meant his release on 31 July, 1891. That the date of his pardon is confirmed by the Joliet Daily News of 13 June, 1891.

Unless these facts are disproved, and Donald Bell does not disprove them, then suppositions about handwriting, similarity of appearance to Ripper suspects, and the multitude of other vague generalisations fall down and Cream is left a poisoner—and not Jack the Ripper.

By Permission of 'The Criminologist'

NEILL CREAM'S HANDWRITING